FOREWORD

In late 1993, I form
with the grandiose i
expression. By spor
collect enough submi ... ogy that would represent
the thoughts and feelings of Canadians.

It soon became evident that the response would exceed my expectations—in the end, over 2,400 submissions were received. Though daunted at first by the sheer number of poems and personal histories submitted, I and my small staff came to realize what a rare opportunity we had been afforded. Each new entry was a keyhole glimpse into another person's state of mind and personal experiences. *Scaling the Face of Reason* includes some of what we consider to be the most moving, memorable and, sometimes, humorous of these glimpses. We hope that readers will appreciate them as much as we did.

Please note that we have made every effort possible to represent poems, dedications and biographical excerpts exactly as they were originally presented to us. In some cases, where submissions were written in long-form, for example, this was a rather difficult task. If inconsistencies are present, we apologize profusely and can only ask for the reader's generosity and understanding.

Regrettably, while reading through submissions, we had the misfortune of detecting a number of instances of plagiarism. While we have made every effort to eradicate plagiarism in this anthology, including having all poets declare, in writing, that their poems are original, we can only hope that our efforts have been successful.

Before undertaking this project, I had laboured under the misconception that poetry was disdained by the masses as the product of a frivolous pastime. I now reject this view and offer *Scaling the Face of Reason* as a testament to the expressive, healing and emotive power that poetry holds over professionals and amateurs alike.

G.P. Hammell
Editor-in-Chief

ACKNOWLEDGEMENTS

The Canadian Chamber of Contemporary Poetry could not have produced this anthology without the help and encouragement of the following people, equally appreciated: Linda, Pauline, Clarisse, Douglas, Charles, Richard, Donna, Chuck, Elicia Marie, Mary, Wesley and "Tat." A special thank-you goes out to Morris Granit for his depth of thought and his expert advice.

The Canadian Chamber of Contemporary Poetry would also like to express its profound appreciation to the Canadian libraries, YMCAs, YWCAs, universities and colleges that were kind enough to hang posters advertising our 1994 poetry contest.

Thanks also to Zoltan Jambor for providing us with the cover art for *Scaling the Face of Reason*.

CANADIAN YOUTH

The Innocence of a Child

(Morgan J. Aho)

I used to think that stars were thrown
    upon the big black sky;
But now I know that, for their presence,
    there is no reason why.
I used to think that, in the sea,
    all fish were shiny blue;
But now I know that, in the sea,
    there are different colours too.
I used to think that in tree tops high,
    I could sing a lovely song;
But now I know that, to get that high,
    takes extremely long.
I used to think that when sun sets,
    it's dark around the earth;
But now I know that, across the sea,
    it must be morning first.
I used to think that when I grow old,
    I'll never really die;
But now I know that, that too,
    is one more great big lie.

Fire

(Tracy Allan)

Orange, red, black, white.
Fires burning in the night.

See the fire bursting out.
People screaming all about.

When will the fire truck arrive?
Will the people inside survive?

The fire fighters have the fire under control.
When they come out they stop, drop, and roll.

The fire fighters have saved the day.
The people who were screaming shout hurray.

Thank God for fire fighters
The fire is out for another day.

In loving memory of my Father, a dedicated volunteer firefighter. I love you Dad.

Untitled
(Starla Antone)

Eternal idol, wither and die
Summer's gone
Silent Sam and porch light lit nights
Mystical thoughts weird purpose

Time to drop
Slumber, wake not
Fall back dance with shadows
Spin, scatter about
Become one

Perfect lips, webs of entrapment
Too soon to be discovered
Too young to grow old

To all those crazy people in Fort Erie, Ontario. You know who you are.

Age: 16
Address: c/o P.O. Box 357, Crystal Beach, ON, L0S 1B0
Born: Buffalo, New York, August 14, 1977, North American Indian. Goals/Aspirations: My goals have yet to be determined, however, I have an interest towards acting, modelling, public speaking and writing short stories/poems. My intentions are to complete Secondary school and two years of Community college. Life Accomplishments: Roles in the Native Community of Fort Erie: I have held the titles of: "Miss Mini" and "Miss Junior" Native Princess, 1989-90/1991-93. I represented the Native Community in parades, talent shows, "Miss Fort Erie" Annual Competition, etc. 1988-90, I participated in public speaking contests throughout the Fort Erie area and was runner-up in those competitions.

The Fish of the Sky

(Jeremy Barbaza)

Like bristles dipped in paint,
Stroking against the sky,
Together while in flight,
They call their awesome cry.

Circling high like vultures,
Double-U's soaring 'round,
Spotting food from above,
Then gliding to the ground.

The sky; like water, blue,
Yet it is always dry,
Birds are swimming creatures,
For they are the fish of the sky.

Dedicated to the fish of the sky . . . and those who admire them.

No Substance
(Troada Bastounis)

Fool with a brain
Love with no heart
Justify again
Your untimely start.

Soldier, you're brave
Doctor, you're smart
Had and gave
Your own corrupt heart.

Fool with a heart
Love with no brain
Do not start
Your slaying again.

Age: 17
Address: 3439 Parkwood Avenue, Windsor, ON
I was born and raised in Windsor, Ontario. I will complete my high school career next year and then hope to attend university. It is my goal in life to publish a book of poetry. The stars of heaven and clouds of the sky take my soul to the greatest heights of inspiration. Every day as I breathe, I see, I feel the world around me, I live a poem.

No More

(Brandy Berry)

There was a time
When everything was secure . . .
When everything seemed perfect.
I would wake up in the morning
With sunlight on my face,
And at night, fall asleep
With the moon looking down on me.
But now when I wake up
There is no sunlight,
Only rain.
When I sleep at night
The moon no longer looks down on me . . .
It laughs at my hurt . . .
Hurt caused by myself
That must be kept inside . . .
Something I have to endure.

There was a time
When everything was secure . . .
When everything seemed perfect . . .

No more.

To Joanne Churchill.

The Mime
(Chattell Blue)

He's soundless,
his motions speak.
He's happy, he's sad,
he seems so deep.
His face is white,
his eyes so bright.
His hands are moving,
his body is grooving.
He stoops down low, he jumps up high,
What I wanna know is, who is this guy?

The Pirate
(Kyla)

The pirate of the seven seas
Has iron joints instead of knees
One leg is gone, so he has a peg
This he calls, "me wooden leg"
He's lost an eye; his hair is long
It's curly, black, and doesn't seem to belong
Around the face so mean and cruel
And he calls everyone he meets a fool
He keeps two pistols and one sword
By his side or in his hoard
The plume on his hat is bright red,
And all he meets are quite dead
The only thing he loves is his gold,
But when he's gone his hoard will turn to mold

To my teacher, Helen Dewell. For help and inspiration.

Age: 11
I have lived in the Yukon bush for most of my life. Except for the two years that I've spent in Dawson City. My parents use large huskies to run our trapline. I've got most of my schooling by correspondence schooling. I can also play clarinet very well. I stay at our friends' commercial fishcamp in the summer. I like to bake fancy desserts that involve beaten egg whites. I've baked since I was six, and I've always used a wood stove. Well, for those who've read this, I hope you've found it interesting.

Behold

(Lisa Boothby)

Behold the beauty of the light,
a wonder in the star-filled night.
A mystery in spangled bands,
a prophecy in maiden hands,
a rose, uncut without its thorns,
a star in which a story's born.
Behold the beauty of the light,
before that beauty takes to flight.
Behold the wonder of a scene,
a mystic tale within a dream.
A fairy's wings of gossamer,
a kitten's soft and fluffy fur.
A maiden beautiful and shy,
a young man preaching to the sky.
Behold the wonder of the scene,
before that wonder turns to dream.
Behold the beauty of the night,
a multitude of shining lights.
In heaven's bed a sun is born,
a shooting star falls weak and worn.
A child gazing in wonderment
is all too helpless to prevent
the mystic beauty of the night
from vanishing from human sight.
Behold.

Afraid

(Kristina L. Burrows)

Me afraid?
Afraid of what might someday be a war?
Afraid of happiness, knowing that sorrow lurks?
Afraid to care, scared that it might never matter?
Afraid of today because tomorrow might never come?
Afraid of friendship, for friendships do end?
Afraid to laugh, in fear of crying?
Afraid to be myself, because I'm not like others?
Afraid of loving and not getting love in return?
Afraid of trying, because I know I might fail?
Afraid to climb and end up falling to the bottom?
Afraid to talk because the right words might never come out?
Afraid of socializing, for people might not want me around?
Afraid of taking chances and ending up in regret?

Afraid of Death?
Or just Life itself?

Well . . . I'm afraid to answer.

whispers
(Erica Butler)

lipstick, skyscrapers, bow-ties,
9 to 5, BigMacs, the new Mustang
minimum wage, pension plan
[These things are not unnatural.]
[It is we who are unnatural.]
styrofoam, smokestacks,
automatic rifles, high heels,
bic lighters, magazines
[It is we who create unnature.]

Lifetime
(Erin Butler)

A dying rose
A bleeding nose
A broken heart
A world apart
A starless night
An endless flight
A need for love
The heavens above
Sinking deep
A restless sleep
A presence near
The sound of fear
Tears in a flood
The copper of blood
A world on fire
Floating higher
Asleep on the street
The puzzle complete
A dreaded disease
The fighting has ceased
Loving your brother
Forsaking all others
Unleashing hate
Learning your fate
A whisper, a moan . . . Ending alone

For you—I know they never really listened. I hope you feel better now.

King Overlooking Linoleum
(Craig Cardiff)

With the earthy smell of
the ancients rushing up from
beneath a pair of half-sitting squatting legs; he
wondered about his life.
Through each peristaltic contraction
of unwanted matter; he
pondered the great Meaning
the problems with the theory of relativity
the spectacular fly-leavings on the bright
wall(flower) paper.
Was he content with 2.3 children?
Was the work ethic so deep, deep
deeply ingrained that to wish for a crown
instead of a name tag brought yellow bile
to his muddy white-blue collared throat?
His vicious thoughts were brought to a murmur
by the slapping of paper and
drowned by the vacuum of water.

For Frank Herbert.

Age: 17
Telephone: (519) 746-3939
My main goal is to learn. I've gotten some stuff published and won a few local literature competitions. I've always held the opinion that I won because the judges saw something of themselves in the poems. I hate this. I don't want to write mirrors for people to fawn. Introspection maybe. I go to high school and slept in a Burger King with an 85 cent cup of coffee in Spain during the Feria celebration.

All Things Are Connected

(Erin Carney)

It is night, and time that I must sleep, yet I cannot.
I lie so still that only the barest breath
Seems to escape my lips.
Outside my window the great tree speaks to me;
And slowly I let the bonds of this Earth slip away.
I join the beings who feel the power of this night.
After all, I am kindred to the wind, protected of the wolf;
I am free to roam the night
And call upon its mysteries.
My sister the Moon calls to me,
And my brother the River serenades the passing of time,
But tonight, time has no meaning,
For this eve is all that ever was,
All that ever will be.
Still, the infinite moments pass in the blink of an eye;
And I drift suspended.
My reality hangs delicately,
In between my mother, the Earth, and my father, the Sky.
I run with the wind,
Howl with my brethren,
And dance with the Fae.
I am the One,
All of they are the Only,
And until the sun
The Circle is complete.

Address: 774 Clements Court, Kamloops, BC, V2B 8C2
Telephone: (604) 579-5565
I realized early what an important form of communication literature could be and began writing young, turning my focus towards poetry when I entered high school. "All Things Are Connected," written in 1993 during the summer of my 16th year, will be my second published work, the first being "Yesterday, She Smiled," published by the Canadian Coalition for the Rights of Children in conjunction with the United Nations Year of the Family. Concerned about a wide range of issues, I plan to receive a degree in Education and enter the field of alternative education, exploring non-traditional teaching and learning methods.

Who?

(Crystal Chaikowsky)

There is a man who's famous for what he does in our world.
Yet no one has ever seen him, not one has looked upon his face.
But stories tell us of this old and bearded man.

Who is this man whom we should give our attention to?
Who is this man who steals our children's hearts?
Yet he is not a thief, he is a good man with a giving smile.

Who is this man whom we trust deep within?
Who is this man who lives so far away, but so close at heart?
How can we trust this stranger who we've never known?

There is a man who gives much more than he receives.
Yet he does not question, because smiles never question.
But who has seen this famous smile? Surely not I.

Who is this man who has lived past his time?
Who is this man who to some has not yet lived one day?
Yet he seems so real to the ones who still believe.

Who is this man who does not reveal his face?
Who is this man who fills our heads with dancing sugar plums?
And who is he to control our minds and wishes?

NOW I ASK . . .

Who is this man whom we call Saint?
Who is this Jolly Nicholas?
          this bowl full of jelly,
          this nose like a cherry.

Who is this Santa Claus?
WHO?

My Kitchen

(Elizabeth D'Angelo)

There's no point kidding myself any longer,
I just can't get the knack of it; I think
there's some secret society which meets in
dark cafeterias to pass on the art
from one member to another.
Besides,
it's so personal preparing food for someone's
insides, what can I possibly know
about someone's insides, how can I permit myself
to invade your body?
I'll try, yes I'll try,
but if anyone watches me, I'll scream.
Maybe I'm handling a tomato wrong,
how will I know?
Confused, I stand in my complicated kitchen
and imagine the salads and souffles that will
never be.

I am a grade 9 student at Lakeshore Catholic High School in Port Colborne, Ontario. My career goal is to be a high school teacher and a writer. I enjoy writing with mystery stories the most.

Anticipation

(Shelly Dawydiuk)

It is winter, and the snow falls
Gently, lightly, from the sky.
The clouds are a soft, billowy grey,
And only time crawls by.

It is late, and the world is sleeping
Peacefully, quietly, through the night.
But listen! Can you hear it?
A tiny voice, so soft, so light.

It is Spring! It is working, toiling,
Pushing its way up through the snow.
It is a quiver, a whisper, forging a path,
Desperately trying for its face to show.

The sun is rising, a cock is crowing,
Nudging the world up from its sleep.
Rays of warm light wash over the landscape.
Is what I hear from the tree a peep?

Why, yes! It is a baby songbird,
Uncertainly chirping from its loft.
Ah! See how it tries to get airborne?
'Tis a good thing the landing is soft!

Look over there! Do you see that glimmer,
Abruptly placed in the blanket of white?
It is a tulip! And there is another!
Basking, warming in the beams of light.
Spring is finally here!

To Mom, because she has always loved spring.

Age: 13
Grade 8 as of September 1994, a published poem in another book, several awards for singing, violin, speech arts, flower arranging, posters, essays, poems, and short stories. Even though a lot of the people I know want me to be a poet or a novelist, I want to be a music teacher or be in an orchestra.

The Snowman

(Jill DeGrood)

I wish I were a snowman
So big and round and tall
I wouldn't have to brush my teeth
or go to sleep at all.
But maybe Mr. Snowman
is wishing he were me.
For I'll be here when summer comes,
but where will Snowman be?

Raven

(Candice Donnelly)

Raven
Feathery, jet-black
Drifting, swooping, resting
Flapping his large wings
Bird

Age: 9

The River

(Lisa Mae Edmonds)

The rhythm of the river flows through my body
Joining with my heartbeat to form a harmonious union
A pulse that is steady and comforting
I feel on my face the mist rolling off the river's surface
And I watch the fog tumble gracefully down the mountain
To surround me at the water's edge
A soft blanket protecting me from reality
I am one black spec in a world of billions
Yet I refuse to not be heard
Emptying out my lungs with a loud cry
I shout to the world of my existence
The river is my equal, flowing determined and strong
I can hear its breathing and listen to its words
For the river, old and wise, has seen many things
By listening to the river, I find out about myself
And the meaning of my life

Tears

(Shari Feuz)

My heart is flowing, no longer does it beat,
for it has melted in this tragic heat.
It's gushing aches inside of me,
causing the destruction of my once sound anatomy.
Throughout the canals of my interior,
pours forth my now liquid core,
racing to escape from its captivity,
as does a river in its quest for the sea.
Even more tormenting now as it swells,
it reaches my eyes, turning them into wells.
And like a pail that can hold no more,
my heart cascades and my face becomes a flooded shore.
Pain has surfaced, there for all to see,
as my innocent flesh bears the evidence of my heart's tragedy.

Abusing Love
(Bryan Fordham)

Take that!
And that, you dear sweet child,
how dare you lie to me!
I am your mother,
you'll give me respect when you talk to me.
It broke the skin.
The bleeding has stopped.
Now you go out to play.
Remember this my little one,
be careful what you say.
Just cover it up with sleeves that are long
and forget that it is there.
I'll never do a thing like that again,
my darling child I swear!
Your broken leg will soon be healed
and you can run and play.
Remember this my little one,
be careful what you say.

Youth
(Renée Friedland)

Youth.
so perilous,
so frightening,
is it possible that years from now this will be a cherished
 and clung-to memory? that I will hunger for that which I now despise,
reaching deep into the depths of my soul for that which I can
no longer have,
Yet here when it is mine I do not welcome or even embrace it,

NO.

i shun it, hide from it,
such is my life,
such is the devil, fate.
i am lost, seemingly forever in this vast world of conformism,
prejudice.
this consumes me,

WHY?

do i have <u>no</u> say?
is it not <u>MY</u> choice?
You have no answer.
i have no answer.

confusion

i am scared.
i am alone.

<u>I</u> am youth.

Who's to Blame

(Amanda Frost-Hunt)

Lazy summer afternoons
I spend listening to the latest tunes
While others try to do the same
They are killed. Who's to blame?
When I go inside for a snack,
Across the world, others are under attack.
Why this happens, how, I wonder.
Their life is ended with a crash of thunder.
When the sun sets, I go inside,
While others search for a place to hide.

To my Father, for always encouraging me to try new things.

Age: 12
Address: 213 Beaton Place, Ft. McMurray, AB, T9K 2B1
Telephone: (403) 743-2876
I live with my parents, my sister, Sandra, and my dog, Banjo. I live in Ft. McMurray, Alberta, and I am attending Timberlea Public School. My hobbies are drawing and gymnastics. My goals for the future are to get a scholarship to university and become a doctor.

Reason of Insanity
(Alicia Garlock)

He grips my wrist, pulls me back and whispers in my ear.
He smiles a lopsided grin the one i found so sweet.
i can smell the whisky on his breath, i don't want him near.
i look for some place to run, but no one's in the street.

He pulls me back into the alley where no one dares to tread,
the grin turns to leer and his look to pure hate.
My voice quivers in fear as i ask if he wants me dead—
his answer? This, my dear, is simply your fate.

i struggle with him, it seems to no avail.
He laughs mockingly at my pounding fists.
i'm whimpering, i hate my weakness, i know i'll fail.
My tears now mingle, are one with the mist.

Everything i ever dreaded has now become so real.
He took my life and mind that night, not just my body.
i forget how to think for myself, or even how to feel.
My life is worthless, mind a blank, self cheap and shoddy.

For Barbara, who always seemed to understand.

Never Thank a Thenk
(Kevan Gilbert)

Never thank a thenk,
'Cause if you do,
A thenk will think,
About the things he thunk.
And if a thenk thinks his thunks,
He'll do the things the thenk has thunk,
And a thenk thinks terrible things.

To my Mom, who inspired me to enter the poetry contest.

Untitled

(Greg Gilkes)

Anger is red.
It sounds like roaring lions.
It tastes like bitter grapes.
It smells like a burning piece of plastic.
It looks like a speeding train.
It makes you feel like screaming.

A Chronic Seduction

(Jocelyne Gingras)

His sharp belligerent voice,
echoed through her crying.
A grin to get in,
no resistance.

His profound breathing,
her loud cries,
both not heard.

Plunged deep in her heart,
a beat too slow.
A chronic ending,
over and over without control.

Burned to ground,
how fast they go.
No one to blame,
but the optimistic minds,
minds of women.

Women,
Women faced with a chronic seduction.

Wonder

(Amy Goerzen)

I have many many questions.
Such as, why are people called pedestrians?

Why can't ostriches learn to fly?
And why can no one touch the sky?

Where is the edge of outer space?
Why does a clock have a face?

Another is why do dogs love to lick?
And why does glue make things stick?

Why are monsters always hairy?
And what, may I ask, is a fairy?

How a web does a spider make?
What is the secret to baking a good cake?

I have many many more.
Questions, questions, questions galore!

A Gift for You

(Christine Gorab)

Floods lift up their voices
Trees clap their hands
Flowers sing their psalms
Rocks stand at attention
Sparkling fountains of mercy immerse the nations
Fires of love call to be quenched
Shadows sleep silently on the snow
Rainbows and clouds dance together
Mountains stretch out their hands
Volcanos stomp their feet
    Just look
        Just listen
It's all for you

I am thankful to God of all creation, beauty and joy.

Age: 17
Telephone: (705) 526-5045
I am a 17-year-old high school student from Midland, Ontario. I love writing, visual art, dancing and performing arts. My other hobbies include painting, soccer, tennis and running. In my spare time, I enjoy working with children, teaching art and trying new activities. I love writing poetry mostly for the enjoyment of words and the love of the art. I enjoy writing and speaking in Spanish and French. I am an avid traveller. I delight in experiencing new and different cultures and viewing exciting places.

Untitled

(Ronda Gress)

The life that's free
    but does not live
The eyes that see
    but are blind as dirt
The ears that listen
    but do not hear
The hands that touch
    but do not feel
The heart that's full
    but is all alone
The sand that flies
    but is still in stone
The love that's full
    but left empty
The smile that's happy
    but deep inside cannot bear
The life that's living
    but will die in despair

My Magic World
(Gabriella Halasz)

In my magic world, time is still.
Colours are vivid and breathtaking.
Children jump and play together.
The sun always shines like fire.
Tears never fall; hatred is unknown.
People of all races are equal.
Unicorns and castles are real.
The trees grow as high as the sky.
The moon is a magician's wand.
The stars are like bright opals.
Birds sing—their melodic voices
reaching to the ends of the earth.
Dreams come true.
There is peace, joy, and happiness.
The road to happiness and eternity is at hand.
Nothing you do is wrong.
Hurt and fear are forgotten.
You are free.

Smells

(Elizabeth Harris)

The perfume of a bank of thyme,
Arises to the air with time.
The smell of leaves in autumn air,
Will send the bear into his lair.
The smell of salt at lowest tide,
Would force a crab to run and hide.

Crisp bacon on the stove to fry,
Sends a subtle smell into the sky.
Aroma sweet of baking bread,
Gets little children out of bed.
Fresh beans of coffee newly ground,
Brings morning toast buttered and browned.

To my friends and family, especially Jackie Worton and my Mom, for their encouraging support.

Dandelions
(Inez Hoeree)

There is an old woman
who lives down the street from me
who wears dandelions in her hair
(she says they make her appear more youthful)

Each morning, without fail, as dawn breaks,
she's in her patchwork garden
picking her dandelions

She arranges them carefully amongst her silver strands
(to make her seem more youthful),
and as she finishes,
her burnished withered cheeks
lift upward

The tangled mass of leaves and splashes of lemon
which we spurn as worthless weeds
Turn this woman, in the autumn of her life,
into a lovely creature

Some days I wonder
what would happen to the old woman
who lives down the street from me
if there were no more dandelions

Hatred War

(Timothy Michael Holmes)

Civilians in the street are weeping;
mothers keep their babies sleeping.
The Elders see the country fall apart,
breaking from the lack of heart.

But the children do not notice this,
blinded by their innocence.
All they view are violent acts,
neighbourhoods demolished, as walls collapse.

People miss the food and healthy things;
still through it all a choir sings,
Deciding to live for today, as it could be the last,
singing of yesterdays, good times and the past.

But never able to forget,
wishing to be caught in the saviour's net.
Will this bad life ever quit?
Answer: "No; not yet."

For as one looks up to the sky,
they witness another plane go by.
And as this one dives to the ground,
he hears an unfamiliar sound:

It's the sound of nothingness,
he's used to screams of chaos.

Has war ended?!

To all the victims of wars past and of present day.

Sans titre

(Stéphane Intraligi)

Ô soleil,
Permets-moi de chanter, permets-moi de vivre.
Ô soleil,
Tu effaces les malheurs des matins de givre.

Ô soleil,
Qu'il ne se termine pas ton règne.
Tu as fait tant de merveilles
Depuis que mon coeur saigne

Ô soleil,
Tu me rappelles les bonheurs d'autrefois
Quand, à mon réveil,
En ta splendeur je me sentais comme un roi

Cher soleil,
Aujourd'hui est mon dernier jour.
Va, brille soleil;
Moi je dormirai pour toujours.

A mes deux profs de huitième année, Rachel Lachance et Elisabeth Jourdain.

La mort du garçon
(Valerie Intraligi)

Là, sur un beau lit de paille, un garçon.
Ses cheveux voltigeaient dans les airs, blonds,
d'une odeur sale et usée.

La lucarne, ouverte, faisait approcher la tempête,
affreuse et redoutable. Le soir-même, le garçon,
habillé d'une chemise déchirée, dormait paisiblement
sur son lit de paille.

Le matin, le garçon était encore couché
dans son lit de paille,
avec sa chemise déchirée.

Il était figé de froid.
Ses yeux étaient entrouverts et sa tête bougeait
de gauche à droite.

Il était là, mort, sans que personne ne le sache.

A tous les lecteurs, à mon professeur, Céline Dufour, et à ma mère, Enza.

Alone

(Emily Jacob)

in a thick crowd
    yet alone
unable to see the faces of adults
    only the staring eyes of children
wheeled past pitying strangers
    not in control of my actions
pushed through a sea of legs
    dependent on the kindness of others
shy smiles
    directed my way
annoyed glares
    as i pass
alone
    in a crowd

Changing Season

(Hasina Jamal)

It is autumn
The leaves are falling
The flowers are dying
And I am crying

But why am I crying? I guess it is because
I had to say goodbye
To the summer
To the flowers
To the birds

And I say hello
To the dancing leaves
To school
And to the changing season . . .

Miss You

(Rangina Jamal)

Thought I saw you in my dream
Thought that you had seen me weep
Hoped that you would never see
All the pain inside of me

Life had pressures and seemed cruel
Love didn't seem to be in reach
Buried our secrets deep
Left our friendship all in grief

As One Planet
(Melissa Kelly)

As we look up and
watch the twinkling of the lights
high up in the thing
we call the universe.

Knowing that there are
millions of worlds
out there.
And knowing that we are
only one little planet in this
great vast universe.

One planet.
A planet being torn apart.
Filled with war, hate, and discrimination
of all kinds, women, children, blacks, and whites.
No real differences, except for minor things.

Some can't even get along with their
families, neighbours, towns, and countries.

We, as a people, a human race
should, must, learn to put these
differences aside, and learn to live
in Peace.

For my family and friends.

Resistance
(Sarah Killien)

Never before have I felt such intensity
As this hatred burning my flesh.
I despise myself for feeling it
And letting him get his way.
He wants to hurt;
And he does.
And I am weak for letting him.
I feel the fire torching my veins,
Begging me to release it.
Yearning to be set free to damage and destroy.
I feel the pain of resistance,
And anger hardens my heart.
I will not let him win!
I will not!

For all my family and friends, especially my Mother and Sister.

Song
(Marla J. Landers)

Voice in a capsule
Fettered and tightened
To spring on a whim
Breaks from its bindings
Shudders and grasps
For a place in the wind
Fills a growing crevice
Mends a rifted ground
Jumps from lame confinements
To charge a ruling tide
Peaks in charmed defiance-
Challenge to survive

To Darcie, Kristal, Heidi, Mummy[2], Melanie, Petra, Melina, Dainty, Figgy Newton—the Psychic Friends Network.

Can You?

(Nicole Landry)

Can you see the water?
Can you see the rocks?
Can you see the sand and the boats along the docks?
Can you taste the salt?
Can you smell the air?
Can you hear the seagulls scattered everywhere?
Can you feel the spray from the waters of the sea?
Can you please come down to the shore with me?
Can you sense peacefulness in the waters of the deep?
Can you tell the memories that you shall always keep?
Can you hear the pounding of the waves upon shore?
Can you perceive the ocean as an open door?
Can you feel the warmth of the gently blowing breeze?
Can you also feel emotions hidden among the trees?
Can you see reflections of the golden sun above?
Can you sense the water is alive with summer love?

To my late Grandfather—Lionel Landry—and all loved ones.

Age: 15
Address: 487 Champlain Street, Apt. #18, Dieppe, NB, E1A 1P2
Telephone: (506) 383-4282
I am a big art lover and also a literature and poetry fan. I spend most of my time practising my writing, but I have other interests such as sports, children, nature and its belongings, including the sea and sea life and my key inspirations—whales and dolphins. I'm currently in the 9th grade at Anna Malenfant, my school in Dieppe, NB, but in school year '94-'95 I will be attending Mathieu Martin High.

whispering dreams

(Naida Lawrence)

whispering dreams
swirl across skyscapes
of a thousand hearts.
the wandering soul
finds solace in the
storms of winter's dreams.
without hope,
empty vessels of violent fear
clamour against
the walls of icy tears,
desperate for belonging.
withered scorn
descends on innocent ears,
corrupting.
the death of life,
the death of love,
the death of truth,
equality gone.

My Dog Sparky
(Désirée LeBrun)

My dog Sparky
loves to play
frisbee, baseball
any day.

My dog Sparky
swims like a frog
my dog Sparky
is the #1 dog.

To my dog, Sparky.

Age: 10

Love

(Sarah LeBrun)

What a beautiful thing
It makes me want to sing
When you hold me in your arms
Your oh so strong arms
And when we go to say good night
You grab me close and hold me tight
And when our lips are forced to part
You say, "I love you," straight from the heart
Now I've learnt my lesson, as we all should,
How not to be foolish, not that you would
How to cherish each moment that we would spend
When we were together, before you were dead
And now I sit down by the river bank
I'll wait forever; forever I'll wait
All is over; all is gone
Without your love, I could not live on.

To my loving family and caring friends.

Age: 11

Finding the Way

(Stacy Li)

Where two paths cross,
  Where eagles soar,
Where candles flicker,
  Where diamonds adorn,
In this place of refuge,
  Away from peril, jeopardy, danger,
Where the ocean meets the sea,
  Where the sun meets the horizon,
The boundary between day and night,
  Perseverance and might,
Where the water laps at the beach,
  Where the palm trees sway,
Where the children play,
  Where the heart beats soundly,
It's where you've hid your solace,
  It's where you smile for,
It's more than a measure,
  It'll take more than a day,
But to have a friend forever,
  Be with them every step of the way,
Through the deepest valley,
  Move mountains as you go,
To have a friend forever,
  You must be one yourself.

When I Look up at the Sky
(Nina Lichtman)

When I look up at the sky at night,
I see tiny specks of light
that shine and twinkle in the sky,
that guide travellers through the night.

Lots and lots of tiny dots,
I feel lost
among the endless skies with countless stars.

Gazing up at endless skies,
I feel like a tiny speck,
a tiny speck of sand along a hundred-mile beach.

And as the night goes on to twelve,
I dream of starlight beams of silk,
that stretch and stretch out through the night.

And once again the morning comes,
the endless banks of stars are gone.
But all the stars will return again,
for you and I to dream about.

Leaving Home

(Laura Light)

When somebody leaves your life, do they also leave your soul?
When somebody leaves you behind, why is your heart left un-whole?
You know some days they'll never leave,
But when they do it's hard to believe.
You think to yourself, you'll always be together,
And when they're gone, it's changed forever.
Your whole life gets turned up-side down,
But still you smile, you don't want to frown.
When somebody leaves your life, do they also leave your soul?
When somebody leaves you behind, why is your heart left un-whole?
A family is a family, and it's never supposed to part,
It just seems that the marriage and family never actually did start.
And when you come to think of it, it all just seems so wrong,
That the feelings between the family members are actually very strong.
Leaving home is hard to do, it's hard to leave behind.
When it comes to love and caring, these are very hard to find.
When somebody leaves your life, do they also leave your soul?
When somebody leaves you behind, why is your heart left un-whole?

To my family through all the tough times.

Age: 16
I live in a small country area north of a large city in Ontario. It is a beautiful area to sit back and relax and write. I am just finishing up Grade 11 in a rural high school. I enjoy English & Chemistry. I was inspired to write listening to the music of Cat Stevens and Canadian singer/songwriter/poet, Leonard Cohen. They both have beautiful voices and know how to put words to music. I hope to be a successful poet in the years to come.

The Lighthouse
(Carmen Loyer)

Massive and majestic, the illuminated lighthouse gleams like gold.
It guards the mighty mirrored seas.
It has saved sinking sailors from drowning in the wind-tossed waves.
It has warned cumbersome cargo ships against the seemingly deeply buried
 reefs.
A hero it is, but no medal has it ever been given.
It is the pentagon of peacefulness.

Attractive it is not.
But wait until storms and tempests shake your world to the foundations—
Then, radiant as an ascending angel, it stands—
Beautiful, solid, real.

Age: 15
Address: c/o 687 Arlington Drive, W. Palm Beach, FL, 33415, U.S.A.
I was born to career missionaries in Haïti. I am the second of four children. I enjoy riding, reading, and writing. I intend to go to university with the goal of becoming a corporate lawyer. I have toured quite extensively through the U.S. and Canada. I have found inspiration in the everyday lives of those people I have come into contact with. My parents' work has allowed me to see the diversities of this world and the need for strength. I hope in some way to change the lives of those around me by being an example.

Masquerade of Fate

(Patricia MacFadyen)

Proud comrades forced to shame,
A face forgotten; let alone a name,
Odd few, evil, led to undying fame,
Those who love are left with blame.
Blood shed through terror, long,
Gunshots fired amidst voices, strong,
Routes travelled with solemn songs,
Screams heard among fatal bombs.
Grief allowed; contradict victory,
Loss not showed; there lives integrity,
Standing tall for existing loyalty,
Bury the young in trenches, dirty.
Misty air, drugged to breathe,
Through the mines, death does seethe,
Grotesque so as not to believe,
The mountains of bodies soldiers leave.
Unity preceded by sad defeat,
Flesh burning in the wretched heat,
Cans of tin out of which to eat,
Triumph is but bitter-sweet.
Haunted by majestic dreams,
In which, perfect, the world seems,
With no gas, or smoke, or steam,
In which, visible, are stars that beam.
Conquered here is masked fate.

Dedicated to my Mother, Sisters, Anne and Melissa, Niece, Victoria, and friends, Sonja and Frances.

Age: 16
Address: 23 Pictou Road, Truro, NS, B2N 2R9
Telephone: (902) 897-0959
I was born in Montreal, Quebec, and lived there until the age of 10. From then on, I have lived with my family in Truro, Nova Scotia. I am presently attending Cobequid Educational Centre and am studying grade 11 courses. I hope to be a successful veterinarian in the future, with a possible career in writing books and poetry. I have won two previous competitions in poetry. One was in grade two, in association with the Laurenvale School Board in Laval, Quebec, and the other was in grade four, in association with the Greater School Board of Montreal.

Remember

(Edwin Mah)

As the soldiers departed,
Their flag was high.
When they arrived to fight the war,
Their flag was high.
Stealthily, they set foot on the battlefield,
Missiles being launched,
Millions of shooting stars,
Lit the sky as never seen before.
Gunshots were never ending,
Like a waterfall making its descent.
Soldiers hiding, waiting, fighting;
On the battlefields grew fear, remorse, and bravery.
Planes roaring and roaming the sky,
Plummeting to the ground like dead birds.
Tanks invading cities,
Carving their roads, and taking control.
Nothing going undetected;
Prepared to do anything.
Hiding, waiting, fighting;
The soldiers fought for their lives and died,
But their flag remained high,
In the shadow of the soldier.

I thank my family and friends who have helped me during difficult times.

Age: 14
Address: 75 Rouge Road, Winnipeg, MB, R3K 1J4
Telephone: (204) 831-6677
I am a person who enjoys travelling to new places; these include Hawaii, Paris and the Philippines. In school, I have performed well in Mathematics and like many of the subjects. Currently, I am in Senior 1 (Grade 9) and taking the I.B. Program at Westwood Collegiate. In my spare time, I read books and play sports. My two favourite sports are soccer and badminton. In the future, I will be pursuing a career in accounting.

Forever

(Nicholas McRae)

Cherries are red
Blueberries are blue
As long as I'm living
It will always be true
That the birds will be singing
In the morning when I wake
The sky will be blue
The grass will be green
And the sun will always come up
As nice as can be
Everything will be there
Still when I die
It will always be there
Like vans, cars, trucks, planes
And especially the animals
That I love the most

For my Mom, Maggie, Dad, Tom, Brother Jamie, and my dogs, Pepe and Rusty.

Haunted Dreams

(Amy D. Morris)

Into the darkness steals the Lady Night.
Filled with terror—an expression of fright—
She fades into the black; they become one:
She's darkness alone fleeing from the sun.
From her blood-red lips, her ebony hair,
And her moonlit eyes comes a haunting stare
That whisks one away to a land afar
Where music's the moon, the song is the stars.
Expressed are true love, passion, and romance
By dreamers, sole heirs to Lady Night's dance.
Venturing out into obscurity,
Deeper, more profound, are her dreams to me.
Then, in a flood of visions from tomorrow,
She is gone.
Her remains are dusky shadows.

Where Shadows Play
(Lisa Morris)

On a silent, dark night
The trees glow green with moonlight
I'm alone in the Dark, dark wood
Where Jack Frost has frozen my foot
For warmth, I walk into a cave
And it sweeps over me like a tidal wave
I have walked to where the shadows play
For nights and nights and days and days
I can't get out, no matter how
They won't release me now
I now belong to where the shadows play
I'm only a shadow for many nights and many days
They won't release me now, or ever

For my friend, Raman, my family, and my aunt Laurie, for helping with my writing.

The Song

(Rebekah E. Panschow)

It begins
A sad soft flowing sound
Conversation comes to an abrupt halt
They quietly glance around
Some move their pencils
Some stare at their shoes
As the bitter-sweet sound grows steadier
The room is filled with song
A sad song
Reminding them of disturbing times
The song begins to fade away
A silence fills the room
They look up
And begin to speak again

To all my friends at school, who helped inspire me to write this poem.

Masters of Music
(Hazel P. Penner)

The fairies' sad music,
Dazzling to hear,
Wafts on the breeze to my listening ear.
It rustles like leaves on a windy day,
It splashes like brooks as they sweep on their way.
It shines precious like diamonds,
It glitters pure as gold,
For the fairies' sweet music shall never grow old.

The harmonious notes drift over the sea,
Rising and falling, they're calling to me.
Regardless of what anybody might say,
I follow the music that leads to the bay.
There by the moonlight, I glimpse a radiant sight,
A large host of fairies is gathered by night.

Singing and dancing the hours away,
Their enchanting colours blend, from crimson to grey.
Slowly, as rays begin streaking the sky,
The fairies hastily wave a goodbye.

Now, their dances with music linger still in my mind,
And perhaps someday soon, the fairies again shall I find.

Heartbreak and Sorrow

(Candice Pickstock)

Is there no end?
Will I ever be able to see the light?
My dream's, future, shattered forever
And no one seems to care.
Heartbreak and sorrow
but still nothing there
In the end I can't despair,
feeling hurt and sorrow.

Perception

(Yolanda Poffenroth)

The silence
The black
The nothingness
A glint of silver
At the moon's illumination
Perceive the virtue
Inhale the calm
All is there
But we are blind
Anchored in all
All is found
All is lost
Anchors away.

For Grandma Marge, who I will never forget, Mom, Dad, and Garfield.

Wonderful Valley
(Krista Ann Power)

In the valley so high up above,
You envision you are a beautiful dove.
Peace is the meaning for this wonderful place.
When you go there you see a smile on every face.

The sun shines by day, the stars at night.
It's so magical it makes me feel bright.
That is why in the valley so high up above
You envision you are a beautiful dove.

A Blind Man's Prayer

(Marie Prill)

Is it true I will lose my sight?
Oh please, God, let me see the light.
I am scared, sad, and forlorn
Oh how I wish I was never born!
Is it true I will never see
A rose in bloom so gracefully,
The sunset as it starts to fade,
The sunrise coming from the shade?
Is it true I will be told
The autumn leaves have turned to gold,
Of the birds in the sky
Flying up there so high?
Oh please will someone say a prayer—
Or is it true, you just don't care?

To my grade nine Language Arts teacher, Mrs. V. Radke.

Mind-killer
(Robin Reese)

It has always been there
Power's cocoon
It waits for the weaker; it preys on the defenceless.
In crackling gunshots, spent mortar,
He, the soldier senses it . . .
Guiding faltering footsteps through enemy lines.

Born from the beginning of time
Eternity's child
Flooding every village and town
Prongs of terror
He, the soldier, prey to the predator . . .
Fortifying firepower to shield himself.

Mourners gather war's graveyard momentoes
History's echoing horrors
It was the engineer of these sorrows
The catalyst of controlled aggression
Gouging hallowed pockets in old soil
And coaxing our tears into grateful hands.

Imp or dictator
It is the mind's eternal menace
Clasping icy fingers
Round our frail spines
And twisting our wills
To its whim.
Fear.

Address: R.R. #1 Sunderland, ON, L0C 1H0
Telephone: (905) 852-9358
Robin Reese spends her free time writing, reading mysteries, doing sporting activities and looking after her animals. She has recently finished her first novella and has already started her second. Last year, she had her poem "Love Is . . . " in Durham Board of Education's *Muses of the Mind* and received a literary award at her grade eight graduation. She intends to continue her work throughout her years at Brock High School and University.

Duty

(Heather Richards)

Devastated by the fate in his presence,
manipulated from the passion he insisted,

quickly she sat, speaking slowly,
humming the unpredictable tune
going nowhere
the song
the woman.

Everything the family was about
he owned—
the game, the name.

Far out of view existed her pot of soup,
which bubbled, spilled sweet and recipied.
Boring it was served today, every day.

Eating, spitting, rude with disagreement
he gobbled her soup and drank her life.
Curiously, behind the desperate eyes
sat a respect for him.

Is it her fault she tastes her tears?

Love and Hate

(William Edward Rush)

Do I hate what I've become
Love what I haven't done
Living unsure promises unsung
Feelings trapped Yesterday's sorrow
Free to live maybe tomorrow

To anybody who finds themselves lost in life, not to give up hope! Kurt Cobain missed.

A Life of the Written Word
(Andrea Saber)

You were created through the toil of my pen.
From the voluminous conceptions rolling over in my mind,
you emerged in all your roughness.
I attempted to perfect you by altering your personality,
structure, and appearance.
I finally saw you through to adulthood; and as I stood
back to observe every component of your character, I
proudly realized that you were one of my greatest children.
You were the creative child among my various theological,
mysterious, romantic, and adventurous offspring.
When the awkward moment arrived, I nervously gave
periodic ownership to another.
From my trembling grasp, you were taken.
I then reflected upon your birth, your infancy, and finally, your
development toward adulthood.
When you did return to me, you had earned only what you had deserved
from you existence.
You were fragile again, with the painful addition of a
bleeding fraction placed upon your slight frame.
As a mother, I had deemed you flawless. Yet, I lovingly
accepted that you were not perfect.
Unique as you were, you would not stand alone. My pen had
given birth to another sibling for you.
I called her "My Poetic."

For Jacqueline, Rosa, Sabrina, Joan, Charlotte, and J. Doan. Thank you for the encouragement.

Existence

(Samia Sarkar)

Fearless, defiant stood the soul,
On a cliff overlooking the sea of life,
Sea breeze mocking his celestial calmness,
The setting sun embracing his homecoming,
All is placid—all is peaceful.

Then, as sudden as a wave crashing onto the shore,
He dove into the forbidden abyss—the sea of life.
Amazed, he looked up into the blue heavens,
Refused, he looked down.

He is no more an unfettered soul,
A mere earthling—no more tethered to the Supreme,
Struggle is the order of the day,
Suffering is its embryo,
Happiness is a distant thunder,
Such is existence.

Alas, he dove into the sea of life,
Alas, he was born.

To my parents, Dr. Sukhamoy and Shubhra Sarkar.

Age: 15
Address: 177 Brooks Place, Fort McMurray, AB, T9K 2E5
Telephone: (403) 743-1650
I was born in Birmingham, UK, in 1978 and have lived in Fort McMurray, Alberta, for the past 14 years. My past accomplishments include an Honourable Mention at the 1992 Canada-wide Science Fair and success at the Young Authors program of Alberta. My ambition is to have a career in the field of Medical Science. My literary inspiration came from my Grade 9 English teacher, Mrs. B. Proctor-Hartley. Among my favourite poets are William E. Henley, Edgar A. Poe, William Wordsworth, and William Shakespeare. I have written several short stories, essays, and poems, and would like to pursue my interest in literature.

Someday!

(Carrie Sawyer)

I lay quietly on my bed,
looking helplessly out my window.
I gazed at the stars above,
I was confused, alone, and scared.
Was my mother up there?
She wasn't in town, the country,
CANADA!
She was gone . . . DEAD!

I thought back to what my life would be like
if she hadn't passed away.
My thoughts ran through my head,
getting scrambled up . . . .
My thoughts were overflowing!

Tears began to make a stream
as they poured down my face.
I didn't get to know her . . . .
what was she like?
What would my life be like if she were alive?
All these questions will be a mystery to me . . .
forever!

I turn my back towards the window,
Someday in my life,
I will see my mother . . . .
SOMEDAY!

Me, Myself and I
(Crystal Schintz)

I am 10 years old
And tall I've been told.
I have chestnut brown hair
And really like to share.
My eyes are blue,
My parents' eyes too.
I really enjoy pets
And admire all vets.
I find poetry fun.
Once I have the title, I'm on the run.
I don't think I'll win this contest
But I shall try my best.
That's what I like about me, myself and I.

To my best friend, Sheri Gagnon, who convinced me to enter my poem.

Age: 10
Address: Box 727, Marathon, ON, P0T 2E0
Crystal is completing grade five. She has been writing poetry since the age of eight. She enjoys reading, pets, being with her friends and crafts. Crystal would like to be a poetic veterinarian when she grows up.

The Creek

(Amber Sheridan)

The creek is a rocky road
for the crystal rush of water,
where the fish all sing, play and
SPLASH!
An old rock gleaming,
wet from the creek,
loves the feel of the water
slipping around his sides,
splashing over his head,
rushing in his ears.
Oh, thc crcck holds many sccrcts
you and I will never know.

To my grade six class at St. Mary's School, Lethbridge, Alberta.

Life's Loves?
(Alanna Sinclair)

The barren desert's foolish winds have sighed,
Their longing, yearning for living begun
But nothing would stir; none have e'er survived
The watching gaze; the vermilion sun

These rancid winds searched all throughout the air
Deaf ears so sharp paired with blind eyes so keen
Ignored the storms of warning—please, beware!
So found the seeds of man, ne'er before seen

Pride, lust, sloth, anger, gluttony and greed,
Born to the motherland on wings of chance,
Once there, took root, grew twisted with need
And writhed through wildly, a civilized dance.

Life's loves had raped the earth; left needs un-met
Yet filled empty winds—to brim with regret

Dedicated to Mr. Finnie, Mrs. King, Mish Carol Murray and Multi-Youth Productions—thanks!

Age: 16

My Father
(Carolyn Sloan)

We stand together
You watch me grow
You protect me from my fears
You're my Father.

Beyond the Gates
(Rory James Soucy)

Beyond the gates lie dreams and hopes and wishes of all kinds
Beyond the gates are creations protruded from the mind
Beyond the gates is laughter and giggles seemingly everywhere
Beyond the gates are beings and creatures all living there
Beyond the gates is peace and joy within everyone
Beyond the gates imagination plays games and has fun
Beyond the gates is where your mind's peaceful thoughts roam free
Beyond the gates things are as beautiful as they can be
But throughout time these gates have closed, lost is the only key
Because people eventually have ceased to believe

Thou Shalt Not Kill

(Kelly Speedie)

God doesn't make the rules,
not any more.
The law is no longer intact
when we go to fight the war.

We go to defend our county;
we do it to survive.
It's an act of loyalty
so we can stay alive.

Once you're sent there to fight,
there's no turning back.
There's no way to defend yourself
from the bullets and the attack.

When you're on the field
the soldiers are all the same;
they fight to survive
in the horrid game.

And when it's done,
have you proved anything?
Did you make them all see?
Did you become King?

As the days go by,
remember still
what the Bible says, "Thou shalt not kill."

Hope

(Julie Sutherland)

Perhaps
with the hope of more
there is something to strive for.
Perhaps
with the chance of better
we'll send that letter.
Perhaps
with goals to achieve
we'll have reason to breathe.
Perhaps
with reachable desires
we'll light our souls' fires.
Perhaps
with dreaming of leisure
we'll get pleasure.
Perhaps
with the determination to succeed
we'll get what we need.
Perhaps
with the yearning from our heart
we'll bother to take part.
Perhaps
with the reward of being content
that letter will be sent.

A Bird's Song
(Heather Switall)

Listen, can you hear them chirp?
They are calling us.

Look, can you see them staring?
They are watching us.

They are trying to teach us,
But they grow weary.
For we do not listen,
To anyone but ourselves.

We call ourselves intelligent,
But the wars have not stopped.

We call ourselves brave,
Yet we put others down.

We must stop the wars.
Only then will we be intelligent.

We must become friends.
Only then will we be brave.

We must listen to the birds.

Proud of What?

(Brooke Tesluk-McDonald)

Lying here about to die,
As sweat pours down my face.
I can't cover my ears hard enough to stop it,
To stop that horrifying scream of others who
wait for me.

Pride?
Proud of suicide.

I can't close my eyes tightly enough to blind it,
To blind the sight of others around me who are
tasting death.

Pride?
Proud of murder.

I battle for whom? They make us hate all.

Pride?
Proud of hatred.

We fight to win and stay alive.
But for whom? I cannot see nor hear
my grandchildren.
I hear only the war and feel only the pain.
The war is over, yet the pain lives on.

Pride?
Proud of what?
Murder, Suicide, and Hatred.

Yes.
They call us heroes.

Reflections

(Tara-Anne Thorarinson)

I look into the mirror,
but I see to my surprise
a wholly different person
looking deep into my eyes.

The carefree little girl I saw
when I was four or five
has now become a young woman
fighting to survive.

It's really sort of scary
that time has gone so fast
for what then I called the present
has now become the past.

I look into the mirror
and looking back at me
is the face of a young lady
where the little girl used to be.

To my Mother and Grandmother, who have always cared.

The Ghost Am I
(Caroline Tidman)

The ghost am I of winds that die,
Alike on land and sea,
O hear me now, O hear me now,
Send one small glimpse to me.

The wind will now to me obey,
The flowers in the garden sway,
The light of moon across the way,
Let me die another day.

I wander here to there at night,
My face is a great ghostly fright,
My body sheds transparent light,
My figures are dim and ghastly white.

For my Family, who inspired me to start writing.

Age: 9
Address: Box 5394, Drayton Valley, AB, T0E 0M0
I'm about 4'6" tall and have brown hair with a hint of red and brown eyes. I enjoy reading, drawing, and playing board games. My goals in life are to become a writer and a paleontologist.

Facets

(Josephine Tidman)

I am the stars' child,
I share warmth.
I am the sun's child,
I bring light.
I am the moon's child,
I reflect.
I am the wind's child,
I bring change.
I am the water's child,
I am pure.
I am nature's child,
I enjoy beauty.

To Debbie, a very dear friend.

Age: 13
Address: Box 5394, Drayton Valley, AB, T0E 0M0
I am about 5'4" and have green eyes and brown hair. My interests at the present time are horses, drawing, reading, writing and music.

If Ever a Fire
(Shannon Toback)

If ever a fire, what would I do?

I'd crawl out of my bed
and onto the floor—
make my way quickly
to the bedroom door.

I'd feel the door
and if it was hot
I'd think to myself,
"Nah, better not."

I'd climb to my window
and open it wide
then jump through
toward the other side.

I'd jump to the ground
and run to the street
then wait for my family
'cuz that's where we'd meet.

Through the doors they'd stumble
to the neighbours I'd run
I know what to do
I'd call 9-1-1.

Dedicated to all little children in hoping they will learn from this poem.

Love of Our Mothers

(Michael Trolly)

Love of our mothers
Living still beyond the years
In memories of care, which could
Ne'er be repaid
Love of guidance, teaching and trust
That patience not forsake
Love of our Mothers
How often we forget
The kindness of their presence, which
Will be until the end.

Love of our mothers which
Guided us through youth
The road be blurred before us
They showed us where to turn.
Love that raised us to adult,
Helped us raise our own.
Love of our mothers
How often we forget
The kindness of their presence, which
Will be until the end.

Written for my Mother (when nine years old) after reading hymn "Faith of Our Mothers."

Do Not Forget
(Anita Turner)

In 1914, men went to war.
It was our freedom they fought for.
They battled with honour, courage and tears
In those cold and broken years.

The peace they died for did not last.
It seemed to slip right from their grasp
And men were called to fight once more.
To take up guns and hear them roar.

Two soldiers sat on guard that day.
Each trained to stay and not give way.
Two men whose lives were on the line.
As thoughts of home helped pass the time.

Men blindly ran and fired shots.
Praying that they would never be caught.
But bullets flew and good men died.
Their bodies rested, we heard the sighs.

And those who journeyed home once more,
Who left the cold and bitter war,
And those who died and don't regret,
Ask, please, that we do not forget!

Age: 12
Address: 116 Mayfair Close, Airdrie, AB, T4A 1T5
Telephone: (403) 948-0078

Harmony

(Josh Turner)

As the river runs into the sea,
In my mind I paint pictures
Of harmony.
There is beauty and pleasure everywhere
But so few people stop to care.
The trees, the birds all as one.
The moon, the stars and the sun.
When it's dark or when it's light.
In the day or in the night.
We need to stop and look around
And listen to the many sounds
Of life.
Take time to look.
Take time to care.
Our faithful world deserves its share.

Age: 14
Address: 116 Mayfair Close, Airdrie, AB, T4A 1T5
Telephone: (403) 948-0078

The Pollution Solution

(Stephanie Vanderweide)

Garbage, garbage everywhere.
All of us are in despair.
We've got to find other ways
To preserve our earth for future days.

Here's a suggestion you might follow:
Don't dump things the earth can't swallow.
Batteries, spray cans, chemicals and acids
Require special handling methods.

So if you love this world of ours,
Be sure to follow the three R's.
REDUCE, RE-USE, RECYCLE!!

To my Family, who live the "Three Rs" daily.

Age: 12
I am a 12-year-old identical twin who enjoys reading and school. This is the second successful poem that I have submitted. The first poem was an award-winner at the Canadian Legion competition. I Hope to be successful writer and actress in the future.

In Memory of You
(Stephanie Villemaire)

The gold box,
the square cards,
hearts red like the fire in your eyes,
diamonds like the jewel you were to me,
spades that drove through my soul
when you left.
The high blue sky
and the flowers
. . . flowers, you remind me of a flower,
and we always loved you.
And at the end you showed
your most beautiful colours,
even to those
who needed to see them most.
And then you were gone,
like a flower at the end of summer,
but
we all know that flowers bloom again . . . .
And I hope to see
your rainbow of love again,
when I bloom,
hoping that when we meet
at the golden gates of Heaven,
we can pick up where we left off
and play a game of cards.

In memory of my Grandfather, sadly missed, much loved.

IT was tragic . . .

(Kyla D. Wendell)

IT was tragic, but then again, **IT** had to be.
The day she decided to tie the rope to the rafters
and then around her neck,
letting her body dangle from **IT**.
The usual note saying how
"nobody understands me,"
accompanied her death.
Her parents who never gave a damn
were consumed by uncontrollable sobs.
The friends she never had all attended the funeral,
as though **IT** was some kind of social gathering.
And **IT** always seemed to me that everybody spent more time
mourning her death,
than they ever did
cherishing her life.

Highway South
(Daniel Wood)

From the bright darkness
There came a voice.

Calm, and slow with
Realization, but without
A hint of fear.

He examined the smouldering butt
And when sure no more smoke
Could be drawn, he scratched his
Bald head and spoke.

The baritone voice carried well,
And even in the reaches of
The corridor,
The others heard.

Though not able to see,
They knew, and were unusually
Silent.

"I'm sorry,"
And then he rode
The lightning.

Age: 16
Telephone: (902) 667-4072

Bigfoot

(David Yau)

In the forest, on the ground,
You might see some footprints
Left without a sound.

They measure about 29 inches long
And 11 inches wide,
When you tell others what you saw
They would think that you lied.

On the mud, on the sand,
You may see some imprints
Upon the land.

Those footprints were surely not made by humans
There is evidence right there,
Stuck in the imprints
Was some long brownish hair.

What could have done this, it must have been a beast,
A beast with big feet
That's what we know at least.

The beast shall be called "Bigfoot"
It's the only logical name.
It has to be non-fiction, unless it was a prank
By some little brat, gone insane.

To my loving Parents, Andrew and Rina Yau, and my Sister, Jo-Anne.

Age: 13
Address: P.O. Box 3425, Airdrie, AB, T4B 2B7
David Yau is a grade 8 French Immersion student currently attending École Airdrie Middle School. At the young age of 13, David excels in both regular school education and extra curricular activities, including: leading his soccer team in becoming the 1990 champs, designing the school yearbook cover for 1992-1993, earning three first class honours in guitar competitions, winning a silver and a bronze medal in soccer tournaments, winning two first-place ribbons in Airdrie's swim club, and getting his poem "Bigfoot" published in *Scaling the Face of Reason*. David plans to attend the University of Calgary, exploring medical sciences.

Past, Present, Future
(Jo-Anne Yau)

Emotionless, unfeeling grey faces,
They come, and they go
Not a word passes through cold lips,
Not a blessing to bestow.

The same ones pass by
Day after day
Yet monotony never surfaces
No one finds it blasé

What, then, is their purpose
Wandering the downtown streets
Through rain or snow
Or sizzling concrete?

While feeding on the 9-to-5 buzz
The pattern refuses to die,
Slaving zombies in monstrous cars
And buildings reaching a bleak sky

To bend over backwards
And still get stabbed in the back
This is our child's destiny?
To be a workaholic maniac?

To bring the zombies back to life
To cleanse their souls, purify
For life's too short to waste as so
And the heart's always too young to die.

With love to my Parents, Andrew & Rina Yau, my Brother, David, and my Friends.

Age: 16
Address: P.O. Box 3425, Airdrie, AB, T4B 2B7
Telephone: (403) 948-6688
Born in 1978 in Calgary, Alberta, Jo-Anne Yau's love for fine arts has won her numerous commendations. At age four, she performed on the piano at the school talent show. At eight, she won a community short story contest. Now, at 16, Jo-Anne has nine trophies from musical competitions and several writings published in the community newspaper and the school literary anthology. A second-year Student's Union Vice-President and an experienced traveller, Jo-Anne plans to attend the University of Calgary, exploring the biological sciences.

CANADIAN ADULTS

The Stolen

(Michael Abraham)

Will you believe me?

Katie,
I knew you when

your eyelids
were chafed with
first efforts.

I've seen
the sapphire alleys
that hide
behind them.

I know that you were stolen:

Gilly hid you
inside her belly
and tip-toed past
the sleeping angels.

Now,
if you go to the window
you'll see, sometimes
they weep
at your absence,

but when
the sun shines hot,
they know
how much
you are loved.

For Katherine Shannon MacLeod.

Fall from Grace

(James D. Adamson)

Cast out of the temple,
I wander alone
In a world where your beauty
Through the shadows shines
Like an angelic beacon
To remind me
Of Paradise Lost.
I hunger for your touch,
To once again feel your form
Beneath my weight,
To be baptized
In the warmth
Of your holy love.
Oh, woman,
Giver of life,
I, man, thy servant
Beseech thee
Restore to me my soul,
That which vanished
With your favour.

Time Heals
(Margaret Addison)

You say you are leaving me,
but you are wrong.
You will still remain here with me
In my mind
When your body is gone.
Your words may sometimes,
By accident,
Slip from my lips
Like long-forgotten echoes,
But echoes fade away
And are lost to the disease of time.

To my ever-patient Mum, Helyn Bulmer Anderson, who is always there for me.

Born in Truro, Nova Scotia. Graduate of Nova Scotia Teachers College. Works for one of Canada's Largest Insurance Companies. Married with two children. Breeds and shows Shetland Sheepdogs under the name of Miamar Kennels.

Casino

(Ian Aho)

Joker smiles, jacks are wild,
52 cards appear before me.
The dealer grins as I win again
the cards seem to flow like a river into the sea.
A number is called, "BINGO!" is yelled,
and the winner smiles with glee.
The dice are thrown, snake eyes is shown
hurry up cash the cheque to pay the fee.
The bass keeps the beat, the beer runs to your feet.
The money continues to flow into a black hole.
The change ching-a-ling-lings, the slot machine rings
and slowly draws you down into misery.
Your last dime, what a crime.
The Joker smiles with no pity.

The Appointed Hour

(Brenda Allan)

Can we get beyond politeness here?
Can we go past the chit-chat
    and the well-modulated voice?
Can we cut to the gut?
To the churning stomach and the why—
To the anger we push down—
    because we still feel "in public."

We wear our public faces
    for the most part.
Every so often they crack
    and the tears run out.
But we soak them up
    and throw them away.
(They belong in the soft shoulder of a hard embrace)

Oh—I guess we hit a nerve.
But the hour's up,
We'll see you next time

. . . next time . . .

Address: 3075-79 Street, Edmonton, AB, T6K 3N2
I am a woman, married, raising four children. I work in a college library, take on-going courses, run, read and write. My writing is mostly a private compulsion.

Robin's Song
(D.L. Allen)

Oh broken wing so painful now
And heavy was the fall
This world all white and colder still
A wish that I were tall

A time to think of warmer days
How gentle was the sun
Bathing in the silver dew
Till morn was all but done

Soaring with the wind so high
An eagle I'd become
And hiding from the dancing rain
So fresh when it had run

"A time to live, a time to die"
How strange that saying seems
Yet not for me, these weary eyes
Must close and dream sweet dreams

Lone Wolf

(Val Allen)

High on a hill-top
Howling to the moon
A lone wolf mourns the passing
Of his mate, all too soon.

With budding life inside her
She stumbled from his side
A hunter's bullet took her life
For possession of her hide.

The lone wolf sent a message
To his brothers far and near
That the one who prances upright
Is a beast they all should fear.

So when you hear the howling
And your child scans the hill
You can tell him its a warning
Of man's greed and need to kill

Human Rights
(Hop B. Anderson)

Why struggle for human rights
Without cease among mankind?
Because there is no good relation
But selfishness and oppression.
The theme of Human Rights exists
Only when bad habits subsist.
That is true but how to stop them?
No way, there is no more confidence.
Force however could be helpful
That the U.N. power is trustful.
Their target is to protect humanity,
We hope true peace will come finally,
Consequently no problem of human rights.
Oh my God! Why wink at mournful sights?
Enlighten the covetous and blind persons,
So as to return human rights to humans.

My best regards to His Excellency Mr. Boutros Boutros-Ghali, Secretary General of the United Nations Organization.

Address: 1414 Aird Avenue, Montréal, QC, H1V 2V3
Hop B. Anderson (White Cloud): Ex-professor, poet/writer, cultural res. analyst. Degree: BA, MBA. Diploma: Eng. Lit., Adv. French. Awards: Winner in Canadian, American & French poetry. Co-author: Anthologies *Toward Freedom & The New Garden's Flowers*. Author: *Trilingually-composed Poems*, *Melodies of the Heart*, *Humorous Stories & Easy Essays*, *The Golden Book*, etc. Works also published in magazines. Ideology: Helping the poor is a real good deed and very needed.

Dreams
(Janet Anderson)

Dreams are something all of us have
    Sometimes it's all we've got
You can be rich, or you can be poor
    It's something that needn't be sought

You can dream of riches, or you can dream of love
    No matter what the extreme
For it may come true, or it may not
    For a dream is always a dream

Grandparents' Day
(Julie André-Dennison)

Today is a special and wonderful day,
When granddaughters and grandsons gather to say:
"I love you Grandpa with all my heart,
Even though we are now apart."
The beautiful words you love to hear,
Instead of my weeping and shedding of tears,
I want you to know that right from the start,
You're hearing the sounds that come from my heart.
I know where you can always be found,
In Heaven's Gates; where I hope to be bound.
I will remember you every day
And always love you in a special way.

To my Grandfather Antoine Boudrias, whose influence still affects my life today.

To Jesse
(W.S. Anglin)

Like sunshine in a mine shaft,
Like a sunbeam in the night,
Like the chieftain Sparkling Water
Or the swallow in his flight,
You're the meaning of my teaching
And the joke behind my preaching,
You're the sadness of the laughter
Of the coming Christ beseeching,
You're the oak tree bearing mistletoe,
The freight train through my night,
The last and only wonderful
To keep me free of flight,
Like the greying light of evening,
Like the dawn upon the dew,
Like bright, warm sun of noontime
Yes, I feel like hugging you!

Address: c/o 2082 Jeanne Mance, Montreal, QC, H2X 2J5
Bill Anglin is a philosopher who sometimes teaches Mathematics. He loves God, beauty, truth, and freedom. He hates religious respectability. In 1994, he published a book called *Mathematics: A Concise History and Philosophy* (New York: Springer-Verlag). In this book he tries to give the human side of the subject. Encouraged by friends such as Esmond and Diana, Bill is working on a one thousand page poem "Journey to the Centre of the Word." It may take years to finish. Currently living on the prairies, Bill often dreams about his home town, Montreal, and he often dreams about travelling in Italy.

Friend or Foe

(Lillian Antoniw)

The night is upon us
It strikes with a vengeance
Surrounding all within its grasp
Is it friend or is it foe?

The darkness brings fear to some
Shelter to others
It lives deep within the soul of us
The essence of evil protrudes from it
Coming closer to all who believe

The streets come alive
The other side becomes real
We try in vain
to take back what is our own

There is comfort in the dark
No one sees us cringe or cry
Wanting help but knowing not where to turn

We try to sleep but cannot
The shadows dance on the wall
They are what we make them

The morning comes slowly
Creeping, bringing with it the sun
Another day—but is it friend or foe?
We all must decide—alone within

Address: Box 203, Rapid City, MB, R0K 1W0
I was born and raised in Rapid City, MB. I received all of my education in Rapid City. I enjoy reading and writing poetry. I would like to be able to travel across Canada and meet other poets.

The Woman in the Moon
(Laurel Archer)

A young girl dreaming in moonlight, hugs herself in peace

A woman reaches for a dark-haired man, masquerading as Pride and weeps

A daughter sleeps, while a mother lifts her eyes in search of the Woman in the Moon

Internal Combustion (Love)
(Arlene Arlow)

I've been a fool for lesser things
than what I saw in you
Each time I jump into the fire
I wonder why I do

Self-proclaimed in pyromania
I watch the fire's glow
Unable to resist the light
That flickers to and fro

As moths are drawn to street lamps
that beckon in the night
Unable to resist their charm
In senseless, endless flight

I watch with fascination
As the fire flickers low
Too soon the flames will fall into
the dying embers' glow

And flung into the darkness
I rest a weary heart . . .
then in the distant silence—
Another fire starts.

Age: 34
Telephone: (604) 785-1806
Aired CBC Radio, Daybreak, Jan 3/90: "1989 Expires." Freelance reporter/photographer, *The Northerner* newspaper, Fort St. John, BC, Feb/89-Jan/90. Education: Honours Certificate, Secretarial and Office Admin., NAIT, Edmonton, AB (1992). Long-term career goal: Prime Minister of Canada. Long-term personal Goals: Literary recognition, friends.

Who

(Connie Armstrong)

Who once lived here
and tended to weed-filled gardens?
Who once fixed
those broken window panes?
Who once tried
to make this place worth living in?
Who once strolled
so gleefully down those lanes?

Who once laughed here
at those special moments?
Who saw
a gleam of hope from behind that tree?
Who once left this place
to be it empty?
Who once lived their life
as you and me?

Age: 21
My eyes were formed in a small town in Southwestern Manitoba. What they have seen is much luck and love from my un-traditional family and my caring friends and husband. As a child, I was encouraged to enjoy reading and writing. As an adult, I have grown to love them both. My past successes in poetry and newspaper reporting will hopefully strengthen my ability to join Canada's literary community—something I consider a treasured aspect of my life.

Bob

(Anthony Arsenault)

People walking quickly through downtown streets,
All you hear is the fall of their feet.
Very quickly so they are not late for work,
Avoiding the alleys, where the riff raff lurk.
But in that alley sits a man named Bob.
Bob was a corporate attorney, until he lost his job.
Now Bob sleeps in a corner, freezing in the cold.
To Bob a dollar bill is like a pot of gold.
Bob had expenses and bills to pay,
Now Bob walks the streets, begging all the day.
Bob's wife left him, took the kids and ran,
Now sitting in that alley is a lonely man.
He searches for food out of hunger and fear,
If he doesn't get his act together, he won't last another year.
So Bob sits in his alley, his outlook very dim,
Watching all the people go by, and wishing it was him.

To my Mother; who lifted me up so I could reach the stars.

red apples

(Raymonde Arseneau)

my wild hopes are red apples
take one bite
and fall from grace

the words keep
drop
ping
from
your
lips

urged the of wind
by motion the

like bleeding apples
stum
bling
in
pain

an orchard of remembrance
beads up
on our flourishing bodies

---

for rps.

The Olde Town
(Simone Asaro)

Catharine come on down to the olde town
And let us find what we once lost
There's nothing gained, no one pays the cost
And there's nothing there that can't be found

The minstrels are out
They've got their tunes
Fading like a dream
And I'm lost in between
A forever changing scene

We'll take a walk to the top of that ole hill
Where memories linger still
Our love was a burning flame
That caused us both so much pain

So Catharine come on down to the olde town
And walk those memories again
I know you got yourself a police boyfriend
But I'm lost in illusions of the end

The Hawk

(Maureen D. Aubut)

For three days,
Each following the other,
Our paths crossed,
Our acquaintance grew.

By the third,
No longer believing it coincidence,
I followed until she lighted a tree.

What had she to teach me; would I recognize the lessons?

My friend was still, observing all.
Betrayed by my body,
At once becoming my prison,
I tried to reach her,
Limited by my vision.

How would such heights be attained?

Then, a direction chosen,
She gracefully crossed the bay.
As my spirit soared with her,
The gods smiled, seeing us at play.

Moon Smile

(Régis J. Auffray)

The moon is bright this night.
It seems to smile sardonically
At me
And tufts of brittle grass on frozen fields of snow.
And in the woods nearby,
Its cold shine greets the black and bony branches
Of skeletal winter trees.
Its spectral moonbeams cast shadows
Under these sleeping sentinels.

So still and silent is the night
That footsteps crushing snow
Seem almost sacrilegious—
A sin to spoil the stillness and the snow.

I turn my footsteps homeward,
And as I do it seems
I feel the cold moon sneer
And hear a quiet sigh
From hushed and speechless sentries.

To all of kindred spirit who seek and strive for more.

The Mysterious Woman
(J.R. Aylward)

There she goes across the lawn,
She's as fresh as dewdrop at dawn;
Her black hair is blowing in the breeze,
She moves with dignity and ease.

She's tall and slender and stands erect,
There are no flaws that I can detect;
Her destination is unknown,
She's a goddess in search of a throne.

She slowly walks down to the beach,
And views the water in the reach,
Then wades in, and with sheer might,
She swims swiftly out of sight.

Now that she's gone out with the tide,
I'll cast my burdens aside,
And dwell upon her smiling face—
My idol—my Goddess of Grace.

Northern Lights
(Larry Bagnell)

Born from the misty tears of Venus
Veils of light unfold
Searching the heavenly spheres above
For places yet untold

Freely flickering phantoms
Of a soul that beckons home
Trembling kiss the treetops
Then burst upon the dome

As spires grow to majesty
They dance the starry skies
Foiling winter's coldest fears
To reach celestial highs

Exploding northern splendour
Of shimmering colours bright
Sends waves of love cascading down
To heal a child's dark night

And as they fade into the dawn
And quietly slip away
They left a gift to all they touched
When night was turned to day

Dedicated to Jane Vincent, a Yukon Northern Light.

Age: 44
Address: R.R. #1, Site 2, Comp. 3, Whitehorse, YK, Y1A 5V3
Telephone: (403) 667-7248 (H) (403) 668-4388 (W)
Larry Bagnell was born in Toronto, December 19, 1949. His most recent job in Ontario was as Director of the Algonquin Experience Youth camp for the Government of Ontario and the Y.M.C.A. He is presently on leave from his job as Director of Yukon Operations for Industry Canada while he is holding the position of Executive Director of the Association of Yukon Communities. He has both a Science degree and an Arts degree from the University of Toronto and started a Masters of Public Administration Program at the University of Alaska. He loves fishing.

Miscarried

(Elaine Bailey)

Forgive a mother who carried you badly
and kneaded unhappily at her belly,
planning to nip you in the bud.
Imagine my sigh, baby, when I awoke to find
red rose petals adorning my bed,
shining rich relief. Under my eyes, they dried
to look like strawberries on snow,
signs of impossible life.

Forgive a mother's dry tearless face.
Blame her only for disgracing
your icy grave with water warm and sudsy,
washing away
all but the faint stain of memory.

Age: 23
Elaine Bailey was born and raised in Ottawa. She attended the University of Ottawa, where she received her Bachelor of Arts in English Literature. She is continuing her studies in Graduate School at Queen's University. "Miscarried" is Elaine's first published poem.

Untitled
(Sue Bain)

Slowly emerging from its roots
Leaves begin to spread
Petals open up
Feel the warmth within
The slight breeze
Altering original state
Strong to the elements
Fragile and Beautiful
It stands
Sprouting its energies
Fully becoming alive

Age: 27
Hi, I'm a 27-year-old "dotted dog" half-owner. I had another dog—he lived to be 18. Anyway, I live in Stratford, Ontario, and I've been here about 20 years—I like it! My formal education is in Recreation, and I currently work for Community Living. I've always used sports as an outlet, and it wasn't until I was 15 that I began writing (this poem written close to 2 years into my hobby). I've continued to use writing as part of my spiritual journey. This is my first published piece.

The Lord of Night

(S. Balcaen)

A white owl came out of the sky
Struck by a ray of light
The feathers turned to silver
And I saw the lord of night.

I saw the scattered star-fields deep
In his eyes of ebony
My soul awoke from despairing sleep
And he cried as he looked at me.

Around his head blue swallows flew
A rosebud stained his perfect lips
His forehead shone in the pale moonlight
And stars sparked at his fingertips.

His wings spread out all caught with light
There colours shone, all seven
And he raised his smooth and muscled arms
And flew with me to Heaven.

Age: 34
Address: c/o 408-2101 Preston Avenue, Saskatoon, SK, S7J 4B5
Telephone: (306) 374-5999

Roses

(Rebecca Anne Balicki)

Your roses haunt me
With their overpowering smell.
They remind me of the laughter
That seems so far away.

Your roses taunt me
With their blood red petals.
That remind me of the passion
Maybe tomorrow but not today.

Your roses haunt me
With their deadly thorns.
Like your emotional wall
That keeps my love at bay.

Your roses taunt me
With a whisper of baby's breath.
Like your words of passion
That make everything okay.

Your roses daunt me
With their blood red petals.
For I know what they mean
And the price I have to pay.

For Hazel

(Brenda Barbour)

Faded image from the lost years
See the jawline, the brow
Familiar and strange.
Lost to us ere you found yourself.
You had a child
          had a child
                    a child . . .
Brightly coloured photograph
See the jawline, the brow . . .
Mother of my mother
Are you lost to us now?

Villanelle

(Jerthie Barinque)

But will they wait until it's done?
The long march through rain in one straight line,
The long rain through March that's never done

Like the March through April; thirty days
Of squares too small for bottled wine,
And only the black numbers repeating—how it never gets done

The sit-ups, the push-ups, the sweaty twelve-mile days
The narrow running through circles that dine
Through strips of smokc, fast food; and thcn oncc donc

Through strips of flicks, rough jokes and ways
To smoke and swear and still keep still in line
Until the long call of names that never seems to get done

Is right away called first thing; 6:00, all foreheads raise,
All shoulders back, all boots and badges shine—
except for some, the laces undone

On feet running crazy with eyes,
The stares that stumble past the "Sir" and the "Fine"
Long rain through march that stops—having finally done,
But never the longer march through rain, tears that never get done

---

Age: 22
I am a University of Toronto graduate with a BA in English. I was raised in Mississauga and am currently living in Toronto, where I continue to write poetry as well as short stories. I will be returning to school for one more year in the fall of '94 to study Philosophy and promote creative spirit in the arts & literary field though the university's English Students' Association.

Taken by the Stream

(Nicholas Barnes)

To the right of consciousness, the fear of being the only one with
a gun pointed to your head. Daydream bullets shattered the inner-world
left cold and empty as the dark spring rain.
Run and hide—there are no answers only more questions.
Follow the thin line of hope, grasp and ride puffy pink clouds into
a dreamy tomorrow where all is real and love is yours.
Forget desperate flights of horror down dark alleyways and through shadowed wood
where pools of silver liquid tempt fingers to dive into its depths.
Watch the wake as it races to the shore; unsure of its flight of fear,
it goes back again to caress slender fingers.
Driven to dance wildly in the rain, laughing and singing,
damp and soaking hair glued to the face's surface.
—Forest creatures hide in the trees—
Falling through layers of conscious steps, eyes open wide to
greet the day.

Grandfather, I try to understand more each day. Rest easy.

Age: 22
Address: Box 155, Steady Brook, NF, A2H 2N2

My Life

(Rosa Maria Barroso)

My life;
The accumulation of things gone wrong.
As to a movie my eyes gripped reality.
As a sense of desolation sank in
No material achievement will ever repair the damage.
The damage of a prank of nature:
The damage of a God not willing.
My life has little by little
Lost the childhood dream of babying a life,
Of caressing the miracle of nature.
Looking into the watering eyes of innocence
Must be the most outrageous adventure.
The passing on of dreams, thoughts and teachings
That must bring the willingness to breathe to live!
And as for the reason of why I can't or shouldn't,
That shall never be unveiled or known to anyone.
Life becomes the ultimate destroyer of dreams.
My life shall never life another;
And I shall never know the pure love of innocence.

Thank you for believing in me and making me smile. I love you!

$7 Million (Tom Brokaw's Annual Salary)
(Elena Basevich)

3 thousand potential Chernobyls sigh heavily

floods consume states
one at a time

hurricanes are taking roofs off houses
and burying towns in early graves

impotent soldiers march home
to hang from bridges

starving Somalian babies
get prepped for T.V. commercials

someone has raped her daughter,
beaten his wife,
cut up their neighbour,
and forgotten to turn off the tap

letting chemicals pour
so fish grow extra eyes
and children grow extra fins

i'd change the channel
but it's 6 pm
and this is all that's on

Rhythms of Life
(Freya Bates)

There is the lapping of waves at low tide
And the crash of the surf at high,
And the sigh of the breeze is matched
To the cry of the gulls in the sky.

And the eagles which soar move their wings
To the rhythm of life in the air,
And the patter of rain meets the rocks
To form the rivers there.

And upon the shore hoof-beats
Tattoo the sand so white,
And from quarter to new to quarter to full
The moon smiles in the night.

So the seasons run their course
From cold to warm and back so soon,
And the rhythms of life are matched
To the beat of drums 'neath the moon.

To my dear English teacher, Mrs. Merilee Gaudin, who has always encouraged my writing.

Age: 18
Address: Box 13, Site 4, Hythe, AB, T0H 2C0
I was born May 14, 1976, in Peterborough, Ontario, the youngest of four children belonging to Ann and Bruce Bates. In 1985, we moved west to Alberta, where I fell in love with horses, choosing to centre my career around them. My time apart from high school is divided between riding and writing. I plan to become an Animal Health Technologist and perhaps someday instruct young riders. Writing will always be a part of my life.

I Am
(Crystal Jardin)

Something stirs within me.
The child awakens
She begins to sing her imperceptible song
Like so many times before
Quietly
    Faintly
        Wait! Listen!

Quietly
    Faintly
        Getting stronger . . .

It is beautiful!
    It is unique.
        It is I!

I am a song
    that dances in the night.

I am a song
    in search of the light.

Socrates
(Jonathan R. Beggs)

Barefooted through the ice and snow,
alone the man inside.
Who sees in himself one way to go,
one path his life to guide.

Among the crowded streets,
and people who all stared.
The man alone and dignified,
the wise man did not care.

Truth and justice both stood by,
while he surely conveyed
the will of man to seek and try,
to find knowledge to obey.

"Virtue then is Knowledge,"
and Knowledge no one knows.
Forever seeking what we can,
to our spirits find and show.

From ancient times, until this day,
I strive to understand.
That I do not know anything.
Thus, my beginning as a man.

Age: 20
Address: R.R. 12, Fredericton, NB, E3B 6H7
I was born and raised in Fredericton, which happens to be the Poets Corner of Canada. I never planned on becoming a poet, I simply enjoy expressing my unique point of view. I attended Fredericton High School, played football and rugby, and eventually became an All Star and played Junior Rugby for my province. Now I attend UNB (Biopsychology) and play rugby for UNB RFC. I write much more now. It seems to me, the more you know, the more you realize you don't know. That intrigues me.

Porcelain Words
(Marion Carol Bennett)

Even before the Great Wall was built, women in China
invented a secret language hidden from men.
Maybe it started in the fields, as ripe figures stooped
days before birth, and slapped rice and wheat kernels
like the infinitesimal patterns of letters into heavy baskets.

While red-robed boy scholars sat stiffly,
sealed for years behind tiled pagodas
until their skin was white as porcelain,
and calligraphic shapes flowed from their pens,
women secreted words in ricepaper journals.
The careful brush-strokes of men built cities of geometry,
penned mixtures of gunpowder, drew Buddhas into cliffsides.

Women arranged their words in careful flowers,
in the placement of bowls and fish, in bright fabrics
they dyed and hung outside like flags:
semaphore beacons from village to village.
The baby who wouldn't quit crying, the husband
who beat and sold them; women fixed silently
on the secret design in a conspirator's scarf.

A language pulled from the earth like wet clay,
shaped into the womb of a jar to hold
all the walls and maps and broken roads.

Address: 1616 Earle Street, Victoria, BC, V8S 1N5
Marion Bennett lives in Victoria, BC, and has just completed a degree in Creative Writing at the University of Victoria. She has been published in the Seventh Wave and was awarded the Millen Undergraduate award in poetry from the University of Victoria.

love is not
(Russell Milton Bennett)

love is not high

love is not a need
for us

love is not counted
or an old coat, discarded
or a memory, lost

maybe love is dancing
with the hopes left by worn-out sorrows

love is not soon

death is not it
a single rose? no,
love dies every minute

and if all of us were to ascend
we'd leave behind
between every rock
below every cloud
beside every bird
            and tree

if there's nothing left for it to be, then
love is not
love is not

I guess it must be something else
that makes me want to sing to you

For Monica.

Age: 23
Russell Bennett lives in Montréal with his four roommates and two African cats: Mr. Man and Lady Babe. He enjoys singing, dancing, reading, his friends and, most of all, just living. "Pizza makes you happy."

Winter Sun
(Marie Bernardin)

I lay stretched out,
The winter sun blinding
    and gently warming,
The room cool,
    except for this space
Just long enough.

My skin, my soul,
Cries out for the light, the warmth,
The hint of summer's kiss.

The warmth reaches into the core
    of my being,
Caressing, warming, soothing,
Transporting to a warmer day,
    a warmer place,
Not hot and burning,
Just warm and gently soothing.

Slipping into a light daze, perhaps to doze,
Unconsciously shifting
    into the warmth,
And as the sun creeps on,
I awaken . . . cooled but refreshed,
A knowledge of the warmth to come,
Able to face the remaining winter
With the sun's respite,
Sun-warmed and comforted.

Untitled
(Christopher William Bestward)

Take this man.
Take all he has and is
and accept it.
Stand tall his lanky frame
and streaked face.
Scars of time,
of life,
and at long last
scars of innocence.
Bring forward this man for all to see.
Lay their eyes upon his last wisps
of World War I hair,
his nostalgia-ridden smile
and thick-rimmed sight.
Look and see his brown tweed
three-piece competence,
his toothless Ellis Island smirk,
and lastly look, receive, and respect
his importance.
So stand up, old man.
Stand with the power of youthful limbs.
Your time is finally at hand.

Age: 23
Telephone: (905) 734-3273
I am currently a fourth-year English student at the University of Windsor, taking time between classes to write for the school newspaper's music section and read as often as possible. With a fondness for the American South, I find myself directing my attention toward post-modern poets such as Dave Smith and James Dickey, hoping to someday piece together my own work in a collective form.

Destiny Awaits!
(Yvonne Bevan)

As I move from darkness
to light
I feel the warmth of the
Angel's embrace.

As I stand on the edge of the universe,
looking into the depths of my future,
I have no fear.

Where there was once doubt,
there is certainty.

Where there was once conformity,
there is freedom.

Where there was once confusion,
there is clarity.

I see before me a beam of light
which emanates from my heart
and shines directly into the face
of tomorrow.

For Shawn.

Midnight

(Christina Bibaud)

Midnight blackness
Twinkling stars
Moonlight shines
All over us.

The clear sky
And still lake
Mirrored by trees
Set the setting.

Two alone
Sit close by
Watching the lake
Ever so near.

The loons cry
Sending their message
Over the waters
To our ears.

In our tent
We lay side by side
Forever embracing
One another.

Earth Culture
(Gillian Biddle)

The times that I've spent
    in touch with the Earth,
Are times in sweet peace
    and full of self-worth.

I stand in the wind
    and in the light rain,
Nothing can touch me,
    not even the pain.

Now mind and soul clean,
    truly transcended—
Worries and problems,
    all the noise ended.

I ponder my life
    and what comes after.
I am the student—
    Nature the master.

Address: R.R. #2, Site 2, Box 9, Newcastle, NB, E1V 3L9

To My Mother
(Margaret Bird)

I came from love
the joining of you and Dad
With all the odds stacked against us.
Mom, you hung in
Never giving up on me

I know there are days you wished you had
Then, as I know your doubts
I move, giving feelings of hope
When despair is all that's there

Mom, you hang in again, fighting for me
We've never met, but you loved me
When none else would

I know of no way of telling you, what it means to me
But, Mom, I'll try to be the one you want.

Thanks for not giving up
Thanks, Dad, for standing by Mom's side
I know it's hard,
But I love you both.
    Your unborn child

Pen name is Liz Bird. I was born May 25, 1959, in St. Catharines, Ontario. My parents are Bill & Helen Bird. I have two children, Charles & Amanda. I was educated in Pembroke at Fellowes High School. I have been writing for about 10 years. Some of my work has been published in the local papers. I had received an award from the American Song Writers for the poem "There Is No Escape." In my writings, I try to reflect the feelings of the people around me and my own feelings on today's society. I now reside in Pembroke, Ontario.

Knightfall

(Terry Bird)

Tarnished knight in rusted armour,
Limping home, his battle lost.
His bones are weary, his lance is broken,
He wonders, "Was it worth the cost?"

What few companions he had gathered,
With his dreams in dust are laid.
He has no victory nor song of glory,
Only memories of the price he's paid.

It should have had a different ending,
A noble battle bravely fought.
He should have had a hero's welcome,
Having won the prize he'd sought.

This jaded knight, bent low in failure,
Empty-handed has come home.
The scars he wears were all for nothing,
His quest has ended, he's alone.

God Cares

(Crystal Bisson)

When my nights are spent alone in the cold,
And my defense, the truth, just won't be told;

When grey skies fill my empty days,
And my mind is lost in a maze;

When no one is around to talk things through,
And my heart is weak from being so blue;

When my thoughts are haunted by the mistakes I've made,
And the reasons for living are beginning to fade;

When the world is full of hatred, and I'm scared,
It is then, that I shall remember that God Cares . . . .

Memory of Mr. Tony Creede: Teacher of Life—you gave all to all, Thank you.

Age

(Brenda L. Bjelan)

Bent with age, time confines him to a wheelchair.

A mind, once keen, now trapped in a framework of hopelessness.
Stale, idle and obsolete.

Merely existing—taking up space within his dim, dispirited dungeon.

Brittle bones barely prop his frail body. Falling prey to a cruel world of blind robots.

He's a victim of the vicious circle of life. Forsaken.

To God; for my genuine respect for our elderly, and wanting to wake up the world!

A Theme of Understanding
(Elizabeth Blackwood)

There's a sphere of understanding
that can only come, in part
from the caring and the sharing
of a true and loving heart.

In our quest for worldly treasures
it's oh so plainly seen
that we've lost the understanding
of what life's supposed to mean.

In our age of new technology,
we've lost the human touch
and the care and understanding
that used to mean so much.

If we would just imagine
ourselves in others' shoes,
we'd be more understanding,
not judge them, nor abuse.

We don't know what tomorrow holds
we only have today
to be the best that we can be
in thought, and in word, and way.

The future of our planet
is precarious, at best
only with respect, and understanding
can we hope to pass the test.

For my parents, Walter and Lillian Hodder, who first showed me love and understanding.

The Search

(Doris Block)

when the evening is full of silence,
the verse slowly winds its way
throughout the page
like a gentle stream,
I follow closely
searching for the final stroke
of love
you forgot to paint
in the picture of my life
missing, like a lost child,
instead, a ghost appears,
the kind that looms
when one is writing verse
takes me by the hand
pulls me onward, upward,
faster, faster
my breath is laboured,
as we stop somewhere, nowhere,
lost, the ghost has disappeared
will I ever find my way back
to discover the final stroke
of love

For Eva—who put a light on my poetry.

Children
(Carolin A. Blythe)

Give them everything they want,
AND
They'll never have enough;
Give them everything they need,
AND
They'll always have plenty.

Astral Projections
(Edith Bottomley)

Last night,
Around thought's crystal orbit
Asleep within the lonely circuit
Of a dream,
Your essence soared again
Like the memory of a well-loved fragrance,
And I gazed upon the sleeping
Architecture of your soul.

I woke to strange murmurings,
But the voice of the city was still.
This is the mind that bends,
the listening intellect:
For you come without speech
Or affluence of gesture.

To my dear friend, Rufus Onyewuchi.

December

(Brian Boudreau)

The last autumn leaves, December's sorrow,
Descend from heights to the ground below
Where silence and solitude swallow.
Drifting in a whirl of dizzying madness,
Strokes of stark red strewn and scattered to rest
In contrast to barren earth, shrieks a protest.
For once we dreamt of a bright future,
But now we leave memories on a temporal shore
Where solace is like a warm beast in winter.
So when you see the last leaves of December,
Touch again the etched pain, but remember
The laughter, the hopes and each strand of hair.
For in the fullness of time, spring will bring
The loved ones we've nestled in our remembering.

In memory of the victims of the Montréal Massacre.

The Greatest of These Is Love
(Gerald Bouey)

Love is always patient, and love is ever kind
Love is sacrificial, sometimes love is blind
Love is bold, courageous too
Love is always there in you
Love resides in a hug, it is in a simple word
Love is the sweetest music that you've ever heard
Love is in faith, beauty, peace and joy
Love starts to grow inside every girl and boy
Love is a feeling deep within
    can you feel it in the air?
Love reaches out to others
    promises always to be there
Love is not expressed in anger
    nor is it hiding in fear
Love is in a gentle smile
    sometimes a sparkling tear
Love forgives others fully, love is ever true
Love perseveres when all else
    is chaos around you
Love waits patiently, love always prevails
Love is a powerful emotion, love never fails
Love believes the best of others
    because it always must
Love is found in friendship
    and love forever trusts.

To the One above, who created love.

Gingerbread Men

(Paul G. Boultbee)

Tread lightly now, hushed be your voice,
one mustn't disturb the dead.
And yet, with dead eyes they look upon us,
silent screams echo in the room
and only chilled laughter answers their prayers.

Why? For what end did they suffer?
Freedom?
In a way, it is theirs.
It lives on with their memory.

Ovens!
But no tasty Saturday-morning smells here.
Only the stench of crisp, burnt flesh wafts from the baker's inferno.
Paraded in two-by-two, naive yet fearful,
not knowing what to expect
and frightened of the unexpected.
How many hundreds of thousands died?
Who knows?
Only just so many gingerbread men.

The chapels,
silent sentinels stand in grave respect,
the camp of death at their feet.
Their cool interiors refresh parched souls,
remind us of the horrors that have been,
the love that succours
and the peace that may never come.

Simple Life

(Jan Bourdeau)

I remember when the paths led to the creek
when the trees towered above
I remember laughing
running through fields of long sweet grass
I remember when flowers smelled of bees' honey
when powder-white clouds looked like cotton balls
I remember when warm mud squished between my toes
when summer was young
and I was free

Free to run

Free to laugh

Free to be a child

Not a grown-up
not a member of society
who cannot remember when

For my son, Thomas Grinnell, who leads me down the paths of the simple life.

Where and When
(Sandra Bowers-Laabs)

Where will we meet again,
and when?

How long must I wait

to touch your lips
with mine

to feel your breath
on my neck

to become one with
you again.

But most of all,
where and when?

1958

(Tim Bowling)

a little blood left in the wheelbarrow
after my father pushed the last
of his salmon home from the wharf
mixes with the falling rain
this September evening:
the canneries aren't buying
so he buries his catch
load after load
in the garden for fertilizer;
the sky around his hands
is dark and sweet as the blackberries
dying in the fields nearby
as the blade of his shovel
sloshes deep in the earth
again and again and the rain
dilutes the blood in the wheelbarrow
a lighter red then pink
then almost clear
until there is no trace of blood at all
only the reflection of a young man's eyes
peering out like stars
beautifully indifferent to the dawn
and the lonely swimming of the long long years

A Sense of Freedom

(Bernadette Braun)

As the dancer leaps to musical notes;
As the driver spins circles in wild fun;
As the actor breathes life into dead quotes;
As the athlete bounds easefully in run;
As the girl sits bareback in endless lope;
As the boxer steadies himself to fight;
As the boarder anticipates a slope;
As the surfer braves the waves out of sight;
As the stuntman hurdles out of a plane;
As the sailor sets flight with the wind's whip;
As the drummer finds rhythm in the rains;
And as one hangs from cliffs by fingertip;
So is our freedom in His perfect will.
This gift from faith is the only that fills.

For my Heavenly Father and for Zack Finley, with enduring hope for his freedom.

The Storm

(Caroline Bridges)

Turrets of snow-capped peaks
Top the heaving ocean grey
Who can still the mass
No-one even today

The flashing of the lighthouse
Continues her toneless way
Calling to the shipping
Stay away today

Billowing quickly to and fro
The wind will have her say
It's her turn to counsel
All of today

The Island has gone from view
It's missing in the sway
We too stay indoors
Until another day

To Derek, the first poet in the family.

Mutant

(Joanne Bristo)

Soiled wings stretched
away she did fly
off into the deadly
poisonous sky

Leaving her unhatched eggs
late in the fall
when cold winter winds
came to call

A mutant she is
many you can find
blame not nature
but merciless mankind

Looking for food
doesn't take long
there's plenty of fish
on shore to feed upon

She met her destination
the last it will be
life for her ended
most unnaturally

Words Shaken from the Tree of Sadness
(John Broome)

Have we come thus far and must we now lose all?
All our great wonder?
Where now the canoe of painters,
   the solitude of stars,
   the apple-green of skies at evening?
Beauty has faded on the eye,
   and gentleness,
   and the sweet arts of peace.

Fearless
The Marathonic march of stone and steel,
The dirtied streams and air . . .
—O the wood is down that parted my fair Pyramus and me—
Dear God!
Is greed a Deadly Sin no more?
Must we sing of scorn and envy forever?

I peep above the lip of my grave
And see them stand in line before me:
The tricksters, the smilers, the foul of mind,
Men of loud opinion and little taste,
Living with rancour and daily with wrath,
A line, a stilled wave, a frozen sullied sea . . .

Tell me,
Did he who made the perfect Lamb,
Did he, my friends, make thee?

Island Preserves

(Matthew Brown)

My wicked Great-Grandmother delighted in the tale
of how the glands of her body produced a sweet odour
that attracted all manner of spiders.

Whatever room she was in, they'd crawl from webbed corners,
to a spot above her curlers, slide on silver threads
down to her gaseous lap, and scurry amongst her knitting.

In time, and with great patience, she would catch them all,
crushing each one between thumb and ring-finger,
"Because," she said, smacking her lips, "their bellies
contained such lovely yellow custard."

I now have a dreadful fear of Island homes in mid-August,
the older ones, the rural ones, the ones set sadly back from the road
on a slope of red farmland, or grassy field,
all owned, I imagine, by wicked old widows who smell as sweetly as she did.

Flowered dress, swollen ankles make a slow, wheezing ascension
up the narrow twist of staircase, to that narrow, slanted room
and that coarse, stained bedspread.

Antique springs moan with the weight,
old dresser photographs absorb what light is left,
the clock's tired pendulum ticks heavily down to sleep
the geese, back from the feeding,
are loud in the marsh.
And everywhere, custard spiders quicken.

A Woman's Cheek

(Evelyn J. Broy)

How many times have I sat like this,
cheek on hand, deeply pondering?
Today my cheek rebels at other thoughts
and claims some thinking of its own.
O, it has known the heartbeats
in a husband's breast, and
his loving, curved hand;
and how many times
have I carried his hand
to my cheek, with love?
Now that he's gone, it knows the glass
in a photo-frame—but I thank God
my cheek has also known the silk
of a daughter's hair, and the wandering
infant fingers of a son.
Lips and eyes are themes for
lovers' love and mystery,
but this, my cheek's a book
of secret history.

Age: over 50
Address: 3810 Queen Strett East, R.R. #4, Sault Ste. Marie, ON, P6A 5K9
I am the widow of a Polish doctor. I have always written poetry when my feelings were deep in sorrow, or in joy. My outlet is double-headed—I paint as well as write. I have won many prizes with my poems and had them regularly accepted by *Canadian Forum* and *Canadian Poetry Magazine*. I had a book of poems published in Windsor, many years ago, *Almanac of Absence*. I have lived in England, Gibraltar, Scotland, Trinidad and the rest of my life in Windsor, Ontario, 'til now. I have come to live with my daughter in Sault Ste. Marie.

Christopher John
(Gloria J. Bryce)

Child of the desert reborn in the night
Child of the desert, eagle take flight
Fly o'er the mountains, forests and seas
Conquer those mountains, follow your dreams
Sand o'er the dunes, blown o'er the times
Fill up the hollows level the mind
Eagle of the mountain fly like the wind
King of God's country, magnificent
Christopher John fly on.
Shine like the sun, not too bold
Clothe not your body but dress up your soul
Dust o'er the mountain is not, but the goal
Search for the riches buried in soul
Fly o'er the mountains, forests and seas
Meadow below you search there for me
Christopher John fly free.

Untitled

(R. Buchanan)

With
the expulsion of Eve and tag-along Adam
the anti-lord Beelzebub
appeared as an apple-worm and
approached the bastard couple and
blessed them with the highest gift of all:
He taught them to speak.
The worm gave them tongue
and the maggot gave them voice
and the Earth wept until the deserts bled
but none
could stifle their cries.

Spintharis
(Stephanie Lanaro Burnett)

Spring down and up with me
          Through azure-cradled suns
Run wild through shimmering
          Forest leaves at night
Watch iridescent
                    darting
                    little orbs
                    shine with the moon
Then when Dawn slowly
 Glazes the Sky with its
            Velvet ether
As one timeless Spiral
Let us sweep over Orcus
        and bound out of bounds
                into the Cerulean Blue
                                        Unknown.

Age: 21
Address: 3843 Marlowe Avenue, Montreal, QC, H4A 3L9
Valentine Daughter of guru/mentor Parents: Artist **Louise Lanaro-Burnett** and Psychologist **Edward Burnett**. Quadrilingual (English, French, Italian, German), 10 years of **Violin** at McGill Conservatory of Music, 6 years of Saxophone. First Short Story published in Trafalgar 1987 Yearbook. Studying Film & Communications/Cultural Studies at McGill. "**Spintharis**" inspired by love/life/reality & **37** Times at Marianopolis, **27/8/1991**. Exploring and merging film, video, poetry, art, music, nature and life.

Untitled

(G.M. Burns)

Like some corporeal sigh
Or an amorphous diamond caught
Shimmers in the eye
Another tiny drop

Quivering and shining
As it overwells and flows
The cheek the drop has jaded
To fall so far below

How doth the gleaming sparkle
Befit the eye bereft?
Once full of life and simple song
Now joy the heart has left

Why Me?
(Victoria Burzese)

The candle's light
Disturbed not
The stillness
    in her room.

Tears of Heaven
Fell upon the world
    outside.
Numbed eyes stared.

First love.
First time.

She had offered him
    her heart.
He had taken her soul.

Cherished images
    faded,
Hands fell to her
    stomach.
In the dim light of the
    candle,
She cried.

And the world,
Cold and dark,
Continued.
Shedding no tears
    for her.

Tropic
(Colleen Buscarini)

Cold expanse of sparkling blue
Stretching t'wards unknown
Dreamy clouds float 'cross the sky
Whither they be blown

Elemental works of might
Hidden from the eye
Quickly build crescendo theme
Focused then to die

Surface calm and lolling free
Rippling mode of grace
Skipping gently into shore
Showing sun-glint face

Sea-gulls screeching overhead
Sending out alarm
Rising far above the churn
Instincts sensing harm

Swirls of heavy mist appear
Frowning dark array
Rush of wind in growing force
Carving new-found clay

Sculpting paths through quiet trees
Shaking once serene
Vicious in its fixed onslaught
Nothing left of green.

Absorbing swiftly
(Boyd Bush)

eVERYBODY'S wISEMEN gROWIN'
tICK tOCK dISPLAYS fROM tHE gROUND
aND tHE lOCAL fRIENDLY cANNIBALISTICALISMS
pLAY quietly oN
hAMSTRING gUITARS,
sLOWLY
wORSHIPPING tHEIR eLDERS wITH kNIVES
tHAT fEED bY oSMOSIS
wHILE tHEIR sTARVING (never dying) cHILDREN rIDE
tHE bLOOD gUTTERS tO
wonderland

wHERE tHE fOLIAGE iS tHICKER tHAN iT
ever
sHOULD'VE
been.

For Rebecca Fenwick.

Soul Searching

(Anny Bussières)

Mighty as a mountain, as the wind strong,
On a stony wall I sat and waited;
The endless ocean spread down my feet, long
And silent and serene and blue it bled.

Behind closed eyes my mind started searching
For an anchor, a motive, a reason;
I thought I could stay still, dreaming, breathing,
But the sea breeze held me in its ribbon.

Loneliness seemed to weigh on me; silence
Filled my days, my nights, empty soul, bare, cloud.
Required was, out-of-the-blue, a scream, loud.

I, too, was looking for something on which
To rely, to live, to breathe and to feed;
Fulfillment became an idea, a need.

Sole survivor of a tormented road
My soul longs for a friend, for a partner;

To share the freedom, the pain, the passion,
To feel useful my soul needs a lover.

Morning Ride on a Dublin Bus

(Judith Butler)

A scruffy man on a Dublin bus
Drops his change, causing a fuss,
Disturbing a student who's trying to write
An essay he should have finished last night.
A man in a trench-coat and tasselled shoes
Frowns as he reads the business news.
A stylish lady, pinch-faced and prim,
Adjusts her hat with its upturned brim.
By an open window, a sombre nun
Squints as she faces the morning sun.
The lady beside her, old and infirm,
Sways whenever the bus makes a turn.

A handful of people on 18A
Travelling to town on an autumn day,
Sitting together, yet strangely alone,
Anonymous faces with thoughts unknown.

With screeching brakes, the old bus stops,
And up the steps a little girl hops,
School bag swinging, she smiles with delight,
Holding a teddy bear, hugging it tight.
Flashing her freckles the driver's way,
She says with a twinkle, "Must Buttons pay?"
And for the first time, the ghost of a smile
Passes over the faces lining the aisle.

Miss Interpreted

(Michael J. Cahoon)

Acid tongue
hides
little-girl thoughts.
Stern facade
protects
tender heart.
She wasn't always
thus.
Time and circumstance
have done their
deed,
and often,
late at night,
she cries

alone.

To my Wife, Lenore, who keeps me from crying alone.

The Storm
(Joel Calabrese)

The storm licks wildly about me,
Howling and biting in the darkness,
The wind whipping my coat,
Rain drenching me—
Hair plastered to my head and face,
Clothes clinging tightly,
Little rivers flowing down my body,
Soaking socks and shoes.
Walking on—
The liquid darkness swallows me whole.

To the angel maid, a ray of sunshine.

It's Colder Tonight
(D.M. Callan)

It's colder tonight than it's been in years.
Your words cloud the issues, I can see them from here.
We drop by degrees whenever we fight.
If you don't turn around, I could turn to ice tonight.

For years I never noticed the snow—
Never sat by my window, just to watch the drifts grow.
How did it happen?
Once we were young.
It's almost over now, yet we haven't begun.

Waiting there all this time.
If I took you for granted, didn't mean to be unkind.
Searching for the future,
Missing out on what's here.
If you wanted more, you should've made it clear.

Woke to a killing frost.
The damage is done, and all has been lost.
Wonder when spring comes, in soft wistful rain,
If we'll thaw enough to feel the warmth again.

And it's colder tonight than it's been in years.
Your words cloud the issues, I can see them from here.
We drop by degrees whenever we fight.
If you don't turn around, I could turn to ice tonight.

To Family, partners, friends and anyone who has begun again—DMC.

Telephone: (613) 384-3394
I am honoured that "It's Colder Tonight" has been chosen for publication in this anthology. Writing is a large part of my life. Poetry comfortably combines with my career as a performer/composer with the award-wining, contemporary folk and children's band GOPHER BAROQUE. I am a graduate Behavioral Science Technologist with a diverse employment background. Current projects range from children's books to a collection of anecdotes and poetry based on Canadian folklore. For a copy of this poem in its musical form or to chat, contact me at: 902 Braelorne Place, Kingston, ON, K7P 1N4.

Life is Like a Sunset
(Tina Camilli)

You appear, I emerge.
You're small, I'm tiny.

The morning sun is but a glow,
As my mother gives birth to me, I know.
The sun, like me, too small, to show.

You change, I grow.
You're lovely, I'm cute.

The sun, I know, gets bigger as I grow.
Its colours so beautiful, my childhood does show.

You brighten, I prosper.
You're gorgeous, I'm gay.

The sun, now beaming, my adolescence aglow.
The sun, so lovely, my beauty does show.

You decolourize, I wrinkle.
You're seasoned, I'm old.

The sun, now is darker, as I wrinkle, I'm told.
The sun has its season, as I grow so old.

You fade, I drift.
You're gone, I'm dead.

The sun is a glimmer, as I am so aged.
The sun fades away, as I drift away.

To Will Garrett-Petts—the one who encourages me to write what I feel.

Age: 18
Address: Box 688, Chase, BC, V0E 1M0
I was born April 20, 1975, as Tina Camilli. I finished grade school with honours and am presently in College; after College, I will go to University to become a surgeon. I enjoy collecting bookmarks, dolls and unique things. I love problem-solving, theatre and art. I hope to continue writing unusual pieces and always dare to be different.

Cast Away
(Mike Camp)

Cast away, cast away that vessel gently,
Why should we harbour such regrets so tearful?
It sailed to us on windswept waters,
A fleshy envelope for our hearts and minds.
As the salty crab burst his mantel temporal,
Eager for his next new home,
So, too, let us wait so ever faithful,
And cast away, cast away that vessel gently.
We know not what the next will be like.
It's best this way, for, sure to tell,
For like the present which we see not well,
We could this precious matter conscious,
Handle not in our daily, humdrum spell.
So cast away, cast away that sensuous shell.
The next one coming will be much better,
I honestly believe and hence do foretell.

Dedicated to the memory of John Barry—gentleman and patron of the arts.

Age: 46
Address: c/o Box 143, Ucluelet, BC, V0R 3A0
Since graduating with a degree in Fine Arts in 1972, Mr. Camp has been working seriously as a painter and sculptor. In 1992, he published his first book of poetry and short stories. Is currently working on his second volume, which will include three full-length plays and will be illustrated with his own artwork.

In Praise of the Czechoslovak Spirit
(Sean Camp)

Darkness becomes light,
The twilight becomes day,

The dust is briskly shaken,
Revealing a hidden lustre.

People begin to rub their eyes
And discover they indeed have sight.

The spring has finally arrived,
Restraining souls burst forth,
Reaching for the sun,
Knowing this is for what they've strived.

Forty years of silence broken,
The impossible being realized,

Workers, Playwrights, Authors, All Countrymen,
Joined in euphoric pride,
Havel, Dubcek and the others,
Yes, they can change the tide.

Songs of freedom,
Leaching the poisoned air,

The flames of Jan Palach,
Becoming candles, lighting the way,

The blood-red grip of Communism,
Crumbling under a VELVET sky.

The future begins today,
With strength and optimism,
INDEED THEY SHALL OVERCOME SOMEDAY.

To the people in Czechoslovakia who kept flames of hope burning through the dark years.

The Answer

(Thomas A. Campbell)

Sitting there,
I feel her beauty surround me—
Choking off my want,
Or thought for anyone else.

She smiles at me;
I feel my heart starting to pound.
Could this really be
True love I've found?

Talking, her voice,
It fills the air.
Like there's no one else around,
Or no other cares.

The Question is asked,
And I, I wait for an answer:
"Do I have a chance with you,
(Or) Am I just believing in fables?"

She turns around shyly,
Then back, facing me;
But I don't get the answer . . .

Not until she kisses me!

To Peggy Darroch—the one who inspired me to write, and made my writing Reality.

Age: 19
Address: P.O. Box 1016, Westville, NS, B0K 2A0

The Street Child
(Samantha Marie Carsen)

I saw you sleeping in the park.
The white moon raged upon your bearded face.
The stars shone down; the shadows masked your
strange indifference.
I stood and watched you dream, a dream of freedom
from the pain.
And you never knew I wept. For you wandered through
the tangled web of sleep and never lost
your step.
But never so, waking.

The autumn night breeze stirred your unkempt hair.
Your bare feet moved in slumber as you lay there.

I turned away, saddened at the thought that I long to
take you home,
But I cannot
For the Law says that you have a right to sleep here
in the cold and in the wet—
Filthy, hungry, and alone. And only I regret
As a parent, I've no rights left.

Turning, I walk away. Wondering . . .

Is your nightmare worse by day, or mine by night?

My schizophrenic son.

For all street children everywhere and their parents who love them.

Address: 1125 Norma Court, Victoria, BC, V9A 5A4
For many years I have been writing poems and songs. I have also written a couple of novels not published as yet. I was a Psychiatric nurse for a number of years, back home in Kingston, Ontario. My ambition (life-long) is to see my work in print, or hear it on record. Right now, I own and operate a janitorial franchise in Victoria. I am married for many happy years to Alexander Carsen, and although we have no children, our hearts go out to all street children and their parents. I am presently writing a non-fiction book about cats.

Nightmare
(Rebecca Caspar)

The laughter and confusion and mixed-up illusion
The simplicity was exquisitely all rambled to infinity
With that shadowed light that shone with conclusion
And that man just stood there with fearful symmetry

His eyes glowed with horror
And he smiled with fright
And the sweat from his head
Continued to pour
As the moon lit the sky
On a cold winter's night

The snow seemed to glimmer and glisten like ice
And the screams in my head began to thunder
My life flashed before me like the rolling of dice
As he raised his claws and tore me asunder

I fell to the ground
My heart ceased to beat
My soul was now free
The Messiah to meet

In Memory

(Laurie Cassar)

They are the whisper in the wind,
They are the brightest light,
A star that shines above us,
On a steely winter's night

They have not gone and left us,
They have simply passed on through,
To where He waits in silence,
In a world so free and true

Please, do not be saddened,
For they have found a worthy home,
A place where pain is forsaken,
And peace is finally known

They will be forever with us,
And as they did right from the start,
They will fill our souls with courage,
And warm a weathered heart.

In honour of those who gave their lives for our freedom: D-Day, June 6th, 1944.

Haven of Love
(N. Castellan)

I'll run to the beach where I know you will be,
When morning breaks upon the waking sea,
I will answer as you're calling me,
And we will be together.

Footprints fading in the sand,
The waves wash driftwood up to the land,
I will be there holding your hand,
And you will embrace me.

We will share many more days,
By the sea where the mighty palm sways,
I will learn all of your ways,
And we will be one.

The sun will rise and fill the sky,
The seagulls will soar and cry,
The reason we are here, we will know why,
Because we love one another.

Salmon Catching
(Vic Cavalli)

The green of the pines
Pushes through the veiling cloud
As they pull back hard on lined sticks
And silver salmon flexing are drawn
Out and airward and fall to the stony ground.

The canoe manned with spearmen drifts far away,
      across—
A fantastic softness holds it in a mouth
Of river fog above the Tyee.

Turning away from the thwacking of landing fish,
Turning my face from their clubbing to stillness—
From my wild motionless rod and line—
I see the rocky mountains with pines from
      the shore rising
And   there
Fiery blankets of smoking flesh.

Turned On

(Joan M. Ceaser)

I enjoy my Seniors' Computer Class—
It's a thrill like nothing other
When they demonstrate an old motherboard
To this no-longer-bored old mother.

For Grandfather
(Lucia Cecco)

A glass-scratched
photo of you
in uniform
circa 1933
mysterious as a seahorse
to this inlander
not yet touched by time waves
that erode sandcastles
And when the water
ceased
you searched for
that shy, half-blind horse
in the desert
but never brought him home
so you could respect him still
when his bones lay
chalk white
under the buzzards
and the endless arc of blue

Head Held High

(Sophie Chan)

One day I shall return to stroll these hallowed halls
And my ears will hear the soft squeak of my shoes
But my mind will hear laughter, cries, voices
Familiar sounds during my high school years
And I will smile

Then I will stare at the big gymnasium
And my eyes will see the bleachers and the score board
But my mind will see tournaments, victories, gym classes
Familiar scenes during my high school years
And I will smile

Then I will sit in a desk in a classroom
And my nose will smell the linoleum floors
But my mind will smell new books, hair-spray, bake sales
Familiar scents during my high school years
And I will smile

Then I will remember the day I left high school
And my mind will see Grad gowns, diplomas, glowing faces
The unforgettable splendour of our Graduation Night

Then I will remember that I was educated among
    future surgeons, teachers, lawyers, architects,
    artists, writers, politicians, scientists . . .
And I will feel proud
Knowing that these were once my high school peers

Then I will leave with my head held high, bursting with pride
And promising to return.

To the 1993 Graduating Class of Britannia Secondary—Vancouver, BC.

The Farmer
(Jim Chapman)

Bent by the labours of time
A farmer breaks the land
With calloused hands
Sweat on his brow
He leans into the setting sun
Stands still and listens
To the wings of a night hawk
A black bird calling
Shadows of the night
Fill all the low lands
Mist from the lake
Walks across the wild meadows
God immortal who made this land
And placed it into the palm of my hand
Kings with Kingdoms
Had no greater love than I for you

To my wife, Ada, our children and our grandchildren.

Address: 2413-11 Avenue, Castlegar, BC, V1N 3B1
Telephone: (604) 365-8022
Jim Chapman grew up in the Canadian Prairies and now makes his home in Castlegar, British Columbia. Jim is the author of numerous poems, short stories, and in 1989, published his first novel, *The Horseman of Shandro Crossing* (Edmonton: Tree Frog Press). Much of Jim's work reflects his Ukrainian heritage and his love of nature. Jim is known locally as a great story teller and is regularly invited to do readings for various groups. Jim is currently working on a second novel.

An Unfaithful Record

(Sharron Chatterton)

He was a pleasant fellow with aromatic air.
She, late turning in, believed in existenz with flair.
In simple synchrony they rocked the paths for months.
A pair in season, filing things away for keeps.

"You, Sir, have eyes the colour of herb gardens."
"And you, Madam, have eyes like the jay's wing."
"Don't ever tell anyone we had this conversation, will you?"
"Did we have this conversation? Truly?"
They never said such things, you know.

She once proposed that he might have begun the Question.
And he, already much engaged,
Responded, with magician's logic,
That questions are begun in fields.
"Morphogenetic," she stated flatly, having read.
"Resonant," he said, "with tympani, in bed."
They giggled,
Walks were gigglesome affairs
That ended oft with fingertips to shoulder-blades
And hands to hair.

I remember. I was there.

The Walk
(Jacqueline Chen)

I walk this beaten path
knowing this ground is already discovered
knowing these steps will leave no impression
on the already sunken soil.
I walk this beaten path
knowing the air I breathe is stale
knowing the smells that surround me are putrid
that this place reeks of decay.
Feeling the need to make a difference
I'll walk this beaten path
searching for new mountains to climb and conquer
till my spirit is bruised and blistered
as the flesh beneath my feet
and at that point—
I will walk on.

To Pat Machin, who gave me the chance to recreate my world, and explore it.

The Pride of Illiteracy
(Yue Ming Chen)

He, born in northern China,
Is now a sight-seer
In Canton, in southern China.
She, from western Canada,
Is now a traveller
In Québec, in eastern Canada.
Although well-educated, he
Never takes pride in himself.
Although well-informed, she
Is never proud of herself.
Are they both modest to people?
And towards knowledge humble?

Now, when Mandarin becomes useless,
He is completely illiterate (at least half so?),
No matter how familiar he is with the strokes.
Now, when English turns futile,
She is entirely unlettered (at least half so?),
No matter how acquainted she is with the letters.

Do they mind
If the locals take them for low or high?
Haughtily they refuse to see
A truth that they won't admit:
Such illiteracy will lead them
To a life of disharmony.

Sleeping Sickness

(Sean Chhangur)

I can't sleep
I wake up crying
Because I dreamt that you weren't there
And when the tears dry
I look around
And find
You aren't there
So
I cry myself to sleep

To ginger cookie
(Sanford M. Chilcote)

A cabin is like a womb and a coffin, dark in the
Shadow of black spruce with the same strong scent of our
Fathers and birth-kindnesses of our mothers, moss and
Patrimony, truth and matriarchy, the setting of us
Side by side and both raising up our queen's grass banners
That are more than live speech could be, our own beautiful
Recourse, and as I am satisfied with death and birth at
Most times—we are felloes of the rim of the same
Un-spoked wheel, as your grandfather would have said—the
Greatest of our lives' accomplishments exist only as
Secrets between you and me, like roots and buds whispering, yet
We need not use metaphors, bothering instead to become this
And die in this old forest, farewelling the times and
Peopling here among the berries and never alone, filling in
Between hard, wind-worn boards and whittling small.

Our wilderness and ever our friend, our wilderness will assist you,
Satisfying your most searching loves, my dear little ginger cookie.

The Woman Farmer

(Ann Y.K. Choi)

A man owned a fertile plot of land
Country capable of growing sweet corn, sweet peas
His equipment scattered around him
He ignored the potential prosperity
Others shunned him, dismissed him as a fool
His good land was going wasted
Unused, it became worthless

Get the point?

(Yeah, the man obviously never wanted to be a farmer;
he decided to raise children instead)

A woman owned a fertile womb . . .

For J.C.

Address: 5795 Yonge Street, Unit 213, North York, ON, M2M 4J3
Immigrated to Canada from South Korea in 1975. Graduated with a BA in English and Sociology from Victoria College at the University of Toronto in 1992. Presently, tutor English and write poetry, short stories.

Return to the Shore

(Hazel M. Chretien)

I sit at my window, looking out to the street
Where scurrying people hurry places to meet.
Far above all the tumult of the everyday throng
Comes a call to my spirit from a sea siren's song.

I am there in a moment, taste again salty spray
And fresh breeze blows my heartaches to a place faraway.
Golden song swells within me, I'm caressed by the dawn,
The gulls cry my welcome, and the tide pulses on.

Etched eternal in memory, I've returned to the shore,
I again feel it's magic, bid its beckon once more.
All I hold is a seashell, smooth and cool to my hand,
As I sit by my window, watching waves on the sand.

Four days on Rathtrevor Beach near Parksville, BC, changed me forever.

Age: 42
Address: 3407B Sparks Street, Terrace, BC, V8G 2V1
I was born and have lived all my life in BC. I love people and receive great fulfilment working as a health care worker in a long-term care facility. I am mom to five almost grown children. Writing poetry has been a life-long therapy and it's exciting for me to see now, a potential to share my thoughts and perceptions in a public way.

Confrontation

(Donna Christie)

Summoning thundering clamouring herds
Gathering speed in the force
Of the billowing dust
As the distance diminishes
Trampling your words
And screaming in unison at each other we must
Come stampeding to crescendo as a lariat girds
Then the clarity
The contact
The consummate trust

To all who continue to strive for the peaceful resolution of conflict.

Address: R.R. #1, Carp, ON, K0A 1L0
Telephone: (613) 839-2263

Donna Christie (BA; BEd) is a freelance writer, who, together with her husband, K.B. Hranchuk, is raising two young children in a rural setting in West Carleton. Active in gardening circles, she is currently serving in the role of District Director for the Ontario Horticultural Association. Writing and gardening are juggled with this former teacher's third love: world travel. Family is an ever-present part of it all.

Trees in Winter
(Flora Macdonald Clark)

Sumi brush strokes
Sleeping
Dreaming in colour

Hair

(Paula M. Clark)

Hair is probably the most important of my bodily appendages.
I don't really know why, I mean, it's just a bunch of dead cells
that won't let go of my head.
But, I do know when I came to this realization.

It came when the hair got thinner, and thinner—
when it seemed as though my hair would rather stay in my brush
than on my head.
When it got to be making such a mess that I just wanted it gone.
When my scalp made a slapping noise.

I never needed to know the shape of my head.
I didn't want to see the scar I got from that nail on the bottom
of the swing that cut my head open when I was ten and gave me the
only stitches I ever got. The doctor gave me a quarter for being
so quiet about it.

No one ever gave a quarter to my hair—and it was pretty quiet
about detaching itself from my skull.
Not a sound it made.
It just died.

The Garden Dream

(Lee Ernest Clarke)

This garden where I dream the most,
I ride my hopes on falling stars.
The moon has glared her silver ghosts,
Throwing muses from afar.
Impressions of sound from whispered pasts,
Like prayers adrift in blowing leaves.
The pleasing thoughts the shadows cast,
As the sun dies down behind the trees.
A wondrous garden I have found
Where solitude and silence mend.
No troubled tears will stain this ground,
This garden dream will never end.

To my parents, friends, and especially Jennifer.

Age: 24
Born in Lancashire, England, April 30, 1969. Emigrated to Canada in 1974, now resides in Barrie, Ontario. He was educated at Barrie Central Collegiate. His interest in writing, art and literature started from the early age of ten. Writing influences include Keats, Wilde, Frost and Whitman. His involvement with The Barrie Writers Club, he feels, helped to develop his skills in writing. Primary goal is to have a collection of his poems titled "Dishevelled Dreams" published and to further pursue a career as a fiction novelist.

Perspective: North of Lake Ontario
(Mark Cochrane)

Leaves, engorged, rustle like flame.

Slopes of scored
earth, peopled with pumpkin
heads, roll down from the embankment
toward the shore.

Silver as mercury, the water
is a one-way mirror. Submerged
like mermen with tridents, scientists
observe a carnage.

And across the Lake, in their hazy south—
what mirage is this
that travels and can reach so far?
Is that a factory
or does Rochester fall prostrate
yet disdain a woman's hand?

America the octopus
once groped the hemispheres.
Ashamed now, it muddies
a watery retreat.
There, too tall to be a steamer
and invisible
unless I squint—

there, one wavering stack
infuses the sky
with bitter ink.

English Sonnet:

Dresden

(Aaron J.S. Cole)

Light ashes blew softly through the orange morning sky,
burning bright and violent from a pre-morning fire.
A child torn asunder and a mother's mournful cry . . .
Nothing more to achieve, nothing more to aspire . . .

Once beauty and wonderment came to people who saw
Venus' blessings, bright heavenly visions,
this city that was finally open to all—
no dreams of evil, blasphemous missions.

Yet massive explosive bombs of torment laid waste,
causing tissues and muscles to sizzle through cries.
A vision that Pluto might want to embrace:
a boy-child screaming with fiery eyes.
And the pale green grass in the moonlight wept,
with dewdrops that flowed for war's horrid debts.

Night Speak

(Teresa Cole)

Caressed by the hand of God
My body rests, spirit soars.
Leaves rustle. Night crouches
And couches
Me in a silence alive with voices speaking thoughts.
I know how wholeness feels, fleetingly.

Captive

(Margaret R. Comeau)

The air
so chilled,
fresh.

Standing,
hypnotized: watching
the horizon
melt into black.

Returning to the time
of a land
rolling green.

Seeing her so close
after all
that has past.

The memories
still clear
and the pain
so accustomed.

Hoping
she understands
why the brine
must always be
more dear.

Where It Comes
(Trisha Consunji)

If I show you something conscious
Is the surface where you'd play?
If the breath uttered by me,
Rigorous and vocal, held souls
Untainted among poetic vipers,
Would the smoke still linger
So I stuttered stifled;
So I held sibling hands less intense?

The scheme I see goes further than
My mother to her father
A louder voice I never hear inside
If I told you I recall every inch
Of Him, from his head to
The tip of his less-long leg,
That his veins and bones
Position my nakedness
  Towards
            the
                  height
Would a solitude expel me?

In times of gentlement,
If I show you something conscious
Could you notice the despair?

For my Mother's Father.

Daddy's Dream
(Elizabeth Copland)

Fifteen years ago today, a baby girl was born.
Her mother cried, "I'm full of pride"; her father was forlorn!
You can't take girls to baseball games or teach them how to swear.
They're busy talking on the phone or doing up their hair . . . .

"Just wait," her mother told him. "Be patient and you'll see.
She'll grow up much too quickly, right now she's only three."
Her dolls and things were lots of fun, and she played with all her toys,
But as she grew much older, her interests changed to boys . . . .

Then one night she sat beside him, and clapped her hands with glee.
Her words pulled at his heartstrings, "Daddy, put on channel three."
"My Blue Jays, they are playing, and they're gonna' beat your team."
Sports had become her passion. He'd missed something in-between,
Though it really didn't matter, she'd fulfilled his life-long dream.

So all you fathers out there who had their hearts set on a boy,
Sit back and let her grow up. She's bound to bring you joy.
For it really doesn't matter if sports are not her way,
She'll still bring you love and laughter each and every day.

To Amanda Patricia Copland—my number one inspiration and guiding light!

Onion Peeler
(Craig Costantino)

this painful
process

of disrobing
and dismantling

has left me
dehydrated

heart less
vein(s)

drifting
out of context

two onions
two Eyes
too many tears

raw touch of
exposed pasts
chafing

stinging remains of
The I

overpowering
    all sense
    and sight

Belladonna
(Eddie Couturier)

Her words pierce my skin, like the prickly cactus
and confusion pours from my open sore
as I sit in silence, with her noisy voice
loud as thunder—she calls for answers
and strikes me with a bolting glare
I shiver at the sound and fury, and stare
out a rain-splashed window

Many pairs of eyes, of asps dance atop her head
Like hair, each twists, and curls, and knots
all tangled in a web

Her eyes flash lightning and burn and spark
I feel them glaring through the darkness
of the room

Her icy breath blows frost and snow
that gather on my brow
and lips move faster, as expectorated
ice forms around her frozen mouth

Now she stops, and turns away, hands on hips
and mutters softly across tight lips
pale as December snow
I wait, until she leaves the room
before I smile

To the birth of the universe and her green velvet winter, cold, infinite, and mortal.

Age: 20
Address: 21 Copernicus Drive, Sault Ste. Marie, ON, P6A 6H1
Telephone: (705) 946-0682
Eddie M. Couturier was born on August 29, 1973, in Sault Ste. Marie, Ontario, but spent much of his childhood in Medicine Hat, Alberta. He later returned and is presently enroled at Algoma University with no decided major. He is interested in fossils and geomorphology, and his favourite place is the badlands of Alberta. His other interests are Astronomy, Physics, Neurophysiology and Mythology. He wishes to pursue graduate studies in science and eventually work for NASA's space program or attempt writing that combines science with limitless imagination.

At Forty-two
(Anna Cundari)

There are no surprises at home,
so you go out looking for them
in a sharp turn of the weather.

Your fortune in a liquid dinner
could not have been predicted,
nor could the unfamiliar smell of leather.

Walk a bridge lit up in the drizzle
like a birthday cake
on no one's birthday.

Say the line that never got a giggle
just to see
a nibble on the back of the neck and
a new bruise.

A quick slip from an aching look.
The choicest alibi does not astonish.
You never liked surprises anyway.

Building Blocks of Noise (Conquering the Silence)

(Trevor Cunnington)

he impregnates the
silence
with his own intelligence,
the intelligence of apes
who want something
and devise plans to get it

with building blocks
he smiles
and thinks of construction sites:

the noise, the thundering hum,
the occasional staccato human yelps
yet not so human, the machinery,
the building blocks

the raw materials transmute
into finished products
out of factories, the omnipresence of
factories:
big grumbling behemoths sleeping
and waking, sleeping and
awakening loudly into continuous
noise

he lies in bed thinking, building,
then he sleeps
like a factory and offends
the silence

A Sonnet to Soothe the Rent Heart

(Dana Cushing)

One to love and rouse to deeds—
My eyes look forward, that man to find;
Yet still too soon—my thoughts impede,
My heart wants what is left behind.

The heart does not smash like a glass
It rips and rends like fresh green wood,
The ends splayed and exposed, alas!
Slowly wrung of its life-blood.

My heart, given you in gladness,
Slowly sliced its own sweet strings;
Snapping, fraying free in sadness
A bloody and dejected thing.

Seek me not, I won't go back;
My heart better endures this lack.

Poems

(Tyron D'Souza)

Poetry has special qualities.
You don't need an introduction,
a body,
and a conclusion.
You don't have to do any research.
You don't have to worry about using words too often
And you're never wrong.
Poetry can make you think, care, wonder, laugh, cry
And a whole bunch of other intransitive verbs.
You don't need no grammar.
Isn't it strange how a poem can say so much more than a letter?
Isn't it strange that a person would rather write poetry
than listen to their prof?
And isn't it strange, too, that sometimes,
just sometimes,
a gift of materials
Is not as cherished as a gift of poetry?

Past, Present and Future
(Judy Dan)

Today
was a bubble,
bright and free,
'til it burst on a branch
of reality.

Yesterday
was as fine
as a glass of wine,
and as warm as a room
filled with sunshine.

But tomorrow
is a pebble
in my shoe,
small but irritating
because it's so new.

Originally a graduate of Interior Design, University of Manitoba. At present, a resident of Don Mills, ON. Have been involved in crafts of all kinds—weaving, appliqué, basket making, macramé—including some teaching. At present, a part-time poet.

The Prodigal Son
(L.R. Danby)

I live my life without conscience.
It doesn't matter where the next road bends.
I'm always looking for the rainbow's golden end.
And on this road of delusions,
Someone keeps watch as I lose my way;
Someone who holds all the love that I betray.

My father sees all my shattered dreams,
In silence he waits alone.
I'd leave a thousand times yet somehow it seems
That just when I feel I can't go on;
The prodigal son is still welcomed home.

I turned my back in anger
On the one I thought was always wrong.
I left my home just to prove I could be strong.
But all I've shown is a weakness,
To seek a fortune with deception and lies.
My father's wealth is a love that never dies.

He'll still be there tomorrow
He'll still be there when my luck is all gone,
Still teaching me how a father loves his son.

To my Father, Russell Danby.

Loving Touch
(Joanne Daniells)

To touch your soul
How gratifying
So much power to relent
One's mind could ponder
Wandering miraculously
Is it a spirit?

To touch your heart
Would be the power of love
A fervent emotion
A great sense of well-being
And happiness

To capture your mind
Thou wouldst recognize
The energy
The yearning to share
The whole strength in itself

To capture your love
One's body would quake
Sensing feelings
All at once
With no escaping
Just suprême bliss

My Sister Sleeping

(Glory Darbellay)

Flaxen hair silk strands
webbing down
spiralling caressing gently
your padded cheek, tumbling
down the crevice
where the bed and wall
long to meet.
The monster pushes
his hand through, reaching to find your
soul
but hidden behind closed lids
it
flirts with the cherubim.
Morning reveals
the brightness of
its
sky.

To Catherine.

I Saw You, Elementary

(Andrew Davidson)

I saw you dance the air today; you slid
Through it as in a trance, you seemed to breathe
More deep than breath and dream of love forbid.

I saw you light bonfires today to wreathe
The edge of fields of pain where sad men hide
And hope to die in dark now ringed with light.

I saw you lie in sand today beside
A child whom you had found and, with delight,
To whom you gave to mouth milkless nipples.

I saw you sleep in brilliant green, so still
Beside the calm nuzzle of sea. Ripples
Decree you have no need to wake, but will.

Wonder I, Love, if you await to die
So that can you betroth entirely sky.

Andrew Davidson was born in Pinawa, Manitoba, but now resides in Vancouver, studying English Literature at the University of British Columbia. He has travelled much of Canada and hopes to visit the rest, and wants to live in most of the countries of Europe. It is his intention to achieve a Master's Degree in Creative Writing and to support himself financially through writing.

At the Picture Show
(Harold Davidson)

As when, in years gone by, I climbed aboard
My Beaver, and took off from glinting lake
To lift above the trees, whilst engine roared,
And thrilled to know the sky was mine to take:
So soared my soul on that first day when we,
In sweet distraction, to a picture went
And sat together in serenity,
Partaking of enjoyment innocent.
And as, when I would dip a wing to turn
And, climbing still, set steady on my track,
I found myself, with more of you to learn,
Turning myself—my life—to fill that lack.
    And thus began, that splendid eve, our flight
    That led us into realms of wondrous light.

City Rooftops

(Sheila Davidson-Chamberlain)

In David's city where Selah lives
Silhouettes on skyline smartly give
Clear perceptions at even dark nights
Of various things, various heights.

Gabled houses from old-fashioned day
Or rooftop signs present news our way
Pointed steeples have church bells ringing
Trees grown tall nest lovely birds singing.

Clocks telling time to her passers-by
Hidden cameras used by super spies
Lights luminating our whole long night
Chimney stacks smoking grey or Pope white.

Swimming pools absent to roof places
Tiny top rooms have diverse faces
Copters landing with competency
Escape ladders for emergency

City landmarks save strangers from lost
Sunsets beautifying for no cost
Poles bear waving flags at half or high
Angels oversee and glorify.

To my Chamberlain children, Monique, David and Dennis, in dedication.

Age: 49
Address: New Brunswick, Canada
Born and raised in New Brunswick, Canada. HTHS Graduate. Some post-secondary education. Maiden name Sheila Davidson. Married Geoyes Chamberlain (Sheila Chamberlain). Three children by marriage including a virgin birth. Divorced after 15 years of marriage. Member of three Royal Families. Office worker. Religious person who had visitations from many holy people. Writer of prayers, songs, verses, poetry. First published literary work. Sheila's past, present and future is as a Missionary and Angel of God who does good and fights evil. Someday, she might write a book on politics of the world under the influence of Gods and devils.

What It Is

(Barry Davis)

power mowers

wind through trees

chainsaws roaring

flowers bees

hacking engines

lapping waves

honking hooting

silent caves

yelling screaming

sounding loon

pushing shoving

wolf howl moon

hatred violence

gulls a glide

drugs and war

not this side

Good Time Management
(Brad Davis)

Sitting like a stationary object
as grains of time fade away
giant waves of thought
trembling in and out

anything is possible here
imaginations run wild
questions thought of and answered
one's best thinking may happen here
suffering   pain   misery
gentleness   satisfaction   relief
any emotion can take place
as one sits here on the thing
we call the toilet

Blur

(Sean Davis)

I see
  critically, not-
  withstanding my
  ignorance, but things
are not in focus, so
  where does that

          leave me?

Give and Take

(E. A. Day)

I took his hand in trust
I took his person as is
I took him to be real

only to be betrayed
by disillusion.

I gave him my hand
I gave him my person
I gave him all of me

only to be forgotten.

My hands are now fists
unable to give any more.
My person is unknown to me,
unable to live.
All of me is incapable
of feeling

until
I
find
the self
I
lost.

To Dave and Jean—the first to reach out; and to Nora for her awareness.

Address: R.R. #2, Campbellville, ON, L0P 1B0
E. A. Day is a veterinarian residing in Campbellville, Ontario. She and her husband, Al, have two children, Louis and Andrea. "Writing poetry has provided me great solace over many years, but it is only recently that I shared some of my poems with a few close friends. It was their support and encouraging words that led me to submit "Give and Take," my first poem ever to be published. I consider this achievement a highlight in my life, and it has inspired me to continue writing and sharing my poetry."

The Witchwood

(Marjorie Day)

This is my Love
Said I
To the warlock of the wood
All right, said he
As we walked by
And partook of the birds
And the trees
And the leaves and the
Pond and the twitter and
Peck on wood of the
Woodpecker and the
Cuckoo into the night
And day and eventide
And dawn.

Come, my Love
You have never seen
Such as this—
The witchwood
Is teaming with flutes
And hanging with ivy
Thou art welcome here
Said I to my Love.

Address: P.O. Box 2248, R.R. #2, Collingwood, ON, L9Y 3Z1
Telephone: (705) 445-8806

I was born in Killarney, Manitoba, the year 1949. Our small family left this gently rolling countryside and prairie farm four years later, removing to Toronto, Ontario, the former home of my mother. After high school and stenographic jobs for a number of years in the heart of this historic city, which I had come to love, I felt compelled to move, in 1986, to the beautiful Collingwood/Wasaga Beach on Georgian Bay area. Killarney, Toronto city and Georgian Bay have been sources of inspiration to me for many poems.

Candles

(Catherine M. de Cocq)

There are no days like those magical somedays
When hours and eons are measured by heartbeat.
Sunrise is at noon, and it shines down all night.

When weeks and months exist, dead and buried,
Clocks have wound down and sundials broken;
Calendars lost. There is no time.

There is no place like that magical some-place
Where loss and skinned knees are borne by the clouds;
Trees are perspective, and lawns speak of God.

Where inches and miles are meaningless nonsense;
Light years within reach; infinity ceased.
"There" is your "here." There is no place.

"When I Grow Up" lived in Fairy Tale someday.
In conjurer's someplace, you stashed away dreams.
With Merlin departed, you feel there is no one.

But you, child, were wizard, creator of magic
With visions of heaven, feet covered in mud;
Adulthood approaches. Which way will you run?

Time, place, and childhood are taken away.
In death there is birth; in reality, cake.
Wishes are made and candles are blown;
With cord and cake cut, you stand all alone.
The magic dissolves; today's cake calls you grown.

For my children, Ryan, Colleen & Corinne Timbers, and the inner child in all mankind.

TeePee Rings
(J.M. deMoissac)

TeePee Rings
stones going around and around
in a sacred circle

Piles of rocks
once alive with blazing fires
abandoned now
by the shores of this tiny lake
shores protected by Saskatoon Berry bushes
thorny Roses
slender Birch trees

I close my eyes and
imagine how it must have been

close my eyes to piles of broken bottles
cigarette butts
and bits of trash around white and red cans
labelled LITTER, in big black letters

Age: 35
Address: Box 425, Biggar, SK, S0K 0M0
Telephone: (306) 948-2396
I farm in Central Saskatchewan. Raise sheep and chickens and Kuvasz dogs. Has her masters in CBC—a poet and a writer of fiction.

To the Trees
(Julie Dennison)

Squirrels seed the campuses of major universities
but seldom are acknowledged as originators of
contemporary theories—critical and otherwise—
of the towering signifieds from which they scold.

They rate the season's slow administration of a thaw
in language crows and sparrows rarely comprehend, tend
rather to dismiss as idle rodent chatter. But the tree
rats know their trees. These days, when one gnaws

a winter-wasted apple, there are those in the academy
who pause in polishing the final pages of a manuscript
to contemplate the ethics of creation. It is rumoured
certain scholars even dedicate their works to squirrels.

* * * * *

Brighter than the grey-black-browns that frequent grounds
of larger universities, our local squirrels are jocund
signifiers, small but flexible and well-read
in the ways of melting snow. Island-ruddy—red but

never rude—they're welcome in the classrooms of enlightened
lecturers. The chattiest of tree rats can't resist
an open window, leap from branch to ledge to seminar
then perch on tenured shoulders where they dictate

brilliant explications, peeling back the prickles to
the smooth skin of a chestnut. And professors, growing
bushy-tailed in conversation with the senior squirrels
here, if lucky, will retire into the trees.

To My Friend
(Alexis Diamond)

He took her out for dinner
and gave her the bill.
The meals, the maid, shoeshine and polish—
for his shoes, not for hers—
she paid for it all,
paid to close his suitcases open by the bed
teeth glinting.

One day, suitcases closed,
he walked out on polished shoes,
leaving laundry on the floor,
shaving cream and stubble caked in the sink.

She deserves love like a house
with insulation and a fireplace
and bay windows for the light.
She never wanted a suitcase love,
his bags on the floor by the bed.

Dear Little One
(Penny-Lea Disotell)

Dear little one, so soft and tender,
We wonder—what will be your gender?
Does it matter? Not a bit—
Within our hearts there'll be a fit
for all life's little miracles!

Dear little one, so soft and small,
We wonder—will you grow up tall?
Will you become a famous star—
Or will you travel very far
In search of all life's miracles?

Dear little one, we love you, and
We wonder—will the painter's hand
Or music's note inspire you—
To do the things you're meant to do,
Presenting all life's miracles?

Dear little one, now you are grown,
We wonder—if you could have known
How much you've meant to Dad and I—
As all the years have passed us by,
Counting all of life's miracles!

Poem for Silent Moon
(Virginia Dixon)

This is the big picture, Life.
Space with figures
whose spherical faces
change with same difference
as generations and days
evolve and revolve.

You and I are mothers, Moon.
Consanguineous spalls
in purdah watching.
So constantly watching
it's been left unexplored what
unveiled is revealed.

There is an emotion, Love,
like gravitational pull
between star and daughter.
We are heliotropic,
heads bowing to both, we are
moon-flowers, lovers.

We share the same song, Rhythm.
A calendar of days
turning to months.
Oceans swell and recede
while our children are conceived.
We live, we deliver.

Address: 273 Dawlish Avenue, Toronto, ON, M4N 1J4
Virginia Dixon was born in Montreal in 1954. After receiving her BFA from Concordia University, she moved to Toronto, where she lives with her husband and three children. Also a painter, she recently had a solo exhibition at Victoria College, U. of T. Frequently, the poetry she reads influences the imagery in her paintings. Other times, the imagery in her head becomes a poem. "Poem for Silent Moon" was written for a dance/video project choreographed by Leanne Dixon.

Admiration

(Trudy Anne Dodd)

Your serenity amazes me.
You're calm and quiet;
A solace for others.
I watch your beauty
With admiration and awe.
You possess the beauty of the innocent
With no trace of annoyance or malice;
Only a need to help others
Make it through
The perils of life.

Your strength amazes me.
You're ready and able
To defeat the elements
As they try to break you.
You see them
Not as evil,
But as misguided.
And in saving yourself,
You don't try to ruin others.
I admire you,
And your power to make others feel safe.

For Stacey and Reilley, who always make me smile, and my parents for their support.

Age: 22
Address: 9 Dodds Avenue, Guelph, ON, N1E 5X2
Telephone: (519) 767-0057
On February 4, 1994, I graduated from the University of Guelph, with a Bachelor of Arts in English. I now work in the Circulation Department of the *Guelph Mercury*, our local newspaper. I am also to be published in *The Space Between*, an anthology by The National Library of Poetry.

Untitled

(Sandy)

You'd never guess
from my purposeful stride
and my well-pressed suit
my black shiny case
and the swing of my arms
that I have nowhere to go.
You'd never guess
I'm really at home
in bed
under the covers
in a dark room
with my face
to the wall

What you see is my
body
marching
running
to catch up with the
crowd

Address: 34-9045 Walnut Grove Drive, Langley, BC, V1M 2E0

Mourning Exercises

(Margo C. Does)

A baby cries
Alabaster little arms reaching up
Amid the hustle and rustle,
Adeptly squeezing real live oranges
Aleena's brown arm goes out
And carries him,
As she carries everyone
All through the mourning exercises
Already, the Others, the Couple
Are in High Gear
Alert to their part in the Making of History
Aware of Stock Prices over mourning coffee
Always up to the Challenge.
Away they swoop . . . out the door
Ahead of the pack—
Ambition speaks louder than loyalty.
Ah . . . the limo
Awaits and they wave limply,
Almost with joy.
Alas, amidst the fanfare of taxis, goodbyes, BMWs,
Angelic Aleena, children filling the doorframe,
Adopts her dream,
Among the palm trees,
Announces her presence with silence and . . .
A baby cries.

To all those low-wage caregivers who miss their homeland.

Mom's Cup

(Wendie Donabie-Dixon)

Brown circles
line
the once-white porcelain cup.
Stains of experience
layered
one upon the other.

Darkest in the deepest part—
(the bitter dregs);
lighter near the rim
where she still drinks the present in.

A simple common cup,
yet unlike any other,
ringed
with years of laughter and of tears;
a vessel of love,
of pain,
of joy,
of sorrow.

For Johanna Dixon, who now drinks tea with the angels and breaks bread with God.

Address: P.O. Box 465, Station A, Mississauga, ON, L5A 3A2
Have written all my life. I love to paint pictures with words in order to share my life experience with others and to bring healing. My education prepared me as a Social Worker, so I have taken several correspondence courses in various forms of writing. I have been published in anthologies and have produced a newspaper column on dreams and another on healing. In addition to poetry for adults, I have completed a book-length, humorous rhyming story of children. Someday, I would like the opportunity of writing song lyrics and creating interactive stories for computers.

Jared
(Andrea Donovan)

He s p e a k s words
from his jaw
because of birth
right.

He has been
l i v i n g
in moments spent
swept round
his breached mind,
g a t h e r i n g
minute dust.

Quiet love s e e s
his boy and man gentle.

The anger is
i n c u b a t e d
moist
is
rising up from the conditions that grow it—unconditionally.

He w a l k s
carefully, is careful.

Not to diminish the e x p e c t a t i o n s
he selects ripe black berries,
and I cannot help myself to
c o n s i d e r bruises,

he eats bruises

Soft Spot
(Chris Donovan)

My eyes make ordinary men shrink;
My voice makes eardrum-shaking sounds;
My chest is tombstone material;
And my arms can lift a thousand pounds.

I've skinny-dipped in the Arctic Ocean;
I've wrestled lions and alligators at the same time;
I've eaten granite for breakfast;
And I've managed to keep God in line.

But I'm not strong—
Not when it comes to you.

You make my heart defy beat-logic;
Cause my knees to tremble.
And when you touch me,
A Super Hercules I do not resemble.

My enemies could use you as a weapon,
Because you're the only weakness I've got.
You're my Achilles' heel;
My one and only soft spot.

Ode to Liz
(Harold Dowler)

A red-haired girl once was my love.
Her beauty compared to that of a dove.
Her smile gave me life; her eyes gave me strength.
I wanted our time to be of great length.
But alas came the day when she said we must part.
She did not leave alone, with her went my heart.
Now I reflect on mistakes I have made.
The ultimate price I obviously paid.
To lose my one and only true love
And never again see such a beautiful dove.

Morning Whisper

(Linda M. Down)

The sun creeps up
over the horizon,
Gently casting light
on open fields.
The trees and flowers
gently sway in the light.
The open meadow
has a dewy cast,
As lovers embrace
the treasured light.
The warmth of the touch
awakens me.
My senses soar
to reach the rays.
The hope, the life and expectation
of a newborn day.

To Bruce: who taught me to see life from the inside of myself.

acceptance
(Patrick Doyle)

when does one stop *wishing* to become?
with the realization of,

I write; therefore, I am.

I need no one's approval
to justify my conviction,
nor a publisher to finance my inner drive
or to qualify the officiating of a title.
nor do I remain silent,
bolstering my timid passion only
within the secrecy of a private chamber,
safe from the phobia of rejection
and its judgement
as to whether my written thoughts
bespeak an author,
an identity.

I am; therefore, I write.

To all the "Dresser Drawer" poets. Write, be free!

Untitled

(Siona A. Doyle)

An apple can look beautiful
With its cherry-red skin
But that skin can only be beautiful
If there is a core within.

To my parents, James and Deirdre, and to Susan Coyne, my natural mother. I love you.

Age: 23
Address: Box 460, Picture Butte, AB, T0K 1V0
Telephone: (403) 732-4178

I wrote this piece in 1988, when I was 17. An Irish immigrant and adoptee, I have always loved expressing my thoughts and emotions on paper. It's a wonderful escape. My favourite author is the late L.M. Montgomery. Her words are so descriptive I could eat them! Like her, I love the sea. It's the most beautiful place and I hope to live by it some day.

Dallen

(Sheila J. Duncan)

The wait is long,
but the rewards are great.
When you add around the table another plate.

The labour is hard,
but the delivery thrill great.
When you add around the table another plate.

The commitment is forever,
but the love is too.
When you add around the table another guess who.

The face is sweet,
and the soul is brand new.
Tiny trusting eyes looking up at you.

It's me, Mom and Dad,
I've finally arrived.
Sure kept my birthday a surprise.

But now I'm here,
and life ahead looks great.
'Cause I got to choose your table
to set my little plate.

To my inspiration, my family.

Seven

(Kevin M.S.Q. Dunklee II)

You live with this dark side every day.
You stay beside it, but always remember—
it stays beside you.
Who may kill it?
We nail it down and refuse to permit it
and that seems to be enough, but—
we all know that every raisin was once a grape.
(Grapes to wine)—(Ashes to ashes)—(Dust to flesh)
(Flesh to incompetence)
Leslie—you know the words that drive me to sweet oblivion.
Let each bear its own exquisite warmth because
my surrender
to your tender embrace
is close enough to universal truth.
I feel dark passion from the apple we shared earlier.
Watch me kneel—watch me bleed
Enjoy the sunshine
but
don't squeeze my head so I have to change into someone else
because
fantasy is as simple as sipping seven chocolate milk-shakes
through your cruel fingertips—
those talons of truthful illusion.

Kevin M.S.Q. Dunklee is a writer, musical composer, and all-around inept card player who currently resides in a humble museum in London, Ontario. Seventeen very tall people once said of him, "he's shorter than we are." This is his first time "in print," so naturally, his mother is very excited. His goal is to one day forge a career for himself in poetry and music. For now, he is happy just wandering around talking to himself.

Today the Moon
(Jennifer Lynn Dunlop)

Today the moon
was just a slip of white
in a cool, calm blue sky
But last night it shone
with all the brilliance
and energy
of a fierce wintry night
Today, I too
possess less
of last night's
overwhelming freedom—
the sense of having
no earthly ties,
no restraints
Cut loose,
I burned as brightly
as the moon's
radiant white light
Today, the moon and I—
today we sit
and remember
Exhausted,
but carrying
beautiful memories.

From My Heart to Yours

(Richard Dupont)

I know two people, they're artists of life
They raised ten kids, just husband and wife
They took on the world, through soil and sin
So that we would be ready, for life to begin
My dad was a cowboy, then a soldier with sense
He met my mother, and their life did commence
There were fields to plant, and tractors to fix
The first cold winter, their blue jeans did mix
Then our life began, this family of theirs
Each one that they had, must have seemed like pairs
So they walked on Faith, the staircase of love
And watched the clock ticking, with help from above
Now it's my turn to give, right from the heart
I love you always, cause you did your part
So from this little body, to a twosome of joy
Happy Anniversary, from your little boy.

The Hanger
(Henry Duthler)

A doctorate in medicine
A plaque on the wall
A white coat on a hanger
To which he owes it all
A pair of rubber gloves
A mask over his face
Swift sleight of hand
He never leaves a trace
But the blood drops on his coat
And on the plaque on the wall
Slowly dripping from the hanger
To which he owes it all

Untitled

(Kevin Dyck)

Under a crow smiling atop a fence post strung to another by wire that spits orange down upon ignorant drinking blades of crab grass that know no better but to suck the poison and residue of rotting metal from the ground a mouse or mole for it is difficult to discern from this distance from across the field of shivering straw in the tepid country air runs about sniffing the rust and knowing it is foreign even though it is always there stops and hops suddenly back thinking it has evaded or is in a trap and vanishes with relief into the field away from the scent of the interloper

Devo's Words
(Devo Jaiikoah Dyette)

You may tie my hands in chains
Despise me because of my colour
Denounce me because of my attitude
But in your heart, you know me,
Because I am free.

My thinking is mine
My actions are mine
I am free
Like the wind rustling through every tree.
Free like the birds that roam the sky.
Free, until that day, when I die.

You may take away my belongings
And even distort my innermost feelings.
But in my heart I am free,
Free to be what I must be.
So remove your shackles,
Stop castrating my freedom with your manacles.
Because I am free, let me be me.

Age: 34
Address: 552 Frontenac Street, Suite 2, Kingston, ON, K7L 4M2
I have been published in four different books by The National Library of Poetry: *The Coming of Dawn*, *Wind in the Night Sky*, *Whispers in the Wind* and *A Far Off Place*. I have also written controversial editorials published by the *Whig Standard* published here in Kingston. Writing, I believe, is a ceaseless process of self-realization. This love of writing has broadened my knowledge, deepened my awareness and defined who I really am. Through my writing, I venture to bring comfort to humanity, to have trust in my friends and to cherish the beauty of life.

Faithful She

(Kenneth P. Eastveld)

A black and masterful art form.
Willing and determined.
The protector of my evils.

Soft brown eyes tell me of her love.
Happy at all costs,
Even when disturbed from a deep sleep.
Loyal to one.

I believe she holds the souls of lost worlds within.
While running in her desire of the day,
I sometimes see her smile.

Do not kill the wolf or anger my animal.
Threaten my life and suffer the wrath of a true friend.

My companion.
She will follow my empty footsteps to my grave,
Where she will pose untiring for endless tomorrows.

Touched,
Awaiting my return.
My angel reborn into a black dog.
My old friend,
Faithful she.

The Big Picture
(Stephen Edgar)

once
when I was fourteen
I cut class to
go out to the parking lot
for a smoke
*
alone
boots on the bumper
I lay back on the hood
of Larry's '68 Le Mans
soaking up the sun
feeling supreme
*
just before I finished my cigarette
a Monarch butterfly
fluttered down
and landed on my nose
*
honest to God
it landed on my nose
*
go figure.

The White City
(Felicity Enayat)

Come sunset, I look across the bay at the white city—
a parchment glowing in the light—its faint lines and swirls
drawing rows of three-storeyed houses, clay or washed with white.
Now I am within its walls. Winds race each other
in the narrow streets and along the houses, throwing up dirt.
Out the tall, wide, open, once people-coloured windows
blow pale curtains, long as they jerk and wretch in the sky—
sick men who've swallowed remedies for their poisoned bodies,
—drunks falling down when the winds subside—addicts
trembling as the breeze returns; then again dragged in the sky—
prisoners racked between wind and rod, but unconscious
of the prisoner who once was there. No bird no green
writes its name on the town; alone I watch its empty streets,
its houses vacated under the force of winds and time.
Turning to the sea, I glimpse a troop of kerchiefed people;
now they blur with the clouds now they flee in the distant waves,
while nearby waters spring towards shore, tongues tipped with light.

Carrousel
(Paul A. Eng)

I love you on the carrousel,
On the carrousel with jazz trumpet smile
On brazen white horses snorting,
I love you on the carrousel,
On the carrousel, with red wool coat
And powder-blue beret,
I love you on the carrousel,
On the carrousel, with twirl glee eyes
Untouched by mean-faced Troggs
On corner posts windy grey,
I love you on the carrousel,
On the carrousel, like gander and goose south winter fly
Away from lizards atop smoky stacks,
I love you on the carrousel,
On the carrousel, spin and spun
Through snow flakes whirling,
On a carrousel,
In a morning trance,
With ocelots gliding over the deep anxious snow.
And streets behind buses with diesel horns rhyme
With organ toots that crack the sky.
I love you on the carrousel,
On the carrousel, with cotton candy pink in hand
As you toss and float the caravan.

To Stasia Morningstar.

Address: 96 Markham Street, Toronto, ON
Left home at 16 after expulsion from Windsor's Riverside Highschool for being drunk in Geography. Returned to school after a year. Later went to St. Clair College and University of Windsor 2 years. Worked in Alberta, dishwasher, waiter, carpentry. Left my car on the street in Calgary and flew to London, England, because the Montana Border Guards refused entry. Stayed 13 years in and around Germany. Wrote a James Bondish novella at 14, 2nd manuscript lost in Cologne, Germany, February '87. Currently working on a novel.

Mind Traveller

(Elizabeth Enyedy)

Slipped out the door as the town slumbered
Heading for a place known only to him
Blissfully dead to the pain he's causing
Unaware that his days are numbered.

Blues and greens sent to uncover his tracks
In a nation still feeling its past
When soldiers and tanks ruled the city streets
And men disappeared never to come back.

But he's a victim of his mind, not the law
Because it can't let him forget what's gone
Showing his eyes familiar boyhood haunts
Using his body as its helpless pawn.

Now his wife's lost her grip on sanity
And his sister lives in fear for his life
But all they can do is wait this thing out
And hold fast to their faith in humanity.

To my mother, who instilled in me a love of words.

Inyanga

(Joanne Esposito)

It comes to me
that maybe
there is some truth
about the Inyanga,
magic man.

I could hope for
some message
of sweet truth
done up in delicious
spells.

Maybe it would last
beyond today.
A cure that would stick
and feel like my skin—
only safer.

To David Suzuki with the hope his dreams will come true for us all.

Life's Meaning Eludes Me (an acrostic poem)

(M.C. Ethier)

long,
    inquiring
        frustration
            evolves
                slowly;

my endless anxiety needs insight,
not goals.

enclosed labyrinth,
under darkness,
ever shadows

my existence.

Recovery
(Vic Evans)

"The economy,"
said the Finance Minister,
"is basically sound.
Of course, there are
problems—albeit
of a temporary nature.
There is, for instance,
a modicum
of Sustained Consumer Resistance."

Down at thc Mission
Mister Kirby
has finished his soup.
He is now consuming
bread and beans
with good appetite.
This looks very promising.
It may indicate
an upturn
in the Business Cycle.

The process and craft of writing poetry is one I have taken up only recently. I had not considered publishing any of my efforts until I received encouragement from Allan Cooper and Susan Musgrave. Largely as a result of their interest and kindness, I have had a dozen or so poems published in various magazines.

Touch
(Rod Exelby)

Total consent all things surmount and gone through
Awareness chooses an entirely new destiny
As it all goes by nothing to be wasted
Cannot the hungry man savour all things tasted
You and I can fill our hands with both hands empty
Tangent fingers reach out not to break but to hold
Hold on to all things realized not to be forsaken
High clouds witness with an entirely new density
Total light throws shadows against the wall
I stand within sight only to notice that the shadows crawl
And with their hands empty I have seen them
Attempt to reach out to touch it all

Address: c/o 24 Colborne Street West, #415, Brantford, ON, N3T 1K3
(Pen.) Rod Exelby, XLB. (B.) January 14, 1957, Toronto, Ontario, Canada. (P.) Margaret Exelby, Glen Exelby (deceased); (Ed.) 10th Grade, Alternative Education. (Occ.) Lithography.

Joy and Pain
(Rita Fabiano)

A precious gift
Round tiny face, rosy cheeks,
Downy soft hair,
Ten fingers and toes,
What a joy

First steps, first words,
Smiles and giggles,
What a joy

First day of school, first hockey game,
First date, first kiss,
What a joy

First cigarette,
Staying out late,
First words to wound us,

No more a joy,
Only unbearable pain.

Roses on Lace

(Judite Faria)

They grow each in a sacred place
Flowers so beautiful and fragile
They spread their precious petals in space
That with a gentle blow
Land on the mother earth where
They once grew, and lay still.

Time will bring in new flowers
None more precious than the ones before
Like the pleasant feel of lace on skin
The roses' smell will reach your soul
Strike a chord down deep
And steal away a feeling that
There will never again lay.

Like the roses' life,
So is the beauty of any living thing
Here today, gone tomorrow
And all that's left is the
Memory of the petal that is
Left behind, rattling in the wind.

The Geese at the Eaton Centre
(F.A. Savil)

Suavely and serenely
I flap my wings
Soaring towards the roof of the Eaton Centre.

Thousands come and gawk at me
And admire me in all my simplicity
As I languidly glide
Towards the clouds.

You wanted to tie ribbons around my neck
"It's in keeping with The Season!" you said.
Knuckle-head!
Leave me alone!
Don't you see that I am a work of art!
Leave me alone!
Bonehead!
Leave me alone while I soar above the crowds
Up into the skylight . . .

Of the Eaton Centre.

Age: 54
Address: 609-280 Dundas Street East, Toronto, ON, M5A 3W1
The author is a 54-year-old Guyanese-Canadian who has written several short stories, plays and a novel.

Human Constructs

(Susan Maria Farrell)

souls do remember
though perhaps it's faint,
drizzling and fog-like
on some grey business day

wisps and dreams
creep into sleeping heads
set on fibre and fluff
and ebb in armchair talk

just like water
on the back of a goose
dribbling slowly off
droplets left lying around

so like words
hanging in the lofty air
they never got caught
by some misconstruing mind

souls do remember
the shriveling insight
autumn in our hearts
of why we ever made words

Nora

(Ted Faucher)

She weaves a web of substance and thought,
This girl from the east her family they brought.
She strives for perfection,
Her goals and her life;
School can be tough, but she copes with the strife.
Her image is strong; one of sound mind
A quality person, simple and kind.
Her world is young and very her own,
A chance to be curious and hers to roam.
The weight of the world might hit her one day,
Only for a moment then she'll send it away.
A wife she will make, for a happy young man,
Vacations and trips; the kids, the van.
Her parents will be there for all that she does,
Giving her strength for whatever is; and once was.
A great friend, one day, echoed his words to me,
"A very nice girl, this Pyesmany."

Ode to a Bach Fugue

(Sarah Faulkner)

Who else so huge in magnitude
still haunting pipes of organ song,
Today those pounding chords or delicate bird-feet
skittering trills stand undaunted.
A staunch God-force called forth to deafen
any impudent sinner who dares to taunt
His omnipotent melodies.
Who else?

Northern Spirit
(Jake F. Fehr)

A stream of sustenance meandering flows
Through perpetual valleys almost unknown,
Water whose limpid tactility knows
Sacrosanct places purity sown.

Shimmering ripples warmly accented
In the full moon's mystical light,
Sweet scent of pines fomented
On whispering zephyr's capricious flight.

A nostalgic dream phosphorescent,
A fragile stillness unbroken,
By dark factories' screams lamentant
Of a lone wolf's haunting cry spoken.

How sweet the guerdon of nature's preservation,
All virtue retained, exalting a nation!

To lovers of the Canadian North.

Age: 28
Address: Box 21094, Steinbach, MB, R0A 2T3
Jake F. Fehr is a new poet and writer. At age 28, he has chosen to abandon conventional ambitions and embark on a long-awaited odyssey in creative writing. In addition to enhancing his studies in English, he is furthering both his practical experience and theoretical education in journalistic-related activities with a variety of independent endeavours. A striking love of nature and freedom imbues much of his work. He is currently comprising a book of poems and researching his first documentary.

Sense of Humour?

(Hilda Feiner)

A leaf falls lightly from a tree
And dances round the trunk.
It isn't like an apple
That descends with a ker-plunk!

I guess I'm just the leaf-type—
All the lighter thoughts I've *thunk*
And I find them full of laughter
When my grounded friends say "Junk!"

When *I* think that something's funny
Their reaction's very dead,
And I know they think that apple
Must have hit *me* on the head!

The Woods

(Nancy Fischer)

I am drunk on beauty's brew—
such a generous portion has nature poured
that but a glimpse is intoxication,
a sip of this sight, the strongest wine.
I am drunk on the nectar of flowers—
such sweetness is surely the drink of gods,
for this is the liquor that butterflies crave
and in their tawny silk robes devour.
Would that nature could set me a place,
and I could dine in this banquet-hall,
with a sunbcam as a chandclicr
and deep green moss as my carpet below.
Butter cup china brimming with dew,
scarlet berries and mushrooms my fare,
such a marvellous feast it would be,
richest by far of anywhere.
What a symphony entertains—
fine-tuned are these swallows and robins and bees.
What a company masquerades—
creatures cloaked by their curtain of trees!
And when I have eaten my fill in this place,
then I would lie on a grassy bed,
A trickling brook as my lullaby
And a soft earth pillow to rest my head.

To Jim and Nellie Ross for sharing the magic of Pleasant Valley with their granddaughter.

Beyond

(Katie Fisher)

Sparkling tops,
green spikes.
Reflect shimmers,
of distorted
light; shadows,
long, short.
Dancing in the
breeze.

Swaying like grass,
prominent, dominant.
Fathers of the forest,
jungles and bush.
There today,
gone tomorrow.
Hard outsides,
soft inners,
beyond.

Fill the skies,
touch the clouds,
up and above;
beyond.
Joined together,
choirs of harmony;
united as one,
beyond.

To my family and friends, who never let me fall short of doing my best.

Age: 19
Address: 3914 West 21st Street, Vancouver, BC, V6S 1H6
Telephone: (604) 228-1093
I was born in Oakland, California, but have spent the greater part of my life in Canada. Currently, I am going into my second year at Mout Allison University in New Brunswick and majoring in Social Psychology. My goal is to one day write a novel or compose a poetry anthology, but for now, I am quite content with furthering my academic career while waiting for my literary career to begin.

The Pendulum's Arc
(Ellen Joanne Fjetland)

Over the grip of the frozen field
With soil like broken stone
The wind skitters
Through the bones of branches
And the frost glitters
Like a silvered desert.

Above the granite
Of a shadowed escarpment
The full moon rises
Below ice-hardened stars.
Its lonely glow can never ease
The mists of cold
Upon the brittle earth.

And Orion strides in silence
With watchful Sirius
Beyond the horizon
And the pendulum's arc.

Untitled
(Lisa Flasko)

Do you still believe in God, my friend?
I know how hard you tried.
Parting is such sweet sorrow,
'til next we meet on the other side.
A pack of cliches could never amount to what I truly have to say.
Deep inside I know that you know I really want to stay
Beside you in a life of fun, dying wasn't in the plan,
But I guess it's just fitting for a very spontaneous man.
I sometimes sit and wonder why it isn't me,
I feel if the tables were turned the words would all be set free.
Still, this is only just a stepping stone
(One that cuts and tears)
As you step from a confining world to a forever without cares.
But I know that you will wait for me, be with me when I fall
And miss you in the darkness, 'til I hear that Heavenly call
That you are safe and being watched, wondering why I'm sad,
When both of our lives worked out for the better
Since we met; that of which I'm glad.

Demons

(B.A. Fletcher)

sometimes i like to torture myself
by standing naked in front of a mirror
          with the lights on

and i clench muscles, suck flesh in and up—
hold my breath, stand up straight . . .
          but it will not disappear

excess flesh hangs from limbs and torso like shackles;
it forms mounds of disgust on stomach, on thighs
          —on my mind;
its lethargic jostlings are the voices of demons inside—
          multiplying with each second i stare into the glass

possessed by overwhelming repugnance,
tormented by willowy size-5 ghosts,
i am relieved only by the temporary exorcism of a toilet flush
          flushing guilt
          flushing pain
where in my mind i destroy their collective mass
which only truly disappears
          when i shower, alone
                    in the dark.

My Dad, My Friend
(Tiffani Fletcher)

In every sunrise, every sunset,
every rainbow, every star,
I am missing you, yet loving you,
knowing you are not far;
Yet I am not sure just where you are.

Are you sitting here beside me?
Or were you the bird that flew?
I feel the wind blow in my ear,
And I wonder if it is you.

Are you reading over my shoulder?
Are you holding my hand right now?
I want to tell you I love you,
I am not sure if I know how.

I can feel you wiping my teardrops
And asking me, please, not to cry.
It is just the simple reason I never
said Goodbye.

I am loving you so much and missing you more,
but you are gone, and I am left to cry
And wonder why, why you even had to die?

To someone very special,
who in my heart, he will stay.
To never be forgotten
And could never be replaced.

To the memory of Shayne, my Dad and friend, who will never be forgotten.

Believers and Unbelievers
(Violet E. Fodor)

The world that crushes
With political neutering
Castrates Joy's tears.
The sovereign of erased faces
Unfurls their amputated tongues.
Dusk succeeds dawn.
Respect kills the notes of light,
Stops their dark murmur,
Crashing and fragmenting on stone eyes.
Kneel
Or be stoned by love.

In memory of Sylvia Plath, Tami Stransky and Patricia Kubalek.

Age: 19
Address: 191 Brownridge Drive, Thornhill, ON, L4J 7E4
I have been writing since grade five. I also paint, do photography and write short stories. I have just completed OAC at Vaughan Secondary School, and I am planning on attending Ryerson to study photography. I have been published in the school paper, yearbook and *Early Harvest Magazine*. Art has always been part of my life. Words are powerful symbols. In all my works, I try to communicate the vision that I see in my mind's eye. Each piece is an attempt to portray and communicate something visual into words. I will continue to struggle.

Reincarnation
(Deborah Foley)

short
yellow
stumpy
quizzical face, funny face
bark like straw
bite like salt
I swim in the brown orbs

"Grandma," I say
"Is that you?"

"Arf," she says

For Bessie, Cathie and Honey.

The Power Within Me

(Jorie Anne DiFoss)

It doesn't hurt to ask for help to get Me through my pain,
But I better understand it's Me I must retrain!
The power is within Me to set my spirit free,
And I must use that power now that I've found the key!

I've learned not to defend myself—to simply state the facts
And not to take it personally how someone else reacts
I am not a chid who must trust, obey, be good
No longer will I take abuse—no one ever should!

I'm entitled to my feelings; you can't take them from Me
Each time I give in to you I'm only hurting Me
I'll no longer suffer; I have made a choice
After years of silence, I now give Me a voice!

Age: 34
Address: 12 A Jarvis Street, Fort Erie, ON, L2A 2S1
Telephone: (905) 871-9707

My family travelled extensively through the United States during my childhood, establishing my desire to explore the world and write about my experiences. At the age of 16, I moved to Germany. This was an exciting time as I was thrust from childhood's protection into the adult world and a foreign country. I returned to Canada four years later, speaking, reading and writing German. Returning to college, I achieved a life-long goal of becoming a journalist. Because of the enjoyment I get from creating poems, songs and short stories, I desire to share my talent with the world.

The Poet's Quandary

(Stephen J. Fowler)

Within my head these words collect, awaiting their release
I often wonder at their worth; is it a blessing or a curse?
That they should come to me alone, not caring for the timing
Giving way to inner peace, concerned at best in rhyming.
I ponder at the message told, some prophesy revealed?
Though tired body begs for rest, these words, they do not yield!
A simple man of humble birth has power in his pen
Was I but chosen this time round to spread my word to fellow men?
My love of family, God and friend matter more than I can show
But to try and hide from these words within and simply there's no place to go.
Yet somewhere in this life of mine, will these words matter to any soul?
This is the question that I ask,   and the answer?
I must, I have to know . . .

Time

(Karen Foxcroft)

If time is an extra-long ruler
each hour measured and firm
perhaps someone bent it
for I am only
skimming the tops
and time vanishes
in mysterious loops
beneath me

From the Rock

(J.T. Francis)

I have walked in the footsteps of despair
and carried the weight of anguish well spent.
I have faced the Demons that knew my face,
bowed my head and wept at their torment.
I've walked the heights of the highest high
and drunk with Kings in a river of wine.
I've told the truth in my own special way,
maybe not all the truth, maybe not all the time.
I've been to the bottom, and I've climbed to the top,
I've been in and out of doors that should have been locked.
I've kissed the Devil and slapped God in the face
and wept as He welcomed me back to the Rock.

I've seen my face in the bottom of a glass
and wiped the blood from my fists at anger's first law.
I've broken hearts just for the sake of a kiss
then gone back and broken them some more.
I've seen the rivers of Hell rolling down my soul
while Demons swam in the tears of sin.
Nothing's passed without keeping score,
nothing's lost without the need to win.
I've watched the years pass into age
and kept the rhythm to the ticking of the clock.
I walked in anger and slept in rage
but still He welcomed me back to the Rock.

J.T. Francis is a poet/songwriter currently working on his first novel. He has written several short stories and two collections of Poetry titled "Energies of Darkness" and "Gold from the Grave." He is a committee member of the Orillia Folk Society and also a member of Mensa Canada. He resides in Orillia, Ontario.

My Worries

(Nicole Freebody)

I paint my worries
with my insides
I use my fingers
as a brush
my body
as a muse
my memories
as a canvas
and my reputation
as a frame
I paint my worries
with my insides
now, but not again

The Cool Breeze
(Golda Fried)

Sipping lemonade
on a southern swing
up north.
The cool breeze came and
I lost your eyes to
the cool breeze.
It led your eyes to
the tall trees
where birds were flying off
in a hurry.
They shat on the tree
with the carved out heart
and still your eyes were with them.
And so my eyes set on my drink
to see the ice cubes sink
as I am left a girl
who likes to feign
that Southern drawl
in the north
with real guys like you
who drive off in real cars
with real ambition
just when summer is ending.

Escape the Madness
(Mercedes Friesen)

Some secrets are beginning to show
Dancing in the light of the moon
Some secrets are better left unknown
Save me from the tears and breaking sadness

Kiss me with fire, escape the madness
Take me in past your heart so afraid
Don't let me leave this night too soon
Let me remain in your gentle ways
Dancing in the light of the moon

I hear whispers through the silence—
With each other,
Love shouldn't know shame
Imparting minds can bear no distance
Feelings of passion can always remain

All I express, you've helped me find
deep within
Let's escape the madness together

Inspired by Jesse and our purest of loves, love Mercy.

Age: 18
Address: 250 Satok Crescent, Unit #2, Milton, ON, L9T 3P4
Telephone: (905) 878-6195
My poetry and song lyrics have flowed both from the deep sorrow and incredible joy inside my heart, since I was 12 years old. Singing and writing are my passions. Ultimately, together with them, I would like my music to find a greater success.

The Mystical Seasons
(Nadine J. Froese)

ing
y
l
f
Life used to pass me by like a jet
but today I take time to watch the changes pass
And I enjoy the transition

The days shorten bit by bit
the sun splatters the sky at dusk with soft brushes of pink,
purple and flaming oranges and reds

A slight wind picks up and cools the air
while the lifeless dry colourful leaves float and rustle in the
Air then bury themselves for another season

o
w o
Great flocks of birds s p across the skyline headed toward a
warmer climate
I haven't figured out why I'm suddenly noticing these changes
they seem more visible to me now

maybe life is slowing down for me now
I take life one day at a time
I am starting to appreciate the little things in life now and it's
wonderful

To God, my Aunt Linda, Uncle Ron and my Nanny for making it all possible.

Eyes of Eternity
(Cindy Gabert)

I looked into my child's eyes
and for a fleeting moment in time
caught a glimpse of eternity there in her soul.

I saw a wellspring of abundant innocence that,
for the moment,
took the breath from my body.

I saw in her gaze the peaceful ebb and flow of life—
the heartbeat of humanity that lay glistening there
like a tear caught in the last whispers of sunlight.

She took me there—where she was—in her daydream world.
A world of childhood illusions and fantasy.
Forever on the very precipice of understanding.

No questions did she ask of me then.
Instead . . . a tiny knowing smile,
and what followed was a comprehension
beyond our natural realm of understanding,
a spiritual bonding of two souls,
of love,
mother and child,
forever.

To my three darlings, Becky, Tony and Missy.

Age: 27
Address: P.O. Box 3307, Lacombe, AB, T0C 1S0
I am a very busy mother of three beautiful children who account for most of my poetic inspiration. I also hold a part-time position as dispatcher with the Lacombe Police Service. I have a grade 12 diploma, which was attained through night courses. This heralds my first literary accomplishment, and I hope to have more of my work published in the future.

There Was No Weather

(Margita Gailitis)

There was no weather, as I remember,
when we first met. We did not discuss
how hot how cold how depressing
how shall we prolong evade the rain.

You'd enter rooms raw waiting
for my skin to run to you wrap
as cellophane does excluding nerve
ends tied mind ribboned but
that was

before we started speaking
English lost our thees and thous,
before we assumed albino identities,
shielded our fragilities.
Without diminutive

a language

that does not distinguish us
from crowds evading pain.

platonism bears she

(Joanne Galea)

can they begin to understand this concept?how so, demand i?why is he avoiding the obvious gift of truth?why?why is it immensely difficult for him?his denial breeds pain in her.may she justify her intent?or is she cast adrift to float among the rest; those who fell for to submit.what?why?i cry.so difficult, and oh, so full of pain.this strange world, i admit, plain, yet intricate, simple, yet misunderstood.it is like the way we face the world untrue, full of extremities and circumscribed desires, ambitions, motives, and foolish inspirations.because life's expectations differ from one to another.from one between another.foolish tho' preciously implied.platonism is what i mean.it is there if we share, to you from me, to me from you.acceptance, accepted, accepting.accept my friend, this is merely all that i wish.accept, as to be accepted.it's so anxiously difficult for him to accept.why?why?why?perhaps denial he fits.fine by it, tho' i will not submit.then cast under and go adrift shall i.hey hoah, i cry. why, why?why, why?not i!this is the way.the way i know.this is live and live shall i.so be it, if all he does is deny, deny, deny!then this great gift, platonic, i say, shall not exist!simple and there it is.only pain may she reveal, she is aware—strength lies in her path, but can she persist, and prevail?dwelling within him, lie misconceptions and unacceptance.because this he wills; it always has and always is.some day i know shall exist.see?he will accept.i know.a unique era shall be born.she is GREAT.do you agree?accept and you will see.she is great.

For all persons struggling for change in society.

Age: 24
Address: 7864 Swanson Drive, Delta, BC, V4C 5C5
Telephone: (604) 596-9485/521-2413
Enduring law school and raising a family with a beautiful man would be my ultimate goal. I have a Bachelor of Arts, Sociology Degree, and I studied piano under the Royal Conservatory of Music. Writing is personal and intimate for me. When writing, I am in touch with the "inspirational self" within my heart. I hope that people find my writing absolutely meaningful! I want it to do something for you—the individual reader. I wish that people would accept each other for who they are, and for who they wish to become. Hockey is my favourite sport!

A Cossack Bridles His Horse (Russian Winter)

(J.C.C. Gandier)

A Cossack tries to bridle his horse
Where rose is the colour of the morning
In a forest lair when the deep frost bangs

Hands from cold lose their hold and then enfold
The steaming nostrils bold for warmth renew
He takes the bit to thaw tongue-burning frost

Then like a musician tuning key strings
The Cossack to assure a comfort fit
Studies and adjusts the bridle and bit

The trail is jewelled by snow diamonds' sparkle
And cries out in anguish from crunch of feet
While the Cossack mounts with an oath and leap

To my wife, Joan.

Tangle of Vines
(Pablo Garcia)

Everyday, I am reminded of vines.
Thorny vines, vines of fruit, vines of flesh
tangled vines that unfold from the earth
and surround, pulling us
towards Her bosom.
Encircling vines, penetrating skin,
spreading with certainty of colour
like the red of sweet tomatoes,
binding souls to the flesh.

Everyday I am reminded of vines.
I see chestnut vines unravel
from your scalp,
caressing sounds of hair
like a hymn rising from your body.
Entwined, you hold me to your touch,
to the fruit that ripens.

Everyday I am reminded, everyday
devouring vines.

For Margareta.

Pablo Damian Garcia was born on the 18th of May, 1970, in Cindad Evita, Buenos Aires, Argentina. He believes that *it* is simple. In the words of Silvina Ocampo: *El que no tiene coraje de vivir como piensa, termina pensando como vive*. There is no compromise to life.

What Is This Primal Rite?

(Jeffrey T. Gardiner)

I'm encompassed within harmonious violence,
consisting of luminous light,
consisting of melodious music,
and enveloped within a small sphere of silence,
with movements, I passively fight.
In isolation, I am not alone.

Think to myself, that ageless is this primal rite,
as thoughts are broken by my eyes,
as thoughts are twisted and bent out of shape,
I suddenly envision a beacon bright light
which will be my victory demise.
I see the focal point of human beauty.

I observe, motionlessly and in timeless joy
others move between her and I,
others who live in their spheres of silence
and in spite of their strategic tactical ploy
the image I have doesn't die.
She doesn't yet know I exist.

Then I dreamt; What if the ground let her and me fall,
into the earth? Up to the sky?
She'd then look around, and see I was there,
because there would be no pink people partition.
Into my arms, I dreamt she'd fly,
unlikely, I know, it never happens.

To the genius of those who've gone before, those who serve can do no more.

Age: 24
Address: 220 Dundas Street West, Napanee, ON, K7R 2A8
Telephone: (613) 354-3058
Jeff was born in Fort Erie and was raised in Napanee, Ontario, where he attended the Napanee District Secondary School. He currently attends the University of Western Ontario, where he studies History. Jeff has travelled the world and even spent six months peacekeeping in the Middle East. He has written poetry privately for eight years. Some of his goals include publishing a complete book of poetry and pursuing further education.

Bay of Quainty
(Jeff M. Gaulin)

In Saskatchewan, gilded,
she dances near water
(whorly-burly withy-wheaty)
on jaunty June days
before snow, smoke will
make claims, kill.

Froggies on the pond
she tosses us croutons, lilies
green in compost,
a fertile pile
for children's children

slippery sliding
in the sands of Presqu'île
she burrows her toes,
the fisher woman,
reels us in—
the pain in our gills:
her hooks: delightful,
grand.

When she sends us
to the bottom of the bay
we swim, silver gleams
in our gills . . .

Age: 23
Address: 92-94 Stroud Crescent, London, ON, N6E 1Y8
Telephone: (519) 681-5436
Born to a lower-class French-Canadian father and English mother, Jeff Gaulin grew up in London, Ontario. He graduated from McGill University (1994) with a First Class Honours BA in English Literature and a Minor in Classics. He is now an MA student at The School of Journalism at UWO. In 1990, Gaulin won Second Prize in the Grand Theatre's Playwright Contest, for his play "Tea for Two." That year, he also won the Carroll Connors Memorial Award for contribution to the arts in London. His poems have appeared in *Script*, *SansCrit*, *The Pillar* and *The Red Herring*.

Cloaking

(Lynn Gauthier-Baxter)

To answer the thoughts,
He said in silent senses.
To listen to the birds and
Their prayerful praises.
Reach for the sky and seek
Comfort in the softness of clouds.
Taste the rain as it falls from
on high, and thirst no more
for it is the only answer.
But in my weakness, I lost
control and found no consolation
in what was feeling.

For Jared, Darrell, Celtae and Ward.

Hair

(Alisa Gayle-Deutsch)

hair
2 tons of hair
arriving at the museum
so says the New Yorker

hair
2 tons of women's hair
braids cut off
scissors close to the scalp

hair
2 tons of dead women's hair
eaten by moths, brittle in boxes
turning to dust one day

hair
2 tons of dead women's hair
bodies beaten, gassed, cremated

hair
a bag of my own hair
sitting in my room
as i cut off my hair each month
unthinking, unknowing
as i breathe their ashes in the air

Mountain Man

(C. Geiger)

Who are you young man with eyes of grey,
A listener to words of the wind's harsh voice,
While your silence pains me like deafening noise,
And mountains shadow your desired gaze?

Do you belong in a coat of armour
With a sword to match your pride
Atop a Clydesdale to enhance your stride,
Fighting Earth's battles without a murmur?

Or shall I find you amidst the Polar Land
Beneath a parka of seal skin and fur
With solitude as your constant lure,
Chiselling a castle in Nature's glass hand?

Will I find you upon a mountain peak,
Feeding the goats and racing the ram,
Conquering the sky and nurturing the land
In hand with a destiny that knows not defeat?

Like a thousand pebbles over sparse gold,
Which no digger's pick or shovel can find,
(Such tools cannot discover the divine)
You remain this hidden metal, with stories untold?

Who are you young man with eyes of grey?
May I be the one to unfold the stone cover
And find the gold that could no other
And lead you from mountain to valley one day?

Repose

(J. Don George)

The Earth has accomplished—vocation
Summer's labour—foundation for rest.
Tired limbs—weary boughs—have surrendered
All production from Spring's firm request.

The leaves like ribbons of crimson
Ablaze in Earth's gentle breath
Fall to the ground with the absence of sound,
Light gently—on Mother Earth's breast.

Silence untouched—we waver and watch
Playful clouds on a sea royal blue.
They never impede our lantern of need
And scarlet blankets bestow comely view.

The blanket acknowledged by Mother,
She's closing the cycle again.
Tired but complacent she lies there,
Again covered by flurries of friends.

For Namie—my mother.

Address: 549 Rose Avenue, Apt. 12, North Bay, ON, P1B 6V7
Telephone: (705) 476-1931
I have recently received my certificate in the Health Care Aid field and also hold a diploma in Communications. I particularly enjoy helping the elderly in their homes and in homes for the aged. I benefit from their true and genuine appreciation and enlist for conversations that escort me to times past.

He Rode a Purple Rocking Horse

(Linda A. Gerow)

He rode a purple rocking horse
And stole my heart.
He bowed
And offered me his hand.
Prince Charming
In a pair of yellow Dr. Denton's.
He said he needed one more ride . . .
And had one,
While I read him Chapter Three
Of Peter Pan.

Back and forth he rode his purple steed
Humming . . .
On the wooden floor.

He rode through London, Derrytown
Then settled down
Into his trundle bed,
Happily exhausted . . . .

His journey to Never Never land
Waited.
Waited for this traveller, mine.
Waited.
Like the purple rocking horse
That rocked itself
to
sleep . . .

For Tyler, the rider.

Eyes Face Forward

(Karen Geurtjens)

Appearing pensive,
lost in thought.
Eyes face forward,
empty eyes, steady stare.
Head to one side,
then to the other.
Eyes remain forward.
Someone speaking,
off in the distance.
Eyes look up,
then face forward.
Wipe woman comes,
to clean the spittle.
Eyes cast down,
watch as she walks.
Can't reach out,
hands bound to the chair.
Can't cry out,
voices only inside.
Suffer in silence.
Eyes face forward.

Colours of Love

(Dominic Girard)

Cool, crisp air fills my eager lung,
As trees bare themselves for winter.
In the shivering breeze, the fresh summer leaves,
Are changing to gold shades of colour.

And they fall to the ground, making little sound,
No more than a cloud's condensation.
When the hot days take leave, they wrinkle beneath,
The sun's shine, now increasingly thin.

Up with the moon, cries a weary loon,
Mourning the loss of a lover.
With a dreary sad sigh, it climbs the night sky,
Answering cries of another.

Walking through the dead forest, an ironic chorus,
Trees lament their sleeps of infinity
Her soft teary eyes, her sad dreary sighs,
Highlight cheeks, turned rouge with frigidity.

Now on my autumn's eve, I must take my leave,
And allow the passage of seasons.
The snow falls with a shove, the colours of love,
Will fly me, with the loon, to the heavens.

For my pretty lady and her "soft moonlit eyes." I won't ever forget your love.

Untitled
(Michelle Glennie)

But,
she grows fatter,
reflecting off the water.
The mirror is too shallow;
pebbles roll along the bottom.
A finger taps the surface—
like rain on a window.

She vanishes
for a moment.
A facc that will not focus
an image sunk forever—
Or is it waiting in
the water.

Cupping her reflection,
mouth fills with water
growing fatter and fatter
distorting shape
and sound.

Mhairi B. Edmiston.

A Missing Child
(Karin Gloor)

Where are you, my flesh, my own
Where are you, my little one
I miss that twinkle in your eye
I miss that certain smile

Where are you, my flesh, my own
Where are you, my little one
There's that empty bed of yours
No one to play with your toys

Where are you, my flesh, my own
Where are you, my little one
I want to hear your voice again
I want to hold you in my arms

Where are you, my flesh, my own
Where are you, my little one
May God be willing, hear my prayer
Bring home, my flesh, my own, my little one

May God grant all prayers be answered to "bring our children home safe and sound."

After the Olympics, 1994
(Marcia R. Goldberg)

Some are asking for more troops in Sarajevo;
some are looking for a way to arm the Muslims or Croats.

Here in Westmount, we're having bitter sunshine, variable clouds.
Here we see light glare silently across our snowy yards

as if grasses soon grow green and bulbs take flower,
as if trees soon bud abundantly and bloom.

Talks of peace through violated ceasefires,
talks of UN aid to starving victims

seem far from ivies and from sunny spider plants my cats attend,
seem simple as forgetting where we've put the minutes.

A phone call away from disaster? A quiet garden . . .
a phone call away from gunfire? Deforestation?

A fence away from Sniper Alley? Putting war into it—
a fence capped with snow topiaries the wind made—

Some pent-up preparation, like Bomba's dash—
some abstract misconduct slips; some awfully dismal failure speeds

wide of its marks as the gaze of disbelief
widens on the nature of sport.

The First Born
(Harry C. Gooder)

In my nakedness, behold the truth.
Without blemish,
I sit upon the throne, and survey the beauty in all its form.
I deride the lesser primates, in their caressing.

Who conceive, in this, my domain.
Now I ponder, I am not the same.
Moulded in purity.
The first born.

A thousand years, I walked alone, this garden paradise
with all its living form.
No toil.
No earthly strife.

Now I slumber beneath the tree of life.
Amid space and time, in this mystic realm.
Then awake. With love, my eyes behold?
Emerge again. A naked soul, from the potter's mould.

In memory of John Gooder.

A Puzzle I Love

(Priscilla Gopsill)

You are a puzzle I love
You are strong yet gentle too
Your feelings run deep and rarely show
Your heart is battered and scarred but whole
You are my love

You are like the oak, so tall and proud
Never bending in the storms of life
Your face so richly woven
In tragedy and joy
You are my love

You give me love all-embracing
Joy, laughter, sadness, anger
You give me hope to dream
You are my tears, my frustrations
You are my love

So stay with me
And together we will share
Our happiness and sorrows
The frustrations of our tomorrows
You are my love

We will weave together
Our rich coat of love
To keep us warm in the chill of age
You are my puzzle
You are my love

The Girl in the Box
(Lorne Gorber)

Reflecting on change,
She chose not to be a victim.
Not just to walk out,
But make a total change.
To become an 'un'victim—
Take charge.

Age: 20
Address: 1429 Bishop Street, Apt. #7, Montreal, QC, H3G 2E4
Telephone: (514) 288-5961
Born in Moncton, NB, Lorne has attended Concordia University, majoring in Eng. Lit. Currently, he is enroled at the Hollywood Scriptwriting Institute (Hollywood, CA), where he will complete a motion picture script as well as make and market it. A staff writer for a Montreal-based magazine, Lorne hopes to publish his first novel by 1996.

Dreamland

(Chad Green)

Drearily, wearily drifting extreme
by the waterside moon of the deepest dream.
Slip, slide away to the passive world,
intense, be free and cast into submission.
    Direct from the source of the silvery moonbeams,
    a rush of enchantment released without warning
    to carry your thoughts to a realm uncontrolled.
    Know no bounds, believe all is true in your subliminal
    voyage to the land deep within.
    Be free to yourself! Be free to your future!
    Ride with your thoughts and follow your dreams.
Drearily, wearily drifting extreme
by the waterside moon of a deep, deep dream.
Slip, slide away to the passive world,
intense, be free and cast into submission.

Johannesburg

(Lini Richarda Grol)

Your wealthy white borough
glittering with jewels
on the powerful Rand of gold.

Your foundations, black and brooding
where in enormous caves your denizens
sweat and slave while you in comfort sleep.

Jet-black eyes fostered resentful hatred
a festering cancer fed by secret fury
vowing vetoes and making vices grow.

Mighty white, proud golden borough
you stood straight on black man's shoulders.
You made him bend but he would never break.
. . .
In silence he has been waiting
and watching you while slowly gathering
strength for that final moment . . . .

Invalid or Invalid

(Tim Grover)

Invalid or invalid,
could they be a frame of mind?
Situation uncontrolled,
or truly an axe to grind?

Do we capitalize or minimize,
about quality from birth?
What has been our portion,
while working at true worth?

It's too bad, on moods depending,
upon hurt feelings cling,
being offensive and defensive,
to invalidate everything.

Some can claim to be invalid,
yes, their Doctors' word concurs.
'Tis much worse, to invalidate,
no way there is a cure.

Invalid or invalid,
is a frame of mind.
Invalid, still hoping.
Invalid, no hope to find.

To all those who feel invalid, one way or another. You are valuable.

Age: 36
Address: Box 1268, Chetwynd, BC, V0C 1J0
Telephone: (604) 788-9567
To keep it short, I'm not highly educated, yet my life experiences have done me more than formal education. My resume is no longer valuable, but I am. I'm a husband of 17 years, father of 3 wonderful children, the likes of their mother, and proud of them all. My goal is to be the best father my family needs, teaching them values that will last their lifetime. Poetry is my passion; and knowledge is growing. It's been well worth the time to encourage myself, now others, by my new work.

Tammy
(Tina Guenthner)

I know you've been blue
So here's a little something to cheer you!

Good friends are hard to find
Honest ones are of the rarest kind
Some may come and others go away
but you stayed to this very day

You've made me laugh and often cry
And you've always made me go back and try
You believe in me and I in you
No other friend could ever be so true

You've given me the sisters I've lost
And stuck by my side, even at your own cost
We've been through the fire and back
But we always kept each other on track.

So, we're together forever and never apart
maybe in distance, but never in heart.

To Tammy and Curtis. When it's all said and done, there's only you to thank.

Death of a Season

(Laura A. Guthrie)

The forlorn wind of the winter's first snow
sweeps across the land;
to race and dance and turn about
then rest upon the sand.

The beach is strangely cold and grim,
the waves so silent and dark.
The summer days so soon have passed,
leaving no definite mark.

No more the sound of rippling waves
replaced with a frightening roar.
Racing one by one across the lake
to mock a lonely shore.

What more to do
than to sit and accept
the winter's unpleasant burn,
The desolate beach, the villainous cold,
and await a triumphant return?

To my Mom and Dad—my light and inspiration.

Unforgiving
(Allan D.C. Halldorson)

I will let you sit and judge me,
If that's what gets you high.
I'll let you walk all over me,
To soothe your foolish pride.
I'll let you take my dignity,
I'll let you break my will,
I'll let you do most anything,
Until you've had your fill.

I'll accept whatever judgement
That is handed from your throne,
For as I sit and look around,
I can see I'm all alone,
I'll let you kill my spirit,
I'll let you make me bend,
But one thing I will never do
Is let you call me friend.

Geriatrics
(Karen Halverson)

In my hospital uniform
I knelt on the tiles
by the tub
and scrubbed
Mr. Simms' back.
He started to speak
in a quiet voice,
"I was Commander of a ship," he said.
He leaned back.

His eyes closed
meditating amidst
disinfectant and urine   his
body sank   his
chin lowered   his
beard set float
like drifting kelp   his
legs fell open   his
penis rolled like a dying fish.

Karen Halverson is a Nanaimo writer who has had her poetry published in *Portal* and an essay published in *BC Woman to Woman* magazine. She is a creative writing student at Malaspina University-College.

Cost of Subscription
(Robert A. Hamilton)

We shall not be amplifiers
taking in with eyes and ears
and spewing out at increased volume,
The Ideas:
Efficiency/Competition.
Productivity. Trade.
We shall not! agree to trade
meaning in living for the youthful orthodoxy.
We shall be unscientific and refuse
to wait sensibly for proof of the soul.

Subscription is available,
but we shall not.
We shall not agree!
that lips that would kiss
keep their noses to the grindstone!

For my Father.

Age: 35
Address: 192 Ste-Anne, Suite 2, Ste-Anne-de-Bellevue, QC, H9X 1N1
Telephone: (514) 457-5770
Robert Hamilton is a 35-year-old writer, architect and artist living in Montréal, whose interests include comparative religion and philosophy.

Toward May's Bounty

(Brenda Hammond)

Shadow patterns, monochrome,
Only the sky is washed with blue.
Sun glistens on snow, a frothy meringue
Glacé frosting the trees while
Snow's riposte to the sun,
A lancing, icy glance,
Gradually melts with spring to gentleness.

When in this trembling hiatus that lies, chiaroscuro,
Between a Rembrandt etching and
The Impressionist palette of spring's bounty,
Then the dream of summer is yet far.

In March, the trees are not yet green (they say)
Spring truly comes in April (they tell me).
When the soulless winter's white and grey
Like an old photo, fades to beige and brown,
As we wait for the beginning—
The spring of rainbow's gleam.

Colours spread and seep and creep
Outwards from the seeding earth.
Green is the carpeting grass and the first
Brave fingers of the spiking bulbs
Reaching for shiny apotheosis
In yellow, mauve, scarlet and blue.
But so far, in April, the
Trees have not yet leafed.

A Word for the Trees

(Elizabeth Hancock)

The pine, the larch, the mighty oak, the hemlock wild and free.
Who would stand and argue the beauty of a tree.
But we, poor man who lives here, cannot make up our mind,
if they should stay and tarry to stand the test of time.
Despite the words of warning, the medicine they give,
man seems to find it difficult to let the giants live.
The men who work the forest, the families that they feed,
depend upon the chainsaw and not upon the seed.
There must be found a balance, some thinking up ahead,
so neither man nor wilderness will come to mourn their dead.
The willow, ash and copper beech, the Maple wild and free.
Who would stand and argue the beauty of a tree.

Liz Hancock is a freelance painter and writer. Originally from England, she is married with children and grandchildren. She is much travelled and had many adventures. She has had some articles, stories and poems published and works as a "Stringer" for the Maple Ridge "News." Her artwork is on commission and she illustrates and teaches when she can.

Evanescence

(Patrick Henry Hanlon)

A huge green flame
Turns into a tornado twister
swirling wispfully
then hanging in strands from the darkness
a hippie's beaded curtain
spreads across the sky like a dandelion's burs' beard

A yellow cobweb of ligh
I'm inside bu'
daren't breathe
shhhhhut the lighdssss
Dim the stars and strobes for a momen
I wish the snow in this outpost were blag
Like the dargness of my chil'hoo nighss
So I c'see the puridy of this delicad miragle
Shhhhh doan exssssplain
I wan' to wonder

gaze at the sheep's fleece

Too Late
(Gaby Harris)

When I left the adobe ranch,
I waved Adios with my hand
And left in tears my Mom.

She gave me her blessings
That I paid with a million kisses,
And hit the road in a hurry
With my baggage of dreams to carry.

Oh Mom! you ought to know,
Even though I'm far from home
And the clock of life with its tic tac
Had mercilessly told me that
It's too late to go back,
I pour my heart out and swear,
I've never forgotten you.

I know that in my lonely nights,
From a bright star you look at me,
You have departed to heaven,
And here I am to cry and sigh ever
For it's too late, too late now

Lies

(Lenore Harrison)

The big guns roar in morning light
Today there'll be no sun
We have our armour shining bright
The battle must be won
We wade in blood and tears and doom
Our courage never dies
And as the sound of cannons booms
Our hearts believe the lies

Our country, we are told, depends
Upon us all right here
They say we are a few good men
They say they shed a tear
I see the armies falling round
I look death in his face
I see the blood-corrupted ground
Let kings now take my place

High on a hill I sit and look
At death and blood and gore
I know my name's not in His book
I'll not see Heaven's door
Forgive me God for what I must
In the name of Nation do
The call is out, I join in dust
To go and kill a few

To: Darryl, Mom, Verity, Roberta, Dawn, Greg and Mark for your encouragement. Dad, I love you.

Address: Asquith, SK
Born: 1950 in Regina. Daughter of Bill and Mary Smith. Has lived in Regina, Moose Jaw, Calgary and Vancouver. Now residing in Asquith, SK, with her husband, Darryl, and two sons, Lenore has two grown daughters in the militia. Although no longer active on the local boards and clubs, she divides her time between writing, her family, neighbours and all her pets. Lenore is an avid horsewoman who enjoys nature and gardening.

Winter

(Shirley M. Harrison)

snow
falling gently blankets
trees
covered softly by
crystals
filtered down from grey
skies
filled with white dancing
flakes
twirling silently to the
ground.

wind
raging wildly blowing
snow
biting frenzied creatures
coldly
gripping hearts and ungloved
hands
rubbing cozy near sizzling
fire
blazing fiercely in the
hearth.

To Mum, who always encouraged me.

Age: 40
Address: R.R. #2, Brantford, ON, N3T 5L5
Telephone: (519) 756-2899

Although I have been writing for almost 30 years, my mid-life crisis prompted me to try writing professionally. I am presently enroled in a Children's Writing Program, Connecticut. I am married, with one daughter and numerous pets. We live just south of Wayne Gretzky's hometown of Brantford. I am a registered nurse and love gardening, horses and sports.

Blink and Miss It

(Reg Hart)

driving west
starting to turn
                    green trash bag in ditch
                    round soggy bail
                    hugging the prairie
                    and notice no end-
                    gate in the truck
                    dried white clay
                    the   gophers are out
                    there's one on that mound
                    starting to turn
lime-green greens
the golfers are out
there's one on that mound
driving west

Address: Box 562, Daysland, AB, T0B 1A0

BA (Augustana), MA (Alberta). This 34-year-old singer/songwriter was born and raised in Killam, Alberta. After living in Edmonton, Calgary and a brief stint in the USA, Reg returned to his home county and settled in Daysland. He and his wife, Joy, enjoy the peaceful life of small town Alberta while raising their 4 children ages 1-13. Reg has combined his lyrical ability with his passion for music into may original songs. He makes his living as a singer, occasional book-reviewer and songwriter.

Searching
(Joanna Harvey)

Beginning:	I am here . . .
Searching:	Here are two hands. These things are seen.
Existence:	I come into being. The two hands are mine. It is me who is seeing them.
Questions:	How do these hands work? What do I see? Why am I here? Who am I?
Understanding:	These hands remain until the body is no more. My eyes will see for only so long. I am here; a brief, fleeting moment in history. I am Eve—Mother of all, daughter of no one . . . .
Destruction:	Here are two hands—they won't move. These things are seen—it's blurry.
Ending:	Here is a shell of what once used to be. The hands no longer exist. Nothing is seen. I am no longer here. I am no one. I am . . . still searching.

"Here's to the man who says, 'I can,' and holds his head uplifted."—William Margets

Anatomy and Physiology

(Ann V. Harvie)

The velocity of blood varies, strictly
According to the cross-sectional area
Of the vessels' lumen,
For sixty-thousand miles.

Bent under indifferent winds
Wheat turns its back to the evening
And glistens
Pale smoke in the moon.

Statistically, the moon has no effect.
Not proven
That the heart beats faster
And the wheat grows stronger.

But lying in the wheat, on the darkened earth,
With the sun aligned, invisibly
Shining in reflection from the moon,
Does not the wheat impress strong upon the retina and tympani,
And the blood quicken?

Lights

(Nicole Hatch)

Lights
They seemed to be so close, so bright
Lights
An everlasting source of painful eyes
Can I approach?
Will they bite?
Lights
To guide me home like no other can.

For Kurt Cobain, Mom and Dad.

Age: 23
Address: 7560 Colleen Street, Burnaby, BC, V5A 2A6
I am near completion of a Bachelor of Arts Degree from Simon Fraser University. I have travelled extensively using my experiences as inspiration in my work. My musical accomplishments include playing piano for 16 years, playing guitar for several years and singing at numerous sporting events and talent shows. Recently, I created an original draft for an advertisement for Western Engraving Ltd. They have acknowledged its success in rendering new business through its placement in *The Advocate* magazine. My interests include writing poetry and song-writing, one day hoping for the world to enjoy my musical and literary meanderings!

Untitled

(Traci Hay)

Acknowledge to God you're a sinner,
    Receive Christ Jesus, today.
Repent of your sin;
    Then fast, and soul win,
Trust in God's word, and obey.

To win a multitude of souls for Jesus of Nazareth.

The Encounter

(Ethel M. Helgeson)

One day in July, a guy dropped by
in an unbelievable off-white suit.
He looked like a Prince, I assumed that his horse
had undoubtedly taken the wrong route.
I was mistaken—he meant to see me
gave me a bear-hug, then a lingering kiss,
so handsome he was, so trim and MY AGE
he was something too thrilling to miss.
We talked and laughed of days long ago
he could only stay a short while.
He looked good as new, I felt old and used
for he had sophistication and style.
You can bet my heart pounded, my thoughts
leaped to ignite the spark that shone in his eyes.
Did this actually take place?
Was he really my Prince?
or was he . . . a frog in disguise??

My friend, Bill.

Untitled
(Officer Cadet Hernandez RM)

The untamed falcon
sought by man and son
flies with might at heaven's heights;
brings wondrous pleasures to my sight.

High 'bove it circles
one stands in awe in myrtle
admiring its beauty and grace;
longing to offer honesty and face.

But untamed falcon
sought by man and son
answers not to my pleads and call;
with my dreams high I begin to fall.

Untamable she flies, she flies
with my dreams to heavenly skies;
thoughts of passion and fate
with outstretched arms I wait . . .

To Melanie Darlene Lowthers.

For B.H.

(Christopher J. Herr)

You come wrapped in night songs and cool, dark voice
Drips smooth liquid words careful as
Ice melting; I sit legs crossed, gather chills.
Over your shoulder, you wear ribbons of
Singing hair; hands sifting shadow,
Knees and elbows bare, every gesture
Pounding deeper the ancient wedge within—
Division upon divisions.
This night you may come again, drift like sin
Along the edge of holy thoughts,
And insinuate lithe beneath the hushed
Hour when light is winnowed from day.
So I, made not to sing, hear songs drowned in
Your voice; and so, evenings cleft through by night.

Untitled
(A. Herron)

How quietly you ensnare me
skillfully weaving new threads of meaning
softly trimming away disorder . . .
Still, there was that moment
when I laid all before you
tangles, knots, intentions,
naked and apart
You didn't see the way these thoughts and feelings
could refract and shine
or the slender gleam of possibilities
fragilc and finc-strung
You stared, appalled
at the gristle and the bone
at the stretched and torn tendons
that could not contain this base and ugly sorrow
You refuse darkness, combat it neatly
with a silver needle of clichés and condescension
twisting, sewing, tying,
cruelly piercing
through skin and flesh and limbs
Until I am drawn together
conformed, bundled, cut—
left to hide
this unravelling near my mind
this fraying at the heart.

The Flag
(Alex Hewitt)

Fly it high and fly it proudly,
So that all the world may see
That it's flying o'er a country
That is young and strong and free.
Give it honour, give it freedom,
In the east and in the west,
For the men who fought to buy it
Ranked with all who were the best.

Fly it high and wave it proudly,
Let the nations of this earth
Know that all men stand united
In the land that gave it birth
To you who come from other lands,
To peaceful farms and busy town,
We know that you will stand with us
And never let our country down.

Long may it wave and freely fly,
In every kind of weather
And let this flag a symbol be
To bind us more together.
May every one in this great land
Have freedom's right to brag,
That this land is theirs and they are proud
To live beneath this flag.

Traditional Healing
(Jody Hill)

A young boy wanders his heart is filled with puzzles.
Amazed at the world around him, he asks for answers.

One man shows him, makes him believe in the world.
Pulling strength within the man, he guides the boy with pride.

A young man cries, his mind is filled with questions.
Hardened by the world around him, he has no answers.

One man tells him to "open up your heart." Giving with
each breath his wisdom, the man sees him through.

A man of years, his soul empty from disbelief.
Searching for the road he wants, he feels time move on.

One man shows strength, One man has pride,
One man shows wisdom and guides his son through it all.

That man is my father, he is my strength,
he shows me my pride, I seek his wisdom.
For it's his love he gives me, and because of my father, I will be a proud man
to answer my son's questions.

A dedication with love to my Father.

Burial

(Devin Hillier)

You will not find the garden remains
of his withered corpse
resting in fields of winter sparrows
that litter the ground with white metaphors,
it is too fragile to be discovered

Nor will you find his spirit worshipping
on the tops of wind-combed mountains
where shrines to the sun are built
by women who praise the sky with glances,
he does not go to sing there

Neither will you find his words
in autumn poems the sun
nailed to a rainbow as a elegy
when his death was publicized,
there are no verses that mention his name

And not in the secret watery tombs
will you find his clothing
among the drowned lilies
and slow-moving seaweed,
his friends cannot mourn for him there

Down my Beating Heart

(Kirk A. Hipkiss)

Down my beating heart! Calm down.
Let not you rise upon my breast
And pump and knock—What ruthless protest!
To a master who waits on his love out of town.
Save your stir until when we unite
With that angelic beauty that inspires your flutter.
Then let your rapturous pulsating stutter
Revive in its uprising, soar high in its flight.

Here! She arrives! Ah, justly the blood flows,
Unleashed in her presence . . . Go on heart and pound
My inward flesh against my chest; Oh, it throes!
Come, listen my sweet! What you hear is love's sound,
Harmoniously thumping a declaration so true:
Uncontrollable passion at the mere thought of you.

Alone on a Bridge

(Julie Hobson)

It seems cruel
to be poor in autumn

to stand alone on a bridge
feeling at the same time

divided and connected
by a river banked

in golden trees
burdened with change

Age: 34
Address: 4-591 Talbot Street, London, ON, N6A 2T2
Julie Hobson is currently employed at K-104 in Woodstock as a part-time News Broadcaster. In addition, she works at The Grand Theatre in London, Ontario, as a bartender, having left her previous position as Educational Services Coordinator, to pursue freelance theatre and art projects. When not "officially" working, Ms. Hobson continues her university education, taking courses of interest on a part-time basis. She has been writing poetry since she was first inspired by her grade eight teacher, Mr. Brian Taylor. Born and raised in Toronto, Ontario, she has made London, Ontario, her home for the past 11 years.

Surrealism and the Mirror
(Sue Hodge)

Like dancing naked in the sun
Our minds meet and are set free
Time catches us stealing
Crouching in the corner of our union
Drawing pictures in the sand
With broken shells and pointy sticks
And building castles
With turrets and a moat and everything
Emerging like a birthing into the brightness of the afternoon
Squinting and rubbing our eyes
Holding hands
Wondering if everyone knows where we've been
Exposed
Like a newborn crying to be let back into the womb
Feeling like everyone suddenly has x-ray vision
The exposure is too much to bear
So harsh—almost surreal
As though we're in one of those early Canadian films
Where it's always winter or raining
And the memory is always in black and white
A silent communication leads us back to the cocoon
Where dancing naked in the sun
We meet each other and are set free

Telephone (403) 468-2102
Sue Hodge is a singer/songwriter with her own group "nickle finger," as well as being sole proprietor of the Arts Administration company "Aardvark Zeal." Sue's active involvement in the performance & business end of the cultural industries has given her a well-balanced view of Canada's culture. Much of her work reflects this perspective, which explains the "familiar" level at which her writings touch people. This direction is further enhanced by Sue's ability to transcend the "private" by sharing the deeply personal.

Untitled

(Marc Hodgkinson)

Up there on the ceiling
I can scatter all my feelings
between the crevasses of stucco and the shadows from the moonlit trees.

"Do you see it?"
I said to her with a throaty warble that was partly mine from sleep
and borrowed from a Hollywood actor in a sexy scene.

She stared blindly upward and then turned to me,
I felt the cold trickle into the sheets as she reeled them in and in and
round her frame.
She looked at me.
She looked hopelessly beyond me.
"What are you talking about?"
she said and . . .
that was all she needed to say.

We slept five miles apart that night
and I without my covers thought,
how cold for her it must be.

Age: 28
Address: 27 Chalet Crescent, London, ON, N6K 3C5
Telephone: (519) 657-9314

The author is a 28-year-old part-time student and full-time bartender hoping to make his way to Teacher's College in the next year. After finishing a Bachelor's Degree in English, Marc has turned his attention to History and hopes to teach both at the secondary school level. He continues to write poetry and is working on a modern adaptation of Alaxander Pope's "Rape of the Lock." His is also struggling with his first play. An avid sports enthusiast, and Buffalo Sabres fan, Marc keeps fit playing hockey and softball.

Athabaska Glacier
(Marita Hollo)

ice the colour of opal
    of white smoky diamond
looming over our spot
on the lookout point
like frozen lava
    halted, pale and gelled
almost hanging over
the rocky descent to river

haze above
between snow-pocketed crags
like angelic fluff
breath of glacier
like a sigh from Heaven

gathered tears of water
running into a silent river-flow
over stones graded into pebbles
    pebbles into sand
    sand into dust

Revolution of the Soul

(Kevin Hopke)

Fire the revolution within the heart
Turn it over and give it air
Thrust it into the mould and let it cool
This is what it takes

How many long days have we searched?
How many years have we wondered?
Where does our agony for truth come from?
Where do we begin to look?

It is time now to turn the coal
Let it sit a while and turn it again
These are the ovens of discovery
Fire up the revolution of the soul

It sits in the heat without melting
It turns red, then white
The revolution of the soul is ready
It is cast into a shape of its own

It burns within you, it never cools

To the evolution of the human soul.

What Am I?
(Tara Louise Hosein)

To one of darkened flesh,
I am a brother of skin and blood,
But to one of native red,
I am a bond with nature and spirit.

To the young I am of fur or
A figment of the imagination,
But to the elder, I am a caring
and comforting hand,
Reality held tight.

To the male gender, I am
Depended on as a joker or wise guy,
And to the average female,
I'm needed for giggles
and to soothe their cries of woe.

To some, I'm just a phone call away,
Or to others, I'm preferred a distant,
To a certain kind, I am of quantity,
Yet others choose to cherish me as one.

But to all of every kind, size, and nature,
I am a common,
A common that you may call a friend!

The Office

(Officer Cadet Michael A. Hovi)

Here I sit, on duty, again
Service Dress, pen in hand
In the office, by the phone
"Good Morning, Sir. How may I help you?"
Pants chafing, shoes biting
I look out, and smell the air
The grass, the mud, the rain
My home
I am no bureaucrat!
I am no executive!
I am a soldier, a warrior
A wild animal, caged
By the office

There's No Other

(Jason Chipman Howlett)

Is appearance more than what they say?
Can you judge a book by its cover?
Everyone exists in their own way
There's no other:
One who moves like you
Shifts their face the way you do
It's true
There's no other:
One who does their hair
Puts on clothing that you wear
It's fair

This is not necessarily sound
But I'm not considering the colour or pound
There's more to someone than what you see
Still you can learn a lot when you look carefully

How can you explain love at first sight?
Strangers glancing at each other knowing it's right
It is the same when one needs the time
They ask certain people without reason or rhyme

Books and humans are scarcely the same
The cover of a book usually just shows the name
Who compared the two in the first place?
A book can't communicate by changing its face

A person's appearance is their expression to you
Read their cover!

William
(Heather Hughes)

Hold my hand
Look at me
Hold me, while I look at you
Time stands still, while I look at you;
Ever respected
Ever loved!

Touch my hair
Kiss my lips
Share my love, so warm and true
Laughing together, so warm and true;
Wave at me
Smile too.

Time goes on
Learn to wait
Darkness falls, and hearts will break
Let others control, and hearts will break;
Lies are told
Pulled apart.

Love is strong
Rich and pure
Honour you, I always will
I loved you then, and I always will
Together at last
Happy for once!!!

To William: to whom I owe so much; respect at all times; and love so intensely!

the children
(Susan M. Hughes)

who are the children that do not smile?
they have empty hands.
who are the children that are forgotten?
they live in empty lands.
who will awaken the rain from its sleep?
their tears have run dry.

the gods of angry winds blow,
their hunger is stirred.
where the sun is no longer the spirit,
their hurt cannot be cured.
their land is void, its shadows lost,
and the sky gives no life.

who are the children that do not smile?
who are the children that are forgotten?
they are our children.
and who will awaken from our sleep?

Age: 24
Address: #203, 1060 Pakington Street, Victoria, BC, V8V 3A1

Winter Wind
(Dena Hummel)

Around me sweep warm heavenly winds
Down from the safety of the mountains
Grasses dance with changing rhythms
Trees are the audience to the scene

Whispers are echoed through my homestead
Creaking and moaning as old shacks stretch
Soft memories hold my thoughts
Awed by the flow of life then and now

Animals face away from chinooks
Quietly grazing moments adieu
Sunshine warms their winter coats
Peace encompasses like warm hugs

Fields rest from the toiling summer
Gold straw protects the sleeping giant
Stillness is felt here alone
Grey fences watch over tenderly

Prairie winter offers safe haven
Feel the wonderment of completeness
Stirrings of wakening start
Slowly winter wind will birth my spring

To Lucas, my Husband, and Jonathan, my Son. Thanks for your love and support.

Age: 31
Address: Box 222, Nobleford, AB, T0L 1S0
Telephone: (403) 687-2122
Married since 1980. I have one son. I am a certified home support aide. I work with mostly elderly people. Went back to school to get my advanced diploma on a part-time basis. Church organist. I have always loved reading and making up stories and poetry. My life's ambition is to be a great mom and wife and to write.

After Auschwitz
(Dr. Wayne A. Hunt)

No Poetry
Ho History
No Geography

Only poets who renounced their legislative authority
Historians who re-invented themselves as historiography
And a world made to read flat: as a
Book whose meaning is fixed in advance: as a
Movie worked to Formula: as Motion
Without Meaning: as Time without Depth: as
Distance without Perspective: as
A Soul which departs without *trace* of a Shadow.

Wee Wounded

(Alice Hutchinson)

Oh, painted in corners,
How the children cry.
No wings, no wings
But a need to fly.

Forsaken in silence,
Their wee wounds to dry.
No wings, no wings
But a need to fly.

Lost, lonely and weary,
How can you pass by?
No wings, no wings
But a need to fly.

I Believe
(Rosemary Ingraham)

I believe God is a
loving and kind God.
I see His love all around me . . .
in the beauty of creation
in the security of my home
in the love of family and friends.

But what if I were
. . . a Kurdish refugee
facing another cold wet night
in a make-shift tent
. . . a large-eyed Ethiopian child
with my stomach distended from hunger
. . . a Salvadorian peasant
struggling to make a living
. . . a runaway teenager
hooked on drugs and living on the street
. . . a Native Indian
searching for my identity
and a place in the world
. . . a heart-broken mother
grieving the loss of a child
in a senseless war.

Could I say . . .
I believe God is a loving and kind God?

. . . Would I?

Ojalá

(Mark Ireland)

Oh the feel of being on the moon
Entwined with the robe of sensuous night
Impaled upon its dim-lit glare
In time's distant recluse of elsewhere
Silent
Like golden statue of a sun's Divine
Meticulous in its passioned dress!

Oh that you were on the moon
Crazed sun a lucid dream
And I
Receiving of your lover's sacrifice
The tingle of poetry on the brain,
Vibrant, intoxicating in its state
Of ravaging undulate, abounding might!

It is the unbridled cataclysm of instant
The rapturous allure of the thought
The liquor of your poesy I cannot forsake
Palpitating with the pith of storm
It propels my spirit to the end of the elements
Crossing waves, lines and merges
Of sound, water and air!

It is then that I am not afraid of the mind
Being earth human and child of the sky.
I meld and fall, I reach out to the abyss
To touch the realm of cushioned stasis!

To my Muse: if only an angel child could see!

Address: 6 Lawson Court, Fredericton, NB, E3B 5G4
Telephone: (506) 472-0202

Life in a Bottle

(Marc W. Jackson)

Beads of sweat roll down its sides, and then they pool;
A manicured hand pours from a bottle, over sculpted bits of ice;
Two people walk a beach and talk of all things nice;
That's how the bottle is for most, but for me that's not the rule.
Many the time I've tried, just one, to play it cool;
Memories stir within me, of how it was, and could be again;
Just one sip to calm my nerves, or a slug to soothe the pain;
Drown my sorrow; kill my troubles; make me a fool.

Beads of sweat roll down my brow, as I fight this urge;
The road I travel, I know it ends not near;
A cunning little voice tells me one can't hurt;
But I know different, I must summon all my courage.
The voice says wine will make you handsome; there's talent in the beer;
I listen; agree . . . and wake face down in dirt.

Age: 37
Address: P.O. Box 612, Snow Lake, MB, R0B 1M0
Telephone: (204) 358-2887
I have lived in Northern Manitoba all my life and currently reside in Snow Lake, MB, with my wife Leone and two children. I am a community oriented person and enjoy being "involved." I began writing poetry just this year, as the result of a correspondence course in English. I find it a perfect vehicle to express feelings and hope to write more. I am a recovering alcoholic and drug abuser, and I've been clean and sober for the past 15 years. My experiences as such contribute to my view on life.

Tick Talk

(Zoltan P. Jambor)

Tick talk a clock patiently on the wall,
But the time ruling life I want to stall.
Tick talk I am ticked as you talk,
When through your door I walk.

Tick talk, the pendant in your neck,
Swinging back and forth as you peck.
Tick talk a noise so cold, nasty and bold,
As clamps to my conscience you have told.

Tick talk, away from everyone I run,
Searching out ways to find a new sun.
Tick talk an hour swiftly sneaks by,
And you my life, I must abide.

Tick talk a precise gadget for the world,
As in the garden of earth I will grow old.
Tick talk, don't talk oh mighty clock,
Signal with arms to lead your flock.

Walk Around the Lake
(Keith James)

Cold sings in the crisp air
And megalith peaks henge,
Sentinel, about the tarn.
We stop at the shore,
Skate frozen fragments
Across the shrieking ice.
They burst like universes
Sliding to oblivion
In the black water.

Soon comes a low mist
And we know the tarn
Only as we know men,
By the edges we map
And circumscribe;
But the deep keeps its mysteries,
Reflecting from the fronded ice
Inscrutable grainy images.

Then, at dusk, a furnace
Opens beneath the swarthy clouds
And spruce-sparred islands,
Like wraiths of outbound vessels,
Strain to depart.

Prayer of the Non-believer

(Nancy Janes)

Faith, Hope, Charity
Three days of dirt to a shirt
Where is the answer?

The Premonition

(Lori Jauniaux)

While standing at the station, my legs began to tire
My hands began to tremble, I started to perspire
The faces of the strangers looked so cold and plain
Their eyes filled with impatience while waiting for the train

I sharply gazed around; there were clocks on every wall
Each read different times; my skin began to crawl
The voice of a man offered me a seat
I turned to answer him; my heart, it skipped a beat

An overcoat and hat, a briefcase in his hand
Ordinary though he was, I said I'd rather stand
He didn't seem to smile; he grinned but rather slight
This added to my fears; it stirred my swollen fright

I heard a whistle sound and squealing brakes outside
The station lit with faces, waiting for their ride
The train so full of people stopped to take some more
I watched the strangers file out the station door

Somehow so relieved, I watched the train proceed
That was one long journey I strangely didn't need
Baffled and exhausted, I questioned my attack
Until I learned, while driving home . . .
That train had jumped the track

To the late Peter. W. Lennon, who will always inspire my depth of thought.

Age: 31
Address: 3511 Ponytrail Drive, Mississauga, ON, L4X 1V9
Born Lori Mammoliti, May 27, 1963, in Connecticut, U.S.A., I moved to Ontario at the age of five with my family. My gift for writing poetry was first discovered at the age of nine by my grade four elementary school teacher, Mrs. Lawrence. I graduated Glenforest Secondary School with Honours in 1981 and studied Business Administration in college; with all my recognition being in my English writing courses. In 1985, I married Joseph Jauniaux, and we are currently raising three sons and managing a carpentry business. After 22 years, I still enjoy writing and hope to have more poetry published.

Rhapsody

(Jasmine Javid)

Touch my chords of varied hue
Play me until I blend with you
Reach the depths of my arduous soul
Whose moods only your melodies can control
Let our rhythms merge as our music meets
With diverse harmonies, uneven beats
Let our hearts blend and palpitate
With staccato temperament or a steady rate
As winds blow gentle or meander with change
Essence is but one that we rearrange
But no time or composition can shatter the song
Whose message and feeling linger eternally strong

A Night on the Town

(Peter Jeffery)

The limpid lions
Plaguing wars
Genuflect
On startled whores.
Teasing, squeezing
Tissue tonsils
And Teddy Bears,
In silent reverie
Aghast on aching irons
And poison pools
Silly fools
And broken rules.
Lines lately laid
On desperate senses,
Confusion creeps
On lame pretences.
Mine own eyes laugh
A giddy thought
Of making sense
And being caught.

Age: 40
Address: R.R. #3, Lanark, ON, K0G 1K0
Peter Jeffery, once, was a very "moving" person. Since coming from England at age three, he had been constantly moving. With almost 50 moves in all, he had lived from Campbellton, NB, to Vancouver, BC. He documented a good portion of his adult life in words that reflect a gradual transition from angst to angels, loneliness to lovingness, fear to freedom, and storms to stability. Driven by nightmares and drawn by dreams, his life has led him happily to the stability of his own home shared, for the past four years, with his wife and three young children.

A Solitary Soul: Of a Schizophrenic

(Susan M. Jeffries)

I am alone—a solitary soul,
reaching out to you.
But you reject me.

You do not understand me.
You do not listen: you run from me!
You deem me as "mad" and turn away.

You do not perceive the world in ways that I do or
hear the voices that only I hear.
These are what set me apart from you.
Yet these seem to be all I have.

It seems there is nowhere for me to turn.
Doors are shutting all around me.
You do not try to open these doors,
instead you lock them behind me.

How can I, a solitary soul,
become one of you
when you are blind and have empty hearts?

By myself I cannot change the way I am.
I will be forever trapped within myself.
I will forever be alone.

Age: 21
Address: R.R. #1, Lombardy, ON, K0G 1L0
Telephone: (613) 283-2863
I am currently attending Queen's University at Kingston, where I am studying English and Psychology. I have always enjoyed literature—both reading and writing my own work. I hope to continue my education at Queen's and perhaps focus more on my writing in the future.

A Note to the Reader:
(Rita Renae)

read me alone
in cinnamon bath water
I want to smell your
open pores taste your salty
cheek touch your soaking
feet watch your skin flush
I dare you to greet me
the softer you speak
the better I hear
tell me a story
sing me a song
play me a tune
dance me around and
around paint me a piece
rhyme a few things
pretend you and I belong
let's thicken our breath
with sweet red wine and
re-claim our weeping
souls and tongues
a ritual without which
I could easily smoke
a pack of poems a day
make possible the life of me

Fevered Dreams?

(Beau Johnson)

I wish I was green
and had two pairs of wings
a house or a ranch
lots of unneeded things
that cluttered my mind
as I polished my rings

But if I had the power to give myself wings
I'd use it for better, more useful things
I'd cure Cancer with Cancer and burn Aids right out
while retooling my thoughts to a state of concern,
a state of concern we all must learn

Liquefied in a dream
by an old yellow man
that a reason is needed
to lend out your hand

But that man was crazy
his nose purple-hazy
and I am not him
my thoughts aren't that dim

HELP THEM!

To my Mother, without whom I would never have been.

Intercession

(Kevin Johnson)

I come to you for some division*, dear,
As separates the thesis from the rest
To use the sonnet so to commandeer
A metaphor complacent with this test.
Which is to make a harmony from that
Which is divided, willing and extant.
Together, then, we make a better match
Than constituted in ourselves we can,
For it is still impossible, we think,
In antithesis or concinnity
To forge in solitude a better link
Than we together can in amity.
So teach me better than division can
A woman's value to a cogent man.

* Division: Latin for "sex."

Warning: A Modern Woman's House
(L. Johnson)

An immaculate house would be the ideal,
But for a modern woman like me, I feel
It's an improbable fantasy; it's far from real.
There's prehistoric dust on my kitchen ceiling fan
And I've a living room uninhabitable by man.

There's not a thing in the house to cook
And if *you* need anything, *you* have to look.
(You'll probably find me reading a good book.)
There are nasty things lurking under the stairs;
It's not a place to be caught unawares.

Under the furniture are storage places
And of designer furniture there are no traces.
(Would the tidy people please stop making faces?)
Perhaps I'll buy more cleaning supplies
In case someone drops by. Surprise?!

I'll just hand them a broom, a cloth, and a mop
And when they're nearly done, I'll ask them to stop.
Guess I should at least offer them—a cold pop?
But what's the use of putting on airs—
Life is too short—and in the end, who cares?

Because my house has a lived-in feeling
Right from the floor boards to the ceiling.
(And if this fractured prose leaves you reeling,)
Drop by for coffee, to relax and have a chat.
Come to see *me*, *not my house*—and that's that!

Crazy John

(Stan Johnson)

There's a White Pine standing on the shore of Minnitaki Lake,
Its trunk is bent with years of wind and snow.
There's a Heart with names below it, Jessie Grey and Johnny Drake,
Carved in the rough bark many years ago.

There's a mound inside a picket fence, beside the bent old Pine,
The picket's old and falling stake by stake,
The Headboard, bravely standing still, has only one faint line,
The Epitaph reads, "Here lies Jessie Drake."

Each year the same old Indian, they call him "Crazy John,"
Paddles up and stops below the bent old Pine,
He kneels beside the lonely grave, in early morning's Dawn,
With tear filled eyes he reads the weathered sign.

He slowly rises to his feet, and sadly looks around,
The things he sees are from another day.
He turns at his Canoe, to take on last look at the mound,
With head bowed paddles silently away.

This year, the same old Indian, he's getting feeble now,
Knelt down beside the Grave of Jessie Drake.
Although the years had dimmed his eyes, he seemed at peace somehow
His old heart knew the course that he would take.

He stood and looked in memory, at what time could not erase,
Looked once more at the Grave and bared his head.
He lay down by her side, a weary smile upon his face,
He closed his eyes, and "Crazy John" was dead.

Address: Box 606, Dryden, ON, P8N 2Z3
Telephone: (807) 223-2847
I have been writing poetry for some time now. I had a poem published in *Whispers in the Wind*, National Library of Poetry last year.

New Age Man
(Stephen Johnson)

I'm a post-modern
   hypersensitive
new age
   man.
Gender-inclusive
   he/she
herstory
new age

man.

Whose Shadow

(Eric Jones)

A space of worms list in time cracks around the neighbourhood
I spy, they spy, we spy together
Shadows and rippling tense energies of subtlety
Rich veins, varicose intention, spasmodic modal interchange
Holy holes, silent antenna, vague murmurs, no phone answer,
The strangers anywhere, a crack, an unsensed vibration,
Likeness, discord, unreal, improbable, prudent, impudent,
Maligned, designed, programmed, recorded, distilled, discarded,
Plots, trees, window blinds, silent ears, deafening eyes,
Locations, satellite spirit, shadow control and paranoia pronoun.
Hovering, waiting, skulking, combs, pencil heads, pin heads,
Tie clips, belt clips, paper clips, paint chips, pop charts, pop tarts,
Close to the ground, underground, underwear, nostrils, make-up
Time and place, time and time, time again, watch straps,
Pieces of time, held in tune, tuna fish, welcome mat,
Peace tower, peace bridge, pie plate, leaning cutlery,
Suspended, descended, resented, re-rented, crime bag,
Bagman, goodman, rich man, friend, smile, double-cross,
Double agent, single agent, sullen, sorry, repressed,
Control, detect, align, confirm, approach, reflect, destroy
Inhibit, rely, whisper, confy, relate, displace, interface and spy.

To the triplets, both of them.

Age: 40
Address: 36 Spring Street, #2, Brantford, ON, N3T 4M5
Telephone: (519) 756-5430
In the last 15 years, I have written about a million words. I write about everything, anything, something and even nothing. I like people. I believe in enjoying myself, honestly and peacefully. I look forward to more of the same.

Rut Breaker

(Kevin Jones)

Go beyond your teachers,
Let your souls run free,
For there is no law written,
That will damn you for seeking **ME**!

God's Winter Playground

(Shelley Jones)

Sunlight reflects a kaleidoscope of colours
In the ice that adorns the trees
The air is frigid and fresh
I inhale its intoxicating perfume
Glistening white patterns blanket all that can be seen
In the stillness of this country mirage

There are no looming steel buildings to mar this picture
No scent of polluted city air
Absent is the roar of traffic
The scream of sirens and the busy, frantic people
There is only beauty and isolation

A deer and her fawn dart from a cluster of angular cedars
I stop walking, lest they sense my nearness
I rejoice in the splendour of nature
All my senses are triggered
by the unfamiliarity of this rare peace and tranquillity
I can only appreciate the wonder in this land
That is unabused by technology and modern civilization
I am in awe of the rare magnificence of God's winter playground.

With love to my Father, Ronald Jones. He taught me to appreciate nature's beauty.

Thirty-eighth Week
(Nelly Kazenbroot)

So this is what it's like
at the far side: not pinned to the damp
spring earth by the swollen weight
of my rooted seed, but lifted above it

buoyed as a bubble
about to burst upon the flat-faced tulips
and the threaded blue irises
in the fey March heat

my mother-hands weaning out
the running clover and Jacob's
fine green ladders from the sponge
of brown soil, the corners of unmade beds

not a soul daring to breathe
the dust of old yarrow seeds through my clearings
while the window's glint fashions
two of me to close the circle

a foot beneath the white hooped crib
and two in the reflected fringe
of verdant blades, my child slumbers like gold
beneath the fall of arcing colour

This Living Death
(Jean Keddy)

You cannot know
how your empty eyes
and insistent pacing
break my heart.

You are not there—
only in sudden snatches
of recognition
that falsely give me hope,
and break my heart.

I see you down the hall
and hurry to embrace you.
You stand still—
pleasant and polite,
and unresponsive,
and my heart breaks.

You cannot know now
for if I told you,
you would not comprehend,
how piercingly lonely,
how utterly empty
our lovely home, our double bed.
Gone . . . all gone.
. . . My heart is broken.

Oracle
(Ingrid Johanna Keirans)

raped of our magic
we seek the charlatan
to bind up the wounds
under an eclipse
only to find ourselves
spitting out his sham
into the dry well
that can no longer hold water

my arms ache
pouring condensed gospel
into a harboured soul

I stand naked
in your shadow

revealing

nothing

For my parents, Brian and Shannon, and Gregory, for their support in my search for truth.

Address: 4960-55B Street, Delta, BC, V4K 3B9
Telephone: (604) 946-5195
I have been writing poetry since I was a young child. Since I find writing poetry a continuous spiritual journey and catharsis for the soul, having several of my poems published in the past has been an opportunity for me to share this personal and universal journey with others. My goal is to have a book of poems published, illuminating my life's experiences to date in the hope of illustrating that all personal experience is in some way universal—shared by us all.

Mindless

(Cecilia Kelly)

There's a rip in the sky.
I can see it, but why
    Cannot anyone else?

Its wide mouth is gaping,
And my sanity's breaking
    For the wonder of it.

I'm afraid it will swallow
The earth in its hollow,
    And send us to a void

Where there isn't a place
But a cold, empty space
    In location and time.

Filled with nothing and nowhere,
It calls me to go there
    And rest in its peace.

So I give up my being
To the tear I am seeing.
    Lost in its emptiness,

My mind has been taken
From this body now shaken,
    A shell where I once lived.

My Love

(John Kelly)

She eats in the pasture of Endurance
She is corralled by the twinkling Stars
She is shod with shoes of Care

Freedom is her Eyes
Belief is her Spirit
Kindness is her Voice
Truth is her Passion

She's turned away by hate
She's poisoned by the proud

She's found a stable in my Heart
She's resting within my Soul

To my wife, Ruth, who taught me to accept love.

Arms and the Boy
(Penn Kemp)

In our time all the world's
worst clichés are actualized.

I am swimming in happiness—
rain cocooning our window pane

—when TV presents drought
in far-off Somalia.

Foreign arms divide
a proud and elegant people

now starving. The clans, the earth,
city institutions crack, rent
asunder by cold war strife.

Shovels at a narrow grave.

"The image that struck me most
was a fourteen year old Somali boy,

just skin and bones. They were
*bury*ing him when

        [crossed, his last gesture,
an ache up arms' inner

                two tears ran down his cheeks."

[That boy survived.

Downtown Dove

(C.F. Kennedy)

I saw a sign of the dove today,
No branch of olive in its mouth;
Instead, it was pecking at its legs
Which were tied with a bright white cloth

This, on a downtown city street
While nearby, church bells chimed;
This, by an abandoned variety store—
To the discerning, another sign

As I stopped to consider how
To help free it from the snare
It took three, short frightened steps
And then took to the air

This, while an old man passed by
Mumbling, and cursing the day;
This, while the downtown sirens hissed;
Then, the scene melted away

I saw a sign of the dove today,
Here for a moment and gone;
Who tied its legs saw but a pigeon.
Fly on, little brother, fly on!

Age: 50
Address: Box 40, 90 Shuter Street, Toronto, ON, M5B 2K6
C.F. Kennedy has published a children's book, *Against the Grain*, and has published articles and stories in many small press publications in Canada, the U.S.A. and Europe. Also, has published "The Bibliofantasiac," "The Blotter," "Drift," "Found in the Trash." Currently published in *Exhibit B* and *Lower Rosedale Review* and is a collaborative editor of the east coast journal *Capers Aweigh*.

A Wholly Unpleasant Plague
(Greg Kennedy)

Where is the form to this pestilence?
The concrete gory limb, the swollen tongue?
A real and visible leprous horror
Would be brave compassion
Beside these wavering, furtive maladies.

Casualties assemble to pile themselves
Listlessly into mounds of architectural curiosity.
The roads are once again free for traffic.
These bodies have invested so much
In their disease;
It is a cruel apothecary who works to dispel
Their discomfort.

Health lingers guiltily, shame-faced,
Un-flattered by its envied position.
It might even spit a phlegmy wad
To prove its undesirability,
And yet we know, before every tarnished bit of steel,
It smiles and winks to itself.

Of Lowly Self-respect

(Ben E. Kim)

Normal by inspection
Judged the public eye,
No patent surface defect
Could the mirrors spy.

Unfounded causes gather
To form a cruel assault;
Shattered skies drown rising candour
To a mumbling halt.

Cataracted inward eye
Wayward logic's rise;
Cankered dreams, skewed consciousness
Fill a heart with lies.

To Julie Cullen, who inspired, and my special geek Robin Stille.

Age: 27
Address: 6 Crawford Drive, Ajax, ON, L1S 3A8
Born in Virginia and raised in Thunder Bay, Ontario, Ben received his degrees in Biology in 1989 and Electrical Engineering in 1994. He currently struggles with ideas of teaching high school and working as an engineer. His interest in writing did not begin until 1986 under the inspiration of a high school English teacher, and his poems have not been published outside the University of Western Ontario. He has continued to study violin and martial arts in university and also enjoys classical guitar, volleyball and baseball.

Song of Loving Kindness
(Bob King)

May all living things find their peace of mind
And may all living things accept their space and time
And may all peoples of the earth awaken from this dream
And may all people in their search discover what is real

May all creatures in the woods and those who sail the air
Be looked upon in brotherhood and treated with love and care
And may all fruits and flowers, grasses and forests too
Prosper in great abundance, we owe our lives to you

And may all different colours, races, religions too
Learn to treat the other as you'd want them to treat you
And may all men and women come to love each other
And come to regard one another as sister and as brother

And may the skies and the oceans, the rivers and the streams
Be seen as pure and sacred, forever to stay clean
And may we all come to know the earth and all as friend
And put an end to sorrow and sing and dance again

This is dedicated to the awakening of all sentient beings to the reality of love.

Someone Else's Dreams

(Kim Klimo)

He stood at the shoreline
For anyone else it seemed like eternity,
but for him, it was a patient wait.
A wait for his dreams to be granted;
soon his long wait would be rewarded.
Suddenly, through the sunset, a wooden chest appeared,
floating gracefully, overpowering the troubled waters.
He ran to the chest, keeping the desperate thought in the
back of his mind that this could be his chest of glory.
He opened it.
Taking a second look, he sighed,
for this was only the remains of someone else's dreams.
He wept with sorrow in the night,
in the pain,
in the thought of his dreams somewhere out there
with someone else,
someone else with no use for them except to throw them away . . .

Blind Vision

(M.K. Kozma)

Why am I like this?
Never here
Always somewhere else far away
My body remains
My mind escapes, floats off, runs away
Searching, yet not really knowing what it is looking for
Nothing seems to satisfy it
A constant frustration. Anticipation
Like waiting for the gun to go off before a race
And then running, running, running
Never knowing where you are going
Never knowing who is behind you
Or who is in front
All you see is the sky
With the sun in your eyes
And the road just in front of your feet
The world behind you just a confused blur
Of memories, emotions, laughter, and pain
Perhaps that is what you are running away from
Hoping to get over that hill to see what awaits
On the other side
Maybe it will be what you are looking for
Love? Happiness? Who knows
You will only know when your mind
And your body rejoin completely as one.

To my Mother, whose wisdom and love have formed the path I follow.

Shall I?
(Martin H. Kramer)

Sometimes flights of fancy seize my imagination, sending it soaring through lofty realms, and inspiring me to write poems of incredible imagery and feeling, that cannot fail to attract publishers, excite readers, and establish my name in the pantheon of literary immortals. BUT THIS IS CANADA! Shall I burn them?

Doves
(Karen Kubara)

There they are again, the doves
Flying in formation above
The power station
That same way,
This time every day,
Not going anywhere.
Like a two-handed kite they loop,
White breasts flash, and swoop.
Absolutely silent
In circles and eights, they break apart
And come back together by some soundless art.
A few drop out (to rest?) Others join back in,
Rehearsing a strategy of protection.

But today there were feathers—lots:
Soft iridescent down
And various grays with ink black blots,
And one—finely marked
(By teeth? By claw?) lines sketched dark
In blood.
Overhead the kite
Still turns—breasts white,
Then gray—
Away.
The pattern stays, unperturbed.
The loss of one does not disturb.

Life in a Fairytale
(Glen M. Kuiack)

The storybook tale didn't happen at all,
The prettiest princess didn't get to the ball.
She was lured into love and lost in the fog
By a prince she once kissed, he was really a frog.

She couldn't quite see the true demon seed,
That, later in life, would make her heart bleed.
He'd use and abuse her, then throw her away,
He'd take all her sunshine and leave her life grey.

Through struggles and pains and many a tear,
She fought her way back to a sky that was clear.
It took a long time to finally get there,
Then it happened again to her deep despair.

She'll be happy again 'cause I know that she's strong,
She'll find a new prince, a place to belong.
I hope and pray that the next one is me,
I'll hold her and love her and set her heart free.

For Delores: a friend with a special place in my heart.

A Lifestyle to Ride

(Weng Thong Kwok)

Looking at the prevailing lifestyle, our lives are just like the traffic on the street.
Much disturbance every second we all have to withstand.
Tension builds up to a harsh extent that seems impossible to suppress.
Screaming with our horns, we hope to blow out the stress.
With this, we unknowingly add pressure to the rest.

Looking at our prevailing lifestyle, our problems are just like the lights of the traffic.
Like front lights shining on rear lights, they are always linked.
With vehicles turning and crossing lanes, they can never stay fixed.
Trying to solve them, how can we not feel horrific.

For this prevailing lifestyle, I hope I can build a bridge.
Standing on this bridge, I wish that these rapids could flow under our laps.
Although stresses can never die,
but by standing on the bridge, we can sense the
brightness of the lights and not be blinded by it.

Looking from this bridge, I dreamt that it could turn into millions of bridges.
To let us glide above turmoil with pride.
With this, the troubles of our lives we will all survive.

To those with superlative and heroic care: Margaret, Brian, Marie-Lenna, Ooi-Ho (Mom), Yew-Fang (Sister), Shuk-Ha, Edith, and Heather.

Age: 29
Address: P.O. Box 57473, Jackson Station, Hamilton, ON, L8P 4X3
I am an Electrical Engineering student. My birthday is 26 June 1964, thus making me a Cancerian. I believe that there is some truth in horoscopes because my character is closely described by the sign. I am emotional, sensitive and affectionate, but most people are blinded by just taking appearances. I am single now. I lost my first love about two years ago. It was this that drove me into depression last summer, when I started to write poems. Writing love poems is my better hobby than writing philosophical poems. I do sincerely welcome anyone to ask for my romantic poems.

Hope for the Future

(Jim Laird)

Everything was dark
And silent,
Except for a slight pitter-patter.
Then the lightning flashed
And the thunder rolled,
The winds gusted with great dignity!
Like bull-whips, trees bend back and forth without rest.
The Sun's warming rays were held back
By the huge band of darkness.
Everything was in darkness and dismay.
But suddenly, one ray of light
Pierced through the blanket of darkness,
Giving hope that one day
There will be peace.

To my grandfather, whom I loved so much.

Age: 19
Address: 8201-95 "A" Avenue, Fort Saskatchewan, AB, T8L 2W7
Poem written at age 14 during a difficult time in my life. Football and weightlifting central focus in life at this present time. Will be playing at the College level in the U.S.A. Would like to teach elementary school.

Demons

(Jeanny Lam)

Like a breathless wind
they come from every side
mercilessly taunting me
to push me beyond the precipice.

Wicked,
their toothless grins
are clouds in the midnight sky
wildly cackling
            as they moan a dirge
            for the dead.

Their wails haunt me
nightmarish phantoms
forever lost
                        in the night.
I have no light
to guide them home.

With love to Ilia Avroutine—thanks for your help and for being there.

Faith

(Tracey Lamping)

You are my spiritual storehouse; my divine embodiment.
My acts are less than pious; you are my confessional.
My thoughts are less than pure; you are my redemption.
The house of my heart is often empty—
You are my cathedral.

A Life Worth Fighting for . . .
(Wendy Landon)

The souls of lost children are crying to be saved,
The tears of the children begging to be wiped away.

The sick and the elderly are praying for hope,
But they would settle for love and respect to help cope.

The homeless scream out for warmth, food and shelter,
But we offer them less than they need to recover.

The world looks to our youngsters to carry it through,
To regain the hope and make dreams come true.

But how can they reverse all the damage we've done,
With no safe place to learn—so many battles to be won.

Our children are living lives worse than our own,
With diseases that kill and cures still unknown;

With guns in our schools and death all around,
And children abused—more victims being found.

How long will it take before we all take a stand?
How long will it be before safety is a demand?

For a life that we bore into this world—
Is always a life that's worth fighting for . . .

Carley Mary Patricia, born February 3, 1993. My reason to fight.

Angels

(Dana Landry)

I have spent years
beneath the shelter of their wings.
I have grown strong
beneath the blanket of their love.
I have learned truth
beneath their gentle justice.
I have gained life
beneath the warmth of their faith.

Though now I fly free
above wing and blanket,
I do not fly alone.
For below,
catching my mistakes,
comforting my uncertainties,
float the angels
in the heavens of parenthood.

To my own two angels, with love.

Windchimes on the Miramichi

(Gary J. Langguth)

They call me
outside, beyond
the creaking, rotting
unpainted back porch steps:
three metal pipes
painted white
rusted maroon
sway
tinkle together
against windy blue October canvass
and jingle out
subtle hints
sounds of a generation gone.

Conflict

(Tom Lanning)

Sitting on his bunk
Thinking back, Remembering all
those whom he had freed from the world.
Some men get hooked on drink
Others Heroin, or the thrill of a bet
But the monkey on his back was killing

Back home they would lock him up!
But here in the jungle he was a hero
A total reversal of morality
Good men, Sane men
Shot, stabbed, burned and bombed
With no remorse or thought.

The conflict was not in the field
That was reflex, killing was easy.
The conflict was between orders and morality
Between Good and Evil in the hearts of men.

Now he weeps for he was a tool of the
Dark half of the equation

Whirlpool
(Jim Larwill)

Caught between the power of lakes
wood nymphs sing with the roar of falls,
twisting and bubbling in cool water
becoming floating shadows,
reflecting veins of darting light,
fluttering down a rocky cascade
in pursuit of minnows.

Lost Worlds

(Bozena Latincic)

It's night and here they are:
Thousands of "guiding lights" shining gently from above
And looking at them, a thought enters my mind
As gently as they shine:
What if, they are all remnants of worlds gone by,
Of worlds that once existed
And now are but a barren composition of mass?
A sombre feeling fills my soul.
I shudder—
As another thought enters my mind:
What direction is all this taking?
Are we too on our way to becoming
A twinkle of light, yet for another living creation?

Bozena Latincic-Bennett was born in Gora, Croatia, in 1957. She moved to Vienna, Austria, in 1968 and immigrated to Montréal, Canada, in 1973. She studied English Literature at McGill University. Her interests are in writing and painting. "Lost Worlds" is her first published work. She lives with her husband, James, in Laval, Québec, and continues to write and paint.

Lost Love
(Ronald James)

Memories of days long past sometime come to me
Flashing down a twisted road of happier time and thought.
And tho I want to bring them back
I know I never can.

Music fills my haunted soul with love that used to be
Magic moments of a face and heart I knew the gods had wrought.
And as I think of that vanished time
I remember how I ran.

O to bring back the forbidden love you could never see
For I never opened up my heart to things that you had taught.
And often very late at night
The pain's too much to stand.

And so my beautiful dream I know it could have been we
But my heart knew you were taken so my love I never brought.
And as my world ended that day
I fled to another land.

Yes I remember you the special days and he
The reason that I left for I know we would have fought.
But I know now I should have stayed
And perhaps become your man.

But alas my heart I know too well this could never be
Your life and mine could never merge ever were it bought.
But I dream of you as my eyes close
My beautiful darling Ann.

To the vivid memory of youth.

Address: 55 Wellington Street, Port Colborne, ON, L3K 2J6
Telephone: (905) 834-9300
An avid reader, I have probably consumed well over 3000 books on various subjects. Although I plumb the depths of my soul with poetry, I have also written three books (as yet unpublished). Forced to leave school at an early age, I am self taught. I take pleasure in wandering through the woods, my imagination conjuring up inventions to appease my obsession to create. My goals are to continue writing, striving for success and the ultimate glory of being an author.

You

(Troy E. LaVallée)

As the wings of life carry me forward
I look into your eyes and see a life I long to live
The door of reality holds me back
The tradition of the past gives me hope to give
Chains of pain, bring on guilt
Yet, I dream on for the days of old
Forever trapped is the nature within me
Holding on to the dream dripping with ice so cold
Somehow the light still burns
Reaching out into the darkness looking for the source
Like the cycle of life, I too take my turn
Waiting for your soft touch I've yet to feel
The burden of the beast knocks at my door
Faced with reality the pain is so real
As I open the door I see the emptiness
The path to your reality is so clear
The dogs of doubt bite at my soul
Yet the road is bloody with haste and fear
Perched up like an angel I wait at your door
Fear fills me, I can fight no more

A love poem dedicated to Aboriginal (Native) women everywhere—who deserve respect as in past Native tradition—sustainers of life.

Age: 19
Address: 3664 Hazel Grove, Regina, SK, S4V 2T6
Telephone: (306) 789-9592
Troy Earthchild Lavallée (Dressyman) was born in Edson, Alberta, in September of 1974 and was raised in Wetaskiwin, Alberta. He is a grade 12 graduate from the Wetaskiwin Composite High School. He is a registered Cree Native from Red Pheasant Reserve in Saskatchewan. Troy's father is Chie Terry Lavallée of the Cowessess First Nation in Broadview, Saskatchewan. His mother, Marjorie Lavallée (Dressyman) is a professor at the University of Regina, S.I.F.C., Regina, Saskatchewan. He has an eight-year-old brother, Myles, and a four-year-old sister, Samy-Jo. Presently, Troy is a first-year student at the University of Regina, S.I.F.C.

Motherhood or Apple Pie?
(Barbara-Jo Leahey)

There were times when I preferred
the apple pie.
You clean your plate, it satisfies,
it's gone.
Grown children, on the other hand,
come back to visit or, God forbid,
to stay.

The son whose floor I hadn't seen
for eighteen years
now irons his sheets.
We shake our heads and wonder . . . .

Is this our child?
He's taller, but he looks familiar.
He speaks of adult things
in our living room when he visits.

We are proud of this person he's become:
a policeman.
Oh God,
a man/child with a gun.

We listen as he talks
of bulletproof vests and self-defence.
Would you rather I didn't have one, Mum?
Would you rather I didn't know?

We'll cherish the day
when he comes to visit.

To my son, Chris: Here's hoping all your dreams come true.

Address: Box 171, Florenceville, NB, E0J 1K0
I am the mother of two grown sons. I live happily in New Brunswick's "potato belt" with one husband, a perfect dog and an exceptional cat. I teach Junior High English and love teenagers, reading and writing. I firmly believe that the world's greatest professions are teaching and writing. I am lucky enough to do both!

Lucid

(Kate Lee)

Is there a door behind tomorrow?
Are there answers in the sky?
Will existence verify its meaning,
in the moment when we die?

Could yesterday be a prelude
Of what is destined to be?
And if I searched the Earth for answers,
would I find them in the sea?

Can you count an ache in numbers?
How much will infinity hold
When a broken heart remembers
and then burns out in the cold?

Could you count the seagulls flying?
Maybe it was a sign.
While the world still stands waiting,
do the angels lose their minds?

How many dreams are in the ocean?
Could I count them if I tried?
Burn the mazes I've been lost in and
still feel enough to cry?

Decipher a haunted melody,
could I tell you what it means?
Is there meaning to this laughter?
Did I lose it in a dream?

For Kane. Even when I'm as blue as your eyes, you make me sparkle.

Telephone: (902) 892-1832
I live in Charlottetown, PEI, with my two children and cats. I enjoy writing poetry and children's stories and may even some day get around to typing out manuscripts for them. I'm presently working towards a degree in Criminology, and in my spare time, I enjoy meeting new people and trying new things.

Mona

(Edmund Legere)

T'was a wee hint of Heaven, how I knew you so well
Sure I knew you before we were born
When I sensed you were leaving, mixed emotions prevailed
Still I'd meet you on earth some sweet morn.

In what seems like an instant, t'was my turn to go
Mom and Dad supplied corpus to mould
But you were back home in Ireland, an ocean away
Would we meet 'fore life's curfew bells tolled?

Then for a moment, I sat by your side
On the feast of Her born without sin.
You had winged cross the ocean, to visit my town
From the sod of your country, our kin

I hope Jude and Patrick help drive out my snakes
So's in a tridium of steads we will meet
Like a seamrog, the trefoil, green emblem of home
When at last we are welcomed by Pete

Age: 63
Address: 43 Champlain Drive, Saint John, NB, E2J 3C5
Telephone: (506) 696-1905
My last throat operation was in Quebec City in 1957, which a local doctor says makes me the longest surviving cancer patient in Canada. I had a shoulder muscle removed, however I continued to play drums in a dance band until 1980. I graduated from high school in '48. My wife, Toby, is a 10 and mom to our 3 children and *sitti* (Lebanese) to our 3 grandchildren. I have religiously maintained a daily journal since 1972, which I estimate, totals an excess of one million words. Thank you, God, for a fabulous experience here on Earth.

Graceful Man
(Gail W. Legere)

Arms raised in ballerina style,
she leaned her body towards her friend
as they walked leisurely down the street.
The young man, hands in pockets,
grin on face, straight ahead,
conscious of her as she moved
by his side in willowy dance not walk.
Looking at her not looking around
he could no longer resist.
He gathered her to him,
kissed her on the mouth,
then dropped her gently to her feet.

Demoralizzante, Rejection of the First Commandment
(R. Leonardo)

money Originated in the thirteenth century.
An epithet used in ancient Rome for the goddess Juno
was moneta

(derived by some etymologist in the past
from the Latin verb monere "advise, warn," although
this is, in our modern age, regarded as rather
dubious; the suggestion absurd).

Ring around the rosy
pocket full of money,
husha husha;
we all
fa
l
l
down.

---

for Gary Hyland, in gratitude for sagacious advice and presenting doors to be open.

Age: 19
Address: 26-1250, 11th Avenue S.W., Moose Jaw, SK, S6H 7J5
Telephone: (306) 692-5694
Recently graduated from high school and missing the inspirational classrooms (especially English). I intend to keep writing poetry in hopes of further expression and recognition. For the future, I would prefer to stay in Saskatchewan and at the very least would not wish to leave the Canadian Prairies. I desire to own my own business some day that would be in the literary field of interest.

A Stone, a Child

(Alan Levin)

A stone, rough
Washed from the rooty bank
Tumbles, clacks down a glacial brook
Black, white, rubs shoulders with its neighbours
The crowd, the mob; shoves over cataracts
Cascades through milky rapids
Clatters into deep round pools
To lurk
Rubbed smooth by the rush of silt and eons
Clean and fine as a newborn child

A child, smooth
Washed from the salty womb
Crawls, scrambles up a playground slide
Black, white, rubs shoulders with its neighbours
The crowd, the mob; shoves into adulthood
Cascades through middle age
Clatters into dark close bars
To lurk
Rubbed rough by the rush of work and longing
Raw and ruined as an ancient stone

The Wedding Day Thoughts of a Bride

(Cathy Watson Lewis)

This day is a new beginning,
The first day of the rest of our life.
Thank you for sharing it with us,
Our start as husband and wife.

The past has sometimes been rocky,
It has enabled us to learn.
Things change and so do people,
Our values—like the tides—make a turn.

Today we feel so honoured,
Surrounded by family and friends.
Two people—two lives—one love,
Whatever tomorrow sends.

Our future will be a happy one,
Mistakes will sometimes be made.
With God's love and our commitment,
Our love will grow, not fade.

The Cycle
(allan g. lie)

A cold-soul wind
In autumn skies.
A leaf
Drifts slowly
Down.

A soul-less breath
As someone dies.
A heart
Lies open,
Unbound.

A soul-drawn tear
Pain's disguise.
A page
Too often
Turned.

A pure soul born,
A new heart cries.
An echo
Shouts silent,
Unheard.

A warm-soul wind,
Tenacity's prize.
A leaf,
Spring's promise,
Earned.

Creativity
(Corina Lindsay)

It begins as a seed in the form of child,
the soil is the nourishment and foundation
like a mother who is always there for me.
Leaves are the ideas spurting into motion
of endless imagination.
Every branch is a contribution to the growth and maturity
in the form of an adolescent.
Each influence of the seasons
determines all of the ideas forming.
Without the sunlight, there is no energy or encouragement
to continue on with talents.
The tree is the adult, the final masterpiece—
the sum of beauty, aesthetics.
Here is a recipe for all creativeness, which, in truth,
stems from the only source—
the "spirit" in each one of us.

To my newborn Son, Nicolas, for making everything a "first time" again in my life.

Age: 30
Address: c/o #103 Maple Drive, Hinton, AB, T7V 1N4
Telephone: (403) 865-3082
Corina Lindsay (1964-) Born along the Canadian Rockies in Hinton, Alberta, which have been a source of inspiration for many years. Being a vocalist first, an artist second (pastel work) and a poet third, she is constantly pursuing these interests and submitting her best works in hopes of future successes fulfilled dreams and recognition. She is enjoying motherhood and is obtaining a degree in Naturopathic Medicine.

A Mother's Grief

(Nancy M. Lisi)

Of myself I once gave;
wholeheartedly and unselfishly.
Once I sacrificed all to make you happy,
to make you whole.

Now, vile thief,
wretched fiend—You take!
You take until there is no more.
"It is my right," you say.
You, You are an ungrateful thing.
Love has never stopped at your door.
You make him unwelcome
and never will you share his time.

When time takes away your youth,
When your health has failed,
When I am gone,
I pray God remember, and you,
I pray shame follow you—
follow you like your second self.
Then, only then perhaps,
will those words escape your heart!

Age: 20
Address: Box 1157, Golden, BC, V0A 1H0
Telephone: (604) 344-5794
I am of Italian descent; however, I was born and raised in Golden, BC. I am currently attending the University of Calgary and am enroled in the final year of my program: a BA in English with a minor in Italian Studies. I hope one day to write professionally, using both prose and verse.

Yesterday I Met a Stranger
(Kathy Loranger)

Yesterday, I met a stranger
And I thought for a moment
Now why couldn't I
Meet someone like him
For my very own

Yesterday, I met a stranger
He had life
Had humour
He had a smile
Oh, so very bright
And I thought for a moment
Dare I

Yesterday, I met a stranger
He was sweet
He was a dream
He was sheer delight
He was a breath of fresh air
And I thought for a moment
What the heck

Yesterday, I met a stranger
And I thought for a moment
 or more
That no, he'll remain
The stranger I met yesterday.

Thinking of You

(Jodi Lough)

with red glowing knives
you slash through to my brain
skin sticks to the searing metal

you embed there, festering
in that grey mass
I once held in privacy
your growth—my decay

my sanity

Life's Forecast
(Dolores Lynds)

The falling dew is my loneliness
The raindrops are my tears
The gentle breeze is a caress
I feel all through the years.

The sun is my happiness
The moon my glowing heart
The stars glitter from past crises
That once tore my feelings apart.

The thunder is my heartbeat
The lightning is my fear
Black clouds appear to show defeat
That I struggle through each year.

Life's forecast is simple to read
For those who wish to understand—
Try to help those in need
And spread happiness where you can.

Just Like That

(Dan MacCormac)

I've always wanted to be a skateboarder
And a windsurfer a biker and a drummer
A lover and a loner and see the difference
A beach bum and a street kid or maybe someone who
Would only smoke two cigarettes a day

I've always wanted to sing the blues and be happy
Enjoy nature and hitchhike all over it while
All the time not caring if anyone missed me
I wanted to be a writer and never be phoney
Or maybe avoid all of that altogether

I've always wanted to dig jazz and understand classical
Learn to appreciate dance music and dive into the crowd at
A punk concert then not be scared to walk home or
Maybe just not have any music and save some money so
I could buy some Top Siders

I've always wanted to grow my hair long and not look like
You and play the guitar unless I heard a good bass line then
I'd just learn something new and possibly get fed up with
Being talented and just be humble driving around in my Volvo
And maybe not drink alcohol and be proud of that

I've always wanted to feel comfortable around sports fans and
Not be scared of being lazy and play pool at an open table
Then study hard for about an hour and pray for awhile and not
Have people be disappointed in me and wake up with a new
Idea or maybe just be content waking up

Great Grandmother
(E.M. MacDonald)

A long journey by sea and land,
Two small children by the hand
My man I join.

From my country with peach trees in bloom
To this raw valley where mountains loom;
The tears come.

Day in, day out—work like a slave.
The only rest will be a grave and—
I am too strong.

I have ten children. Eight live
And two die. Too tired to grieve;
Numb in my heart.

Children in bed, the man in the mine,
Alone in the house I work in time
To silent screams.

He sells the land, to the village move—
We've worked so hard. The years will prove
If it is better.

People who my language speak—
I'm able to go to mass each week
Ave Maria!

Children grow and are doing well.
Grandchildren come to hear me tell
Sad stories.

Home Grown Children

(Judith MacDonald)

We start by planting rows of PEAS,
Like patience, prayer and pride;
Then LETTUCE add the process
A good parent should provide.

When tender life has just BEAN SPROUTed,
ROMAINE on your finest guard;
Too many LEEKS in the watering source
Can make leaves TURNIP CHARD.

PUMPKINtinously peace and praise,
CUCUMBERsome as it can be;
Precision in placing your pruning
Shall perfect this recipe.

BUTTERNUT SQUASH those tiny shoots,
As they SCALLION their way;
CARROT to come with prudence
For they MUSHROOM every day.

HOMINY days does it take to
CORNer the market on what we sow?
Look for the moment of greatest bloom
SOYA can step back and watch them grow.

This verse is gratefully dedicated to Agatha Gauthier and Joann Gouin.

Age: 50
Address: 160 Askin, Windsor, ON, N9B, 2W9
Telephone: (519) 253-6134

Judith, a former school teacher, currently employed at the University of Windsor Library, Reader Service Department, is married with three sons and seven grandchildren. Her five books of poetry contain 140 poems which incorporate special occasions, commissioned works and messages of endearment. Seven selections were featured on "Patterns in Music," a radio programme hosted by Mike Deja, on WJR, in Detroit, Michigan. American Greetings has purchased several verses for international distribution. Many poems have appeared in Canadian and American publications, e.g. *Thanatos*. Her literary and personal goals are to inspire, comfort and entertain her readers.

I Believe

(Ann MacGillivray)

As I walk through these doors
the promise of tomorrow is within me.
I will treat others with dignity and respect,
and I will honour those who surround me.

I am but one child in a sea of children.
I am a special child, and my gifts are many.
I am the promise in the world of today,
I am the hope for the world of tomorrow.

As I learn, achieve and grow,
I will take these lessons with me
so that each child in this sea of children
may join and bring a world of peace.

To my children, Christopher & Katia, who, no matter the obstacle, never stopped believing.

Religion

(Kathrine MacGinnis)

What defines religion
Is it, of all creation
The heavens and earth
Of all mankind
Nature that walks among us
Everything that can breathe
Feel the wind, rain or sun
To have a true belief
That all was created equal
Everything created unique
Even in a small way
to hold a feeling
A sense of belonging
Within our hearts and soul
To live a lifetime
Just to die and be forgotten
Or return and begin again
It's safe to have beliefs
To help guide and comfort
Knowing that—yes
All was created equal
By a mightier being
Knowing that not one belief
Is always the right one
For all to live by

Alone

(April L. MacKay)

Here I stand,
Alone and free.
I have no friends,
It's only me.

Staring at water,
Water running free.
It must have feelings,
Unlike me.

Untitled

(Duncan M^ac^Kenzie)

Seething, enormous, ultimate rage
Gauged its vices, rhythmically alternating
Like razor-edged wires slicing their
Way down my neck and body—completely
Reducing its parts to a single depleted mind.

Friend

(Paul Macknight)

I walked upon a word or two
To come to meet you here and now,
And I've cast a smile here and there
in order to catch you wonder how.

Still, I stop myself from being here
each time I take a breath of Time;
Yet you should know that fogs of past
Are fleeing to let the sun be mine.

Gift of Glass
(Calabrese)

As a child I was often given glass,
dogs and horses, sleek and still, mine
for a moment before my mother placed them on a shelf
I could never dream of reaching.

But I did dream
and sometimes prayed
to be the child
we saved them for.

I wasn't there the morning
the whole shelf
fell.
But that night,
I gathered what I could
and hid my joy.

My fingers marvelled at the fine white dust.

Three-legged horses ran
across the lavender fields of my bed.
And overnight,
while the dogs slept close,
the horse
with no legs at all,
grew wings.

Dawn Predator

(Sylvia MacNairn)

Turning, gliding, ever in flight
Wings made dark by pre-dawn light
O'er the ocean, in sun's first rays
Searching, searching, for its prey.

Comes a flash of silver fin
Then the waves are still again
Windless morning, moonlit night
End of hunt, is it in sight?

Long, long hours beneath the stars
The hunter searching near and far
And then to spot it, in the east
The treasure trove, an ocean feast.

Are you wondering of whom I speak
And the prey for which it seeks?
A sea gull looking for a meal
A smelt for brunch, what a steal!

To Stuart, Scott, Glen and Mom—my patient, understanding and tolerant listeners.

Broken Down
(Dave P. Madole)

hair that a thousand winds have grown
candle lit eyes that a million sights have peered
sandled feet that endless miles have walked
a lean face worn by a razor coarse beard
clothes that a thousand days have put on
a voice that a million songs have sung
deaf ears that countless sounds have heard
a tired mind that too many thoughts have stung
a life that a thousand deaths have lived
a heart that a million feelings have felt
a body that many lonely places have been
knees that endless hard floors have knelt
all these own the person they came from
his word a thousand tongues have spoken
and now our brother can't even feel used
his will to do anything long since broken

For Sheena Moodie, an inspiration and a friend. For Jill Edwards, my dear sister.

Age: 18
Address: Box 614, Lacombe, AB, T0C 1S0
In my short period of time on this earth, I've graduated from high school, worked and travelled. I've learned just one thing; there's something about having a pen in my hand that sends me into worlds of creative thought. I thank God for that. I hope to one day become an English teacher. In that way, I'll teach everyone how a pen in the hand puts freedom in the heart.

Variations on a Winter Cantata
(Magon)

The sky opened up
with the glow of
blue rose, and the
ordinary peach,
oranges, greens,
pinks, of the

flatlands were open,
also.
You were there
standing straight
and tall,
that ruggedly

handsome, amiable
stance of yours,
waiting for
something dainty
and pretty to waltz
by, which she did,

and you might
as well stay
married; that way,
the ballroom lights
at your feet, beneath
your bodies and within
your souls, forever.

Thanks to writers, everywhere.

Time

(J.L. Makela)

My hand in my grandfather's,
Small and smooth and slim,
Held by a curious curve
Of puffed and stubby fingers,
Scraped and darkened, mysterious, family;
My hand in my grandfather's,
Small and slight and trim.

Age: 50
Address: R.R. #1, Maccan, NS, B0L 1B0
Born: August 3, 1943, Amherst, Nova Scotia. Family name: Landels. Education: Toronto Teacher's College; BA, Mount Allison University; MEd. St. Mary's University. Taught in Ontario, BC, and Nova Scotia. Member: Scottish Cultural Society, Art Teachers Association. Writings: poetry, articles, short stories.

Mr. Andretti Wanna Be

(Sara Makowy)

He twists his steering wheel to the left
to the right
left
right
throwing his passengers,
who sneer and shout perversions.
"I'll report you!" a woman screams and
receives nods of agreement from her co-passengers.
"Mario" ignores them,
whipping through yellow lights,
dodging car doors,
screaming to sudden stops.
"Did you get the number of this thing?" someone snaps.
"Yes I did."
"Me too."
"I did also."
There are persistent dings.
"Let me off this tube from hell!"
He's tuned the din out.
Mario today, Michael tomorrow,
but never who they want him to be.

To Margaret and Kris, as promised.

Untitled

(Archibald L. Malally)

The day is brisk but yet so bright.
As I tread lightly through the snow,
My eyes gaze past the evergreens
To where a stream does gently flow.
Surrounded by peace and tranquillity,
I feel so very warm inside.
To see such beauty everywhere,
It fills my heart with pride.
The silence then is shattered
By the Blue Jays' warning cry,
Informing creatures of a stranger,
And that stranger, it is I.
But all creatures of the forest
Sense this stranger means no harm.
He's only here to view their grace,
Their beauty and their charm.
So with the comfort of this feeling,
They return to nature's way,
And I feel so very fortunate
To observe them as they play.
Time passes by so quickly,
And dusk begins to settle in.
A promise is made as I depart—
I shall return, yes, I shall return again.

To all creatures of the wild—may they always be free.

Alive

(Ellis Manderson)

The ocean came alive last night
I watched in horror,
As it raped the starry beach.

Ocean's strong arms
Caressed the hundred sands,
Screaming with rage.

Sometimes the ocean would leave,
Letting the sands wet themselves
With tears.

But the Ocean
Always came back.
Begging for forgiveness.

To the memory of my Grandmother, Hilda D. Jamieson—for your love and support.

Faintest Glimmer
(Meredith Manley)

From the beginning of my soul,
Where God first began—
                    the beginning of my being,
                    my intelligence; my first
                    faintest glimmer of life—
My love for you begins.
And all barriers it breaks until it is past man
And God only knows—
                    He is everything and all things,
                    the beginning, the end—
He can know the depth and height of my
Love, for you.

For my Father, Mother and Family.

Age: 20
Address: Box 444, Cardston, AB, T0K 0K0
Meredith is the youngest of five girls. She has four brothers. She enjoys family and is a beloved aunt of 21 nieces and nephews. She is quietly kind and modest in nature. She has a strong sense of self. Her educational intent is to get an advanced degree in Physics. Some hobbies are reading, writing, baking and studying. She lives in the present and looks forward to a bright future.

Discard

(Pat Marche)

The Volkswagen groaned past it on the highway.
It was nothing, a piece of rock; But it moved.
"Dad, Stop! I think it's a bird."

The reverse crescendo of the car's motor brought closer scrutiny.
"It is! It is! It's a baby! It can hardly fly!"

Ruffled grey down covered its body.
I felt its heart race out of sync with the motor of the car.
What were we going to do?

Tender hands caressed the frightened ball of fluff.
"Can we keep it Dad? Oh please?
"I'll take care of it. Feed it. Please?"

Somehow I knew life's harsh blow was already executed.
All attempts at rescue would be futile.
But what do you tell a ten-year-old who's known nothing but life?

For days he fed it fresh worms.
Plenty of water, and cosy bedding would ordinarily satisfy.
But this shabby ball was a discard.

One morning nature's darker side was exposed.
He found it.
Its stiff body was belly up.
It's stick-like legs outstretched as if resisting the unknown.

....

That day, a ten-year-old became a little less innocent!

To my son, Ian, for whom this experience helped create a greater appreciation of life.

the last of august

(Nicole Markotic)

remnants. of sun. of that insidious optimism. of you. yesterday I began reading fairy tales. Red Riding Cap and Hansel & Gretel and Snow White. as if they are only possible when I begin to believe in winter again

I discover that in the original version (or at least the earliest recorded), the wolf gets away with swallowing little Red Cap whole: there are no woodcutters standing by, no stones in his belly, no revenge. I have cold chicken for supper and, after, I walk and I walk until I am no longer thinking about not thinking about you. and it's ridiculous, I know, but I never have claimed not to be ridiculous, so I turn around and walk back home and recite ridiculous rhymes to myself: sentimental: everpental; resolution: caroplusion; group dynamics: scoop-eye-lamics and am pleased that every single one is a feminine rhyme and thus makes perfect sense

but really what I'd like is to go backwards, I decide during the night: reverse my whole life so it's one endless stream of yesterdays. a fairy tale gone crazy. august. july. I'm in Red Deer again. I'm in L.A. I'm in your arms again. we haven't yet met

good evening, I pronounce to the building manager as I leave the next morning. well, it's a start

Vitae in Ovum
(Katherine Martens)

Heart beats high;
Pulses race.
Dreams swirl by
At star-speed pace.

Wings beat hard
Against the air;
Breathless, flung
Into Time/Space rare.

Excitement, hunger
Desire spirals.
Eyes flash fire;
Conquer trials.

Now is the Time.
The Moment's at hand.
Doubt and fear
Have both been banned.

Anticipation feeds the flame.
Logic cools the senses.
Love spreads wide its beating wings;
So the Dream commences.

Of Thanksgiving and Praise
(Chad D. Martin)

You are my mother,
I shall not wander.
For fields of home,
I cannot grow fonder.

Unfledged had I left,
Motley currencies to hold.
The yearning for adventure,
Great sights yet to behold.

Miles from you did I Rome,
Versailles in a day.
From St. Peters to Blarney.
A lighted Champs Elysées.

But oh, how I ached
For the place of my birth!
With snow-covered peaks,
My Eden, my hearth!

I longed for the Rockies
Where as child, I'd bound.
To walk in the woods,
With barest of sound.

On this soil I shall remain
For the rest of my days.
And to the Maple Leaf,
Thanksgiving and Praise!

To my friend Patrick, for the days spent travelling I will never forget.

Age: 22
Address: 221 10th Street South, Cranbrook, BC, V1C 4P5
Telephone: (604) 426-4022
Chad Douglas Martin was born in Cranbrook, British Columbia, June 17th, 1972. One of two children of Nick and Joan Martin, he can remember enjoying writing at an early age. Having completed several writing courses, Martin is currently completing an undergraduate degree in Psychology at the University of Lethbridge, Alberta. An overseas backpacking trip to Europe provided Martin with invaluable potential writing material, and indeed was the motivation behind "Thanksgiving and Praise," a poem about his love of Canada. Martin is also engaged to the woman of his dreams, Miss Kristi Robertson of Golden, BC.

Spouse

(M. Dayle Martin)

To give of oneself
To continue giving
Even when you've given all

To sacrifice one's own
Measure of happiness
For the sake of the other

To cope with the
Asked and unasked
To listen to
Everything and nothing

To sense changes
When none are
Apparent

To love and understand
To just love
Without understanding . . .

Lost and Found

(Lisa Mathews)

It is July and I am lost.
The blue sky isn't blue and
the voices I hear create patterns of unease.
I cannot find status amid the wind and waves of existence:
I only drown in lakes of averages,
my youth swept off by static and chaos.

It is July and I am lost
looking for something and finding
but that I am like
the falling bird, the drowning fish:
    lost in my own skin.
My heart pumps blood to various parts of my body,
ultimately reaching my heart again:
    I am running for my life.
    Time is running me towards
    Perspective.
From my vantage point I will then find
each lost moment of my life
from once upon a time until
the end.

It is July and I am lost.
I have given up searching.
Now I only wait to be found.

For A.

Embodiment

(Emily Mayne)

If I were to ask
would you bring me
your tears collected in a glass
so I could taste
the salt of your pains?

Would you bring me
your sighs
contained in a jar
so I could smell
the breath of your contentment?

Would you bring me
your sweat
pooled in a basin
so I could bathe in
the product of your labours?

Would you bring me
your blood
spread on a palette
so I could paint
the anger of your spirit?

And if I were to ask . . .
would you bring me your soul
so I could join you
in your
abyss?

To Mrs. Wade, the one who sparked the fire within me.

Age: 19
Address: c/o Box 40, Marysville, BC, V0B 1Z0
The only thing I was ever sure of growing up was that being a kid sucked—I wasn't allowed to do anything. Being a teenager sucked—I was all confused inside. And now being an adult looks like hard work too. But the key to surviving is this: Find something you're good at and do it. Do it well. No one can ever take that away from you because you won't let them. Go for it! I did.

Lisa

(Maureen Mayr)

Her smile was like the morning sun,
Which warmed the inner soul
With eyes that shone like diamonds
That set the sky aglow.

Vital-energetic, self-sufficient
She had grown,
From the little girl we knew
Into a woman of her own.

She danced with every step she took,
The world was but a stage,
And all the Love she had to give
Lit up her lovely face.

She's gone but not forgotten,
Her legacy will live on
In the precious gift she gave us,
His name is Matthew,

LISA'S SON

Silent Soldiers
(Robert C. Mazur)

Upturned eyes, now blind,
gazed at the hazy skies.
Peace came to the fields
that will be forever theirs.
They loved. They cried.
They cursed. They prayed.
They fought. They died.
The neat, long rows
and white crosses,
mark their passing.
Not shouts. Not blood.
Not bullets. Not shells.
Not cold. Not mud.
We remember they
who will never grow old.
Beat the drums!
Strike the colours!
Send them on their way.
War is not as neat
as those row upon row.
Glory has its price and
freedom demands sacrifice.
All silent soldiers know.

Age: 37
Address: 82 Lawrence Avenue, Thunder Bay, ON, P7A 6X6
Telephone: (807) 344-7731
Born and raised in Thunder Bay, Ontario. Employed by Transport Canada as a Canadian Coast Guard Radio Operator. Graduated St. Catharines Business College with a diploma in Computer Programming. Married to Janice. Interests include shortwave radio, philately, astronomy, reading and writing. My hero is Terry Fox. Have travelled, worked and lived all over Canada.

The Pin

(Barry McAuley)

I lost a pin in the chesterfield
But don't you fear my friend
For when I sat to think on it
I found it in the end!

The Seedling
(Dave McConnell)

I tempted you
with an apple
in the garden.
You bit into it,
juices mingling,
yet continued to run,
naked
and unashamed across the grass,
stopping here to pick a flower
or there to watch an insect probe.
There was nothing sinful
in these actions
and I longed to join
your celebration
but age,
tradition and
neighbourhood eyes of decorum
returned me to my search for weeds
as you laughingly slithered
among the upturned carcasses of toys
and my lost innocence.

Address: 4 Steffler Drive, Guelph, ON, N1G 3L6
Is currently teaching at a high school in Acton, Ontario. Personal interests include cycling, interacting with his family and cultivating what has become a lifelong regard for literature in its many forms, poetry being one of the most important.

Progress

(Eugene McCoy)

A fall of snow
greeted the awakening dawn
with an awesome hush.
No twittering birds,
nor human sounds,
just an awesome hush.
A soft snow-mantle
blanketed the earth
with whiteness
at morning-time.
Nature's beauty!

The economic man
greeted the day
with a frustrated shrug.
No stopping work,
nor slowing economy,
just a frustrated shrug.
A hard high-tech crust
overlaid the ground
with yellowness
at evening-time.
Nature's master?

To Maudie and Anne, for inspiration and encouragement.

Invisible Me
(Amy McDougald)

I want to be
invisible
and live free,
undetected

to do
and say what I want
without
concern for others'
reply

I want to be
invisible,
but I think
it would be lonely.

Age: 18
Address: P.O. Box 1313, Guelph, ON, N1G 4K5
Amy McDougald is an 18 year-old student who is very much in love with all aspects of the arts. She has won many competitions for her short stories and most recently was a recipient of the Guelph Art Council Youth Award. Her future goals include gaining a post-secondary education and pursuing a career in theatre.

The Dream Catcher

(Teresa McDougall)

Solitude—the empty night wraps around her

But still sleep eludes; the weary mind alert;
And reality is ever a cruel reminder
She reaches out to touch on—
To escape from; and cries out in pained despair.

Then he comes to her; an elusive being
His eyes burning deeply into her soul
Desire so tangible; it splits the atom
Reaching out to touch on—
To be her destiny while she sleeps.

They call him the Dream Catcher
His web of intrigues transcending
An unbidden lifeline to the lovely woman
Who lies innocent of his coming.
He reaches out to touch on—
Her body an extinguished flame.

He halts in his reverie—
Recoiling when she turns with yearning
Loneliness and fear gave birth to the nightmares he feeds on
But now the nightfall is her freedom.
And the Dream Catcher remains impotent;
    a frozen exile!

Wonderful

(Glenn McFarlane)

Warmly sweet
Only more of a feeling
Never mistaken or confused
Demanding, yet pleasurable
Entertaining and amusing
Realization of needs
Fulfillment of joys
Understanding
Love.

Glenn McFarlane was raised an "army brat," with roots in Eastern Canada. He is a 31 year old software engineer in the aerospace industry. Most of his poems are either light and humorous or very strong in emotion; however, he insists "Wonderful" was written merely as "an exercise." Glenn is unmarried and lives in Brampton, Ontario.

Untitled

(Tamy McKay)

What we have in common
You will always know
For the reflection in our eyes
Show the yearning of our soul
And the unity we find
Will bring us peace of mind
For you are one with me
And without your love
I cannot grow
And when you hear the universe unfold
in colours that flow through
I'll be there for I am one with you.

The Hands of a Carpenter
(Jennifer McKenna)

The hands of a carpenter now lie so still.
The hands once so busy are now marred by his skill.
These hands built us shelters and provided for us all.
This man with such strong hands was busy;
Yet at our beck and call.
Always time for fishing, hockey games and ball.
Poppy gave us each so much, the greatest love of all.
For in his example we find a wealth of good,
A wisdom and more answers to live life as we should.
He made so much more than wooden crafts and dreams.
He made a part in each of us so eloquently it seems.
For Poppy in his strength was gentle to the bone,
And as long as he's in our hearts, none of us are alone.
If we each carry with us a special memory or two,
No one will forget the Poppy all of us knew.
There was never any time I can remember when his presence was not felt.
Or an evening when I was little without rosary and prayer we knelt.
And I know now he is happy and praying for us all,
That we may meet in God's Kingdom when we answer His call.
Poppy's gentle hands will dry away our tears.
And his memory will live on in us for years and years and years.

In memory of my Grandfather, Louis McKenna, who died December 13, 1993.

From Dawn 'til Dusk

(S.A. McLennan)

In the youth of the morning
As the first dawn shows
A slight brightness creaks
The vast mountain glows
As it shines over the white covered peaks

As the quiet morning glistens
And the dew embeds in the ground
As mother nature wakes
And the beautiful atmosphere can be found

Now the earth has wakened
And the bodies are alive
The day carries on
And still continues to thrive

The night comes near
The sun goes, as the moon sets in
It is nearly midnight so soon
And a new day will begin

Mountain Life
(Geraldine McLeod)

We bought a home in the mountains. What a beautiful, serene place.
A stream twists and bubbles endlessly through the bulrushes.
The black-headed chickadees and blue-winged jays scramble for the box seats at the feeding stations.
White-tailed deer roam under the apple trees.
The lone coyote howls consistently at the moon.

Here is where the moon and earth join in holy union.
The sun peeking ever so gently through the crimson leaves of the maples.
The stars hang as if suspended in mid air high above our heads, casting their brilliance unaware.

Snow plunging from heaven to earth so fast that within hours, fields, roads and house tops are concealed by blue-white folds of fluff.
Rain pelts on the tin roof of the garage with a rage of inner turmoil that will not be satisfied until every living thing has become a victim of its ferocity.

Listening to the tree frogs burst forth in sweet harmony after the ice descends down the steep incline, refreshes my faith in God.
This is what life is all about. I think I'll stay.

Cathedral Poem

(Leslie J. McNab)

Yawning doors expel the blessed,
descending into waves of
grasping, reaching hands

fighting   dirty   unloved,

crouched in shadows of your might,
gathered not to breast but thrust
outside strong resolve,
puddled at your feet.

To Jeremy, for understanding.

Leslie McNab is a Toronto-based freelance writer. After graduating from the University of Western Ontario in 1989, she spent a year backpacking in Europe and Asia. Currently studying Journalism at Ryerson, Leslie is a regular contributor to *Onset* and *Venue* magazines and is working on a feature-length film script.

Good or Bad
(Nancy McNair)

Good or Bad
merely a judgement
no more no less
merely a perception
no more no less
merely an attitude
no more no less
Good or Bad
Bad or Good
Who knows?

Prism

(Evelyn A. McTrowe)

It sits in light—white
and sends out light—delight,
    red and blue
    and purple and green.
Its heart gives out
what's not been seen.
Though quiet, alone
in dark unknown,
it shouts of life
when sun is shown.

Prairie Spring

(Jean M. Mercer)

The prairie spring is harsh
Old winds erase new furrows
Windrowing fertile topsoil to the fenceline.

Late snows conceal all indication
Of the earth's renewal.
Battle lines thus drawn pit hope against despair.

Romance and flow'rs bloom late.
Nor warmth, nor fragrance
Stir the sensitivities
'Til May, by chance one day meets June,
And there, accompanied by bird-song,
Spring weds Summer
Suddenly.

Faces

(Duncan Mercredi)

standing next to a face frozen on rock
hidden by centuries of dust and snow
only to be revealed
by the explosion of intrusion
drilled into its side
stuffed with dynamite and rags
ignited by ignorance and fear
face frozen in time
standing next to clear cut forests
listening in vain for voices in the wind
hearing only the mournful cries of the past
stripping the bark off unwanted trees
left discarded on dying ground
revealing the agony of death
etched into its side
the memories of its life
exposed in its roots
standing next to death
bloated by water
child's beauty erased
replaced by anger and fear
did you test the water before you jumped
face frozen rock earth water
mother hast thou forsaken us
we remain exposed

Address: 109 Evanson Street, Winnipeg, MB, R3G 2A1
Telephone: (204) 774-7497
Inninu (Cree) born in Misipawistik (Grand Rapids, MB). New book of poetry titled *Wolf and Shadows* to be published this year. Published two books of poetry: 1) *Spirit of the Wolf* and 2) *Dreams of the Wolf in the City*—both by Pemmican Publ., Winnipeg, MB. A poem in Theytus Publ. A short story ("Blue Collar Indian") by University of Saskatchewan—Extension Div. A poem in *Absinthe*.

The Wells of Time

(J. Kelly Ramsey)

Shimmering and glistening they lie, submerged in the depths of the wells of time
Long-forgotten thoughts and memories of ages past,
Amidst veiled images of that which is yet to come.
Suddenly the handle begins to turn, the mind wanders back to yesterday.
The pail of memory rises slowly, occasionally banging against the rough wall
When it does, fragments of thought—obscure details—splash over the edge
And tumble back down into the hazy depths, but the essence remains
And continues on its upward journey towards conscious remembrance.
The top is in sight, the mind rejoices as the images it sought come into view.
The years melt away, and for a moment the curtain is lifted between *then* and *now*.
Then just as suddenly the mist closes in again,
And the pail begins to lower until it is summoned again.

Walking
(Maria Micuda)

Walking alone late at night in the streets of the city, I think and meditate.
Thinking how pacific and lonely are the neighbourhoods, sidewalks, and houses when people are asleep.
So, walking along on an autumn night through the streets
of the metropolis, I think and meditate,
while crushing thick carpets and piles of dry leaves
amidst an almost pristine solitude.
Then, after awhile, I hear some other steps crushing leaves behind me.
So, carefully, I hurry away with fast fast steps,
And turn all of a sudden with great curiosity to see
what it is that follows me.
And what do I see?
A big black cat coming my way, silent and recollected like me.
Then I break into a smile and wait for him to pass close by, to caress, hug and talk to it, but the cat is antisocial, unsympathetic, and hostile and runs away from me, crossing the street with the speed of an arrow.
Ah, that cat, unfriendly as unfriendly can be, reminds me
How the world treats me sometimes.

The Cosmos; Christmas; The Child
(Doris Moran Migus)

I love you snow,
I love you rock,
I love you rain,
I love you sun,
I love you dew,
I love you light,
I love you wind—
You healed my friend
with your breath that night.

Bells are ringing
Choirs are singing
Santa's ho-hoing
but wistfully sighing
"I'm short of some toys tonight."
People are scurrying, partying, buying.
. . . .

But was the North Star not shining tonight?

Enlighten, pursue,
and guide me, O God,
as I sift thru' the choices
that your season brings.
Yes, jolt me from my insanity
the insanity of "things."
. . . .

But was not the manger meant for a babe?

Eleanor McKim; John Jackson; Margery Coffman.

Age: 75
Address: 2 Water Street East, Elmira, ON, N3B 2H5
Telephone: (519) 669-3885
Birthplace: Blackhead, Conception Bay, Newfoundland. Attended Memorial University for 1 1/2 years—Arts and Home Ec. Grad. from St. John's Gen. School of Nursing. Specialized in Psychiatric Nursing. Music: U. of T.—1st Class Hon. Grade II Rudiments, and Grade VIII Singing. Still studying. Environment Affiliations: Ont. Toxic Waste Research Coalition; Great Lakes United; Citizens' Clearinghouse on W. Management; Sustainable Development Community, Elmira; SNACC (NF). Goals: May the beauty, mystery and yes, the mess of this emerging creation, ever attune and humbly alert me to my responsibility. May my two sons, spouses, my three grandchildren and All Creation thrill and thrive!

Continuing Search
(Cathy Mihowich)

I am breaking down;
Struggling against failure, fighting sleep and battling mass media.
Looks change, I cannot.
My time has passed, like a fad.
Moons glow smugly overhead, occasionally winking sarcastically through the filmy night.
I wonder if I will make it.
Stars blink innocently while I watch for some sign.
They know.
I am tired
Of asking and no one listening.
Am I heard, just scorned?
Sporadically I learn answers whispered in the soft night,
Like a gentle caress, sometimes soothing.
The faintness of your voice has me looking,
Searching for the truth.
I realize it's out there, I can see it cloaked vainly in your eyes, masked by your forced smile.
Chaste sunlight burns into my eyes,
Screening reality from my mind.

For Andrew, who always eludes me.

The Labourer

(Tanya Dawn Milheron)

Thoughts of a young man, watching his mother
Mend his worn-out
Winter jacket . . .

Kindness is your daily guide,
What you touch is sanctified
Let all your dreams be ever sweet,
Your joys and comfort be complete.
Mother,
My spirit of springtime . . .

To my Mother, Connie, and all Mothers of the world.

Legs and Sandcastles
(Nadine Lee Miller)

tripping over my bare feet
a determined sea wind
drives me to the spot
i drop to my knees
wet sand slucks at their boniness
blue flowers on white cotton pleats
fade into nothing muddiness
my hands tremble as they scoop and scrape
my heart pounds in my ears
or is it the tide
and will it wait for me to finish
before it swallows my castle
and will it hurt
when i dissolve into foam

Mom and Dad—for providing me with sand shovel, bucket, etc.

Age: 23
Address: Apt. 1507, 1375 Prince of Wales Drive, Ottawa, ON, K2C 3L5
Telephone: (613) 225-1015
I have been writing poetry ever since I learned how to spell in elementary school. I have had a newspaper column in *The Caledon Citizen* and poems published in school literary reviews. I am currently enroled at Carleton University, English Honours.

Upon Receiving a Hideous Gift

(Rhonda M. Miller)

The foil of appearance deludes the receiver upon first contact.
Trespassing through unknown territory, the owner proceeds, confused, and wondering.
Up stairs, up stairs, until the final landing is claimed with certainty.
The mystery of the wrapping exudes beyond comprehension into a dimension unknown to a mere joiner.
Unattached to the mystery, the joiner stands astride the brown paper claim.
The joiner enhances the separateness when opening the mystery, finding simple irritation.
Disconnected from the mystery, the joiner resists acceptance of this token of good will.
Instead, the receiver proceeds, annoyed, painfully pleased, and marvelling at the audacity and wit of others.

For Ellen.

Today
(Victoria Miron)

I cannot live in the past;
I have no influence there.
I cannot live in the future;
I am unprepared.
I can only live today
And adapt through experience.
I am thankful
For what I have.
I accept loss
And avoid greed.
What I have
Is far greater than virtue,
Far greater than desire . . .
For I have hope
Of adapting and flourishing.
I do not feel unfulfilled;
For each day breeds success,
As I survive and advance.
I live in the present,
A place where I have
Control and influence.
I learn from the past
And prepare for the future.
But I will always
Live for today!

Regularity
(Molly Misra)

In his head,
the clock ticks
and chimes

In his heart,
she moans
and
cries

In his veins,
the blood ebbs
and flows

In his thoughts,
mother croons
a song

In the world,
his time
has
come

In the distance,
the gong sounds
thirteen times.

Molly Misra is a student at the University of Toronto, pursuing a specialist degree in English Literature. Molly was first published at the age of eleven in the poetry anthology *Samplings*. Her writing has also been recognized by The National Library of Poetry and Canadian Authors Association. In 1993, Molly was deemed one of the top student writers in Peel and became that year's recipient of the Woodhouse English scholarship. Molly is extremely grateful to her high school teachers for exposing her to the beauty of the English language and for encouraging her to wield the pen.

So Silent

(Alison Mitchell)

As the moon flows softly through the misty shadows of the falling rain,
A beautiful night has become one of pain.
To see the tortured souls asleep alone on the street,
To hear their cries so loud from the children that we meet.

So silent is the evening, as a baby cries throughout the night,
The hunger that he feels, his mother knows is not right.
The woman lay there sobbing with her hands upon her head,
So desperate is she to find a way to get her baby fed.

So silent is the night, screaming with the anger of a young boy's pain,
Desperately searching to find his way home once again.
Just a young runaway, with no way to get home,
Unwillingly, once again, he will have to spend the night alone.

So silent is the night, secretly searching for the man laying in the gutter,
Where the wine that he holds in his life, is the only thing that matters.
A father of three children, whom he hasn't seen in years,
Each painful day, represents one of a thousand tears.

Though the night is dark, the moon offers a ray of hope,
That through all the pain and agony, these people will be able to cope.

For the people in our lives who are most often forgotten.

I was born on the coldest day of December 1967, which happened to be the 29th. This special event took place in a town called Humboldt, SK. At the tender age of 16, I married my husband of today, John Mitchell. Throughout our ten years, I have experienced the three greatest joys of my life:
John Mitchell Jr., Suzi Mitchell, and Jesse Mitchell. Now in Regina, blessed with the best of family and friends, we're living our life richly with love. For this I extend all of my love and thanks to the person who made it all possible: my Mom.

Fallen Angel
(Miss Sam Mitchell)

I . . .I,
I kissed you.
I wanted you to feel
an angel's breath,
a perfumed, lingering
nudge.
But
my lips had not
acquired their wings,
and so, I flushed hot against
your face.
I . . . I kissed you.
I wanted you to feel and angel's caress
upon your cherub cheek;
a soft pressure.
But
I fumbled,
like a nervous chicken;
a starved peck.
And so,
I blushed and looked away.
I kissed you
and left.

For the Pastor's son . . . it's your loss.

Untitled

(Tony Mohr)

And now we're sitting here
Crayons in hand
Smoking paper and inhaling life

I'd get out of here, can you show me how?
Is the way there or over here?
What is it that we really fear?

You, you may talk in illusions
Images and confuse the mind
Under some time and joy
You reach and seek to destroy
What won't die and always loves

You're just an image of what isn't real
Is that you or do I dream?
Few are honest, lost in smoke
Chasing their ghosts in spirit accidents

For Paul Hewson, who searches for God with questions all of us need to answer.

Age: 18
Address: 1 Tanager Street, Elmira, ON, N3B 1C8
Telephone: (519) 669-8421
Poetry is writing down your emotions without bearing your soul. I discovered this in grade seven when I was assigned a poetry project. Since then, I have written many poems that convey personal beliefs, emotions and thoughts. Presently, my poetry is used mainly in the songs I write. I am the singer and songwriter for the band U4EA. The poem "And now we're sitting here . . ." was included on our demo tape with a musical accompaniment composed by a close friend. My goals are to continue writing lyrics and poems that may someday make a difference in someone's life.

Impressions
(Margie Molnar)

Beyond the twisted embers black
I saw a weary yellow cat
Upon one foot beheld the mark
Its slanted eyes betook a spark.

Its tail it swished so ever high
I heard it laugh, I know not why
Its eyes were crimson, it laughed with glee
It was waiting, watching me.

I did not move, could hardly breathe
There seemed to be no escape for me
the can tipped over, I heard a crash
It disappeared within a flash.

Upon one foot beheld the mark
And yet I search within the dark
Someday to find the yellow cat
Beyond the twisted embers black.

Show Me Where Truth Lies

(Vic Moran)

Her words said,
Please be at ease, I am not threatening.
His words replied,
This is what I've done, I am worth knowing.
They sat close together,
Her slip and tenderness showing.
Excited and in tune,
With each other's needs,
He waits for the opportunity to arise.
When his expectations,
Have come back down in size.
He sees her as she would like to be seen,
She tells him what he said,
They think of what to say
They think of lying in bed.
They want to embrace
But feel awkward instead.
The evening ended, they part
Morals intact and honesty dead.

For a Friend Who Committed Suicide

(Lance V. Moses)

When I heard that you'd gone away,
I knew that pain in my heart was here to stay.
Through the dark, long, lonely night,
I wonder why you gave up the fight.
Then the rumours began to spread;
I can still hear them in my head.
As children, we were never apart;
Now I keep you in my heart.
And as the rules of life twist and bend,
I'll grin and bear it, until the end.
Remember those notes that we used to send?
This one is my last, Goodbye,
My Friend.

To my family and newborn child.

Thick and Sticky
(Keith Muldoon)

The bread was fresh—it had just been bought.
Each slice was set in just the right spot.
I buttered each piece with skill and precision,
And then I approached my next big decision.
There on the shelf I reached with great haste
For that delightful jar of sticky brown paste.
I'd eat it at breakfast, I'd eat it at noon,
I'd eat it at supper, and I'd be eating it soon.
I took off the lid and dug in with much vigour—
Each moment I waited, my appetite got bigger.
I spread it real thick, at least half a metre,
'Twas specially made for one hungry eater.
At last I was done, said grace and dug in;
The stuff, it oozed out and dripped off my chin.
Soon ready for more, or at least so I thought,
My mouth would not work as I knew a mouth ought.
The stuff in my mouth was stuck fast to the roof;
I struggled, made faces, and looked like a goof.
The stuff was so thick, I could not even mutter—
Guess that's why I'm fond of thick PEANUT BUTTER.

To my daughter, forever my "little girl," Lisa.

Dad

(Kimberly Mulligan)

Because you dared to drink and drive
Your life ended when I was five
There hasn't been a day go by
I didn't wish you were still alive
Mother did a lot of crying
Single parenting can be trying
A college education became a dream
Survival was the ultimate scheme
How dare you, to drink and drive
Leaving us here, to struggle through life
Just think of all the things you've missed
Or how much you have been missed
Giving away your eldest on her wedding day
Or your son's promotions in the military
Bouncing your grandsons on your knee
Grandfather things, you'd know what I mean
Life itself is no bed of roses
But growing up without a father
Makes life's paths even harder
I'm sure if you had known
What lay in the road ahead
You would not have drank that evening
And come straight home instead.

To my Mother, for always being there . . . then, now and always.

My Sweet Syrinx

(Martin Multamaki)

Love, my love,
What spell did'st say
To puppeteer
My soul this way,
That from your grace
I'm turning never;
Pining on thine
Image, ever?
Lend me peace,
Oh blessed Pan,
When I would speak
In fear I ran,
That had I failed
Her heart to sway
My love, like yours,
Echoed away.

For the love of Candy.

A Man Walks Through
(Michael Mundell)

A Man walks through the garden alone
He leaves behind him a past of pain and a future of sorrow.
Destiny, Fate
He knows not where the next step will bring him
    roses, violets, orchids or poison ivy.
Wandering seemingly forever.
A Dove he sees pale with the coming of Death,
A Robin he sees red with the coming of spring.
Sleep, eternal sleep.

Ecstasy of life the passion and thrill
A ball of fire a shivering chill

He lies in the leaves brown and dead.
He watches the sapling strive for the light
What a man seeks forever is a mystery,
He knows not the answer to so many questions.
Pain, oh glorious pain,
Feel the pleasure of the pain.
One day you will feel the true beauty
And thrill of life, for life is the
Ultimate Adventure and Death is the
Prize that awaits us all.

For all the Mirandas in the world.

Age: 23
Address: 11 Cedarvale Avenue, Toronto, ON, M4C 4J5
Telephone: (416) 750-0841
Michael Mundell was born in Toronto and has lived there most of his life. He has travelled around North America, Mexico and England and hopes to continue travelling the world someday. He would like to continue writing, and his dream is to be a pilot, one which may come true soon. Michael is very sensitive, good looking and has great sense of humour. The poem "A Man Walks Through" will be his first in publication, hopefully the first of many. He would like to thank all his family and friends who always encouraged him.

Gone Are They

(Christine Nicholas)

What sadness I see in your eyes.
The pain is there beneath your weak smile.
The loss apparent, to those who know you.
I reach to touch, but, oh so cold your response.
Withdrawn in your shell, sifting through your thoughts.
Looking for understanding to love lost.

They say to look beneath the surface to the soul.
To find comfort in your memories.
To find something for you to hold.
But, there you find no replacement for the touch of their hand.
The simple understanding they had of you, like no one else can.

A parent, lost to this mysterious thing called death,
Is like taking the foundation out from beneath a wall
And you sit and wonder why
You do not crumble and fall.

But unlike a wall, we have roots that run up and down.
Weaving in and out, joining the past with the future,
in the teachings of our parents.
When you close your eyes, you hear them just like yesterday.
But if you listen carefully, you'll hear them in everything you say.
You'll see something that you do,
and laugh within yourself and say,
"My parents are not gone, but are just hiding away."

To my closest family and friends, whose feelings and support I have drawn upon.

The Vulture's Tail on the Lips of the Young Leonardo
(Kelly Robin Nicholson)

Descriptions of bodies are exact.
Take for example the confirmation of your
expectations, which passes for
pleasure. If a woman
she fills one third of the canvas,
squandering with the bare flesh of her
arms the involuntary limits of your uncertainty.
Caught in her hair is the whole Roman alphabet,
all of Horace addressed to itself.

From another angle the same woman
in three-quarters profile. Through the black
background a ghost billows gradually, touching
with its spectral mouth her copper
shoulders like a pile of coins,
the breasts small enough to be
parodic. The fourth dimension wells
from her. It's cathartically white, as a
chessman, or the daylight undressed, dropping
on a mirror's face its discarded clothes,
which we are.

For Beata.

From the City to the Country

(Jane Nicol)

Here I am, residing in the country,
Having sought refuge from the city.
Spectacular sceneries, restful to my eyes
I enjoy the purity of its skies.

I came here on a trial basis
Avid to meet new faces.
I began my search for a new identity,
Wishing to leave behind the city's complexity.

Then I came across tormented waters
For, in spite of the fragrant scent of flowers
And the enwraping sounds of mother nature,
I yearned for the city's unique pleasures.

An inner turmoil intensified.
For my loved ones, I often cried
Alternating my daily life, I tried
But I remained unsatisfied.

But then I reached a final decision
To remain in this lovely location,
Yet to find as many occasions
To return to my former habitation.

Two Standing Souls

(Hal Niedzviecki)

Antlers, forced into
one, buck the solitude.
A face is barely
seen in such a mist.
Arms wrap up the heat of bodies.
Two standing souls
let loose dangle
damp. Lost limbs
must muscle through
this nature battle.

Alone

(Susan Nisbet)

Alone but not lonely 'til you came along;
Persistent, insistent, passionate, gone.

A borrowed lover on borrowed time,
We shared little sleep and a little peace of mind.

Separated by circumstance, philosophy, geography,
Now alone I miss a temporary part of me.

Alone.
Lonely.

To my daughter, Christianna, and Kenton Fast, the permanent parts of me.

Beams

(Louise Gaele Norman)

Dreamer gazing with looks so warm
Through eyes shades of emerald, gold, and desert sands;
Love's distant image is no mirage.
Oasis—from various hands, foreign lands.
Night sky floats fragments of a scene desired;
As wind swirls the pieces, they go higher,
Moving together in a clear crystal prism.

Love in a land white, silent, and cold,
Where the half moon wanders casting diamonds on snow.
Mountain lion stands with steady looks.
Aura—viewed with eyes that know the magnetic glow.
Easily seen is the spark in winter's glimmer;
Pure vision near, midnight stars seem dimmer.
Like cool blue streams in fire and yellow flames in ice,
This love holds all that's true, finding paradise.

Switching Roles
(Ero Nosa)

I laughed!
but watched you with an almost fake indifference
you showed me,
and I did it, out of the frivolousness of my spirit
just to be able to feel the unfamiliarity
of the warm sun on my face.
Out of dilapidated walls of obliviousness
came my emaciated structure.
The fate of the one crying out in the wilderness
would be nothing . . .
when compared to what I would have done for you.
You watched me
whilst I brandished my incompetent skills
alongside those of the strong, living and long dead;
Up into the decaying, dark and dreary globe,
I plunged the cradle that bore my head
only to be met by the claws of fate . . .
You watched me
as I struggled to get out of the choking coop
and in the graveness of my soul,
I look up and wonder:
where have you hidden your warm palms?

To Mum, my source of inspiration; my family, and the gang: Nnakalanzi, Winnie . . . and Kayode.

Nosa Ero was born on the 28th of April 1975 in Nigeria into a family of eight. Her literary aspirations were manifest at a very early age as she acted in plays and wrote many poems in her elementary school days. She is very much inspired by her mother, who is a branch president of the Association of Nigerian authors. Nosa took part in a winning French play written for her high school (Command Secondary School, Ibadan) by her mother in 1992. Presently on a scholarship at Pearson College Canada, she aspires to be a writer in the field of journalism.

Dilemma

(Carol Nyereyegona)

World-famous, fast-paced.
That crisp drive in from the country
To the morning city.
Laugh with your colleagues.
Savour the rush
Of knowing you're good at your work;
That you contribute.
Homeward to change, return, city at dark
With your friends—whom you love—
And dine, see a play.
You give what you can;
The day is too short
To stand front-row centre,
Turn, clock-handed.
Methodically.
To view
Another world.
One of lonely people, homeless people,
                gunned-down people.
To step in, feel real, try to share their world.
And where does that leave you?
What good do you do?

To my beloved family and mairead—they have no dilemma with loving me unconditionally.

The Web

(J.W. O'Connor)

Feather light, finer than silk,
It sways between tall blades of grass
Unseen but for the sun
Shining through dewdrops on radial threads.

And there, by river's edge,
A red-gold spider at the centre of his keep,
In sanguine expectation of prey—
Some careless gadfly settling down
On his gossamer net.

Mother Wind

(Teamhair Cailín)

Mother Wind . . .
I found you yesterday,
And you welcomed me
With your many arms,
Embracing me—soothing me,
Billowing my skirts,
You exposed me.
Making me free,
For only in you am I true.

You entwined me with your silver fine silk,
Coating and covering me,
To transform my mortal body.
Emerging from your cocoon,
I was the butterfly.
Body banished,
Only soul and mind remained.
Your strength made me light,
I soared with you,
High above the world,
No longer constrained by gravity
Or the other laws of men.

Address: P.O. Box 7209, Cornwall, PEI, C0A 1H0
Teamhair graduated from the University of Prince Edward Island on May 8, 1994, with a major in Anthropology. Completely in love with the past, she hopes to continue her studies in Europe in the field of archaeology and to eventually obtain a PhD. Although she has had no formal training in creative writing, Teamhair loves to write. She draws her inspiration from her natural environment (especially the wind and the ocean) as well as her Celtic ancestry.

Spending Life
(George W.F. O'Neil)

What does it mean to *seize the moment*
to grasp experience with both hands
as if I could wrestle an act in mid-stride
pin it in motion catch and hold sunlight
that passes through the boughs of an oak
or net a cold drop of rain from a windy night
without it splashing flat in the palm of my hand

How would I recognize a worthy moment
from an idle hour spear the silver salmon
amongst a school of white fish before
they pass no before they swim into view

I think of the time I've spent renting
this life in search of moments have I
spent it well sometimes lying drunk
in tall wet grass I feel the earth turn
beneath me watch the moon a sleek peel
of silver amidst the milky-way

The Creator

(Martin Odeau)

I am the bell maker
I am the bell
I am the chimes that toll
in the tower at times

I am the ocean
and I am the waves
I am the crest that rides the waves
to the deep in the blues and the greens

I am the baby
I am the babe
I am the cradle that rocks
in the middle of the day

I am the grass that is green
and I am the gold
I am the dunes that blow
and I am the mole

I am the lover
and I am the love
I am the heartbeat
that beats in the dove

I am the blue skies
and I am the midnight stars
I am the warm golden sunshine
that greets you at dawn

To Joni Mitchell, who has inspired me since her early beginnings at Yorkville in Toronto, Canada.

Telephone: (416) 483-8688

Martin has been writing since the age of 10. He began playing piano and continued his writing until the age of 16, when he did some small acting parts for CBC and TVO in Toronto. From there, he worked his way in and around folk houses, with his poetry and music. Finally, after a brief appearance at Mariposa Festival in 1976 and the Harbour Front Festivals, Martin went south to California in search of a publisher and/or record contract. With some success and great consideration, he returned to Canada in 1986 to continue his writing and poetry.

Shadows of the Inward Mind

(Doni-Marie A. Oliver)

(on sub-conscious thoughts)
Cat's-paw shod,
With shadow stealth,
They glide through musty, dusty passages.
With fluttering fingers,
They touch a volume
Or seek a chapter
From among the many shelves,
And if I snatch at one
It seeps through my fingers,
Like water that swiftly evaporates.
How like phantoms they whisper
Just beyond my reach—
Untouchable—haunting.
In moments of silence
They speak like gentle rain,
Lulling me into tranquillity
With a song my ears will never know.
At other times,
Their footsteps echo
Like thunder in a lonely sky.
If I could but once hear their voices,
Would it be Bliss
Or would I wish I had left
Their Meanings
Undisturbed . . . ?

Address: 185 Oxford Road West, Lethbridge, AB, T1K 4V6
Telephone: (403) 381-7828

Empty Playground
(Jim Overton)

Empty playground, monkey bars, like lifeless cages.
Joyous cries of children past—they echo with the thought.
Empty playground, rusty swings, well-worn paths to tread.
One dark day, a monster came, and clever words he said.
One lost child, the trusting one, stolen from the life.
Taken cruelly, savagely, cut down by a knife.
A parent cries, the will to live, taken in a moment.
Children leading sheltered lives, filled with fear and torment.
Empty playground, burial ground, never used again.
Empty playground, sorrow sound, jungle from a garden.

Momentum
(Clifford Oxford)

Calmly, the water begins its mysterious journey
Slowly weaving a path through Nature's plush garden.
Gently rolling over the naked form underneath,
It softly caresses this wondrous beauty as it moves.

Courageously, it explores the aged depths,
Carefully searching for this foreign land.
Ultimately, this probing mass will encounter,
A force much greater than it has ever known.

Freely, it travels God's pre-determined course,
Gaining intensity with each new wave it recruits.
Commanding more control, the battle is soon won
When Nature surrenders Her fragile banks.

Oh, mighty river, rush to that abundant ocean—
That bountiful sea into which you must eagerly plunge.
Thrust forward towards that vast oasis and
Deliver yourself unto that precious soul!

Only God knows the path a river will take
And the resting place after its momentous journey!

To the beautiful angel who has been my inspiration!

Age: 26
Address: P.O. Box 57, Marathon, ON, P0T 2E0
Telephone: (807) 229-3254
Born Trent Stephen Pittman in 1968, I chose to write using the pseudonym as a tribute to my late grandfather. In 1991, I received a BA in History from Memorial University. A desire to help people quench their thirst for knowledge, as well as an enthusiasm for doing research, led me to enrol in the Library and Information Studies program at Lakehead University. It was during this stay in Thunder Bay that I "experienced the most wonderful two years of my young life."

Dead Trees and Poisoned Water
(Darren Page)

For as far as we can see,
There is waste and pollution
To the first degree.

We cut down trees; it is a slaughter:
Dead Trees and Poisoned Water.

For pulp and paper we do not need;
I think we should plant another seed.

Cutting, cutting, all for greed?
To the next batch of forest with all due speed!

As they clutch their axes in their hands,
They scan and search the barren lands.

What will they see?
But a last and lonely standing tree.

We cut down trees; it is a slaughter:
Dead Tress and Poisoned Water.

For a drink of water we must pay—
Don't drink from the river; it is polluted they say.

Streams of red, yellow and green;
Streams of all colours can now be seen.

There is no place to swim for the Brown Otter:
Dead Trees and Poisoned Water.

No end in sight, it is sad without doubt,
But there is hope, no reason to pout!

To <u>Conserve</u> is the key to our salvation,
For all of us and every nation.

Swirling

(Shannon Pardy)

Swirling brightly,
shining,
glittering
like a great tiara.
How beautiful you are!
While you dance,
life rushes on.
Being born
living,
dying,
over and over and over.
So magnificent!
They call you
Galaxy.
Do you know? Do you care?
No.
You just dance your endless dance.

To my family, who always encouraged my dreaming.

Age: 20
Address: Box 145, Garnish, Fortune Bay, NF, A0E 1T0

Adolescent Girl 1958

(Linda Parker)

Bobby socks and saddle shoes
Pink poodle with rhinestone eye
On flared, felt skirt and
Fully-fashioned sweater set
Or cardigan, back to front
Over cone-shaped size 32AA bra
Proud points crammed with doll socks
Stolen from Woolworth's
At the plaza on
Saturday morning

To Cheryl, Chryl and Sheila . . . partners in childhood mischief.

Ghosts of Desolation
(Rena Patrick)

You who walk softly
beneath the towering trees
in the deep dark forest
where you may not see the sun
for four months at a time.
You may go away,
but oceanic rain
is falling in the depths of your soul
as you move out over
the waters of freedom.
May you always have your place
in Desolation Sound.
And when your time is over,
may they throw you overboard
to feed the ocean that once fed you.
May your body drift over the same beaches
you walked when you were alive,
and may your spirit be the wind
over Desolation Sound.

Umbrum
(David R. Pauwels)

Hissing speak softly denizens of night
the city parodies the rolling sea
and winds whose circles crack the balmy gloom
of window shutters rasping like the trees
then penumbrae steal into the heart's
unspoken dusky mirrors, opium fog,
the nests of wasps who settle on their darts;
presuming wise to steal an upward glance
a clock ticks soberly at settled chairs
whose rests unvarnished brown the haze reflect
a swollen, open eye uneased and bare
to dark unseen in patches covered up
or stolen from the mark in pairs, tattered,
embalmed by night air brushing in their lungs
crisscrossed by dread and warmth along by patterns,
to doom the silken ears never to shut
the fears of undead houses or peat-moors
in umbrum dwelling, shading stocks amend
the spaces flowing in amid the doors.

Age: 23
Address: 22 Chestnut Avenue, Brantford, ON, N3T 4C1
David Pauwels was born on Hallowe'en in a hospital. After being forced to read books in school, he would like to try his hand at writing them. His goal is to be a professor, a musician, a writer and a gentleman. Although he has travelled extensively, he has yet to witness the perfect meeting, on a dissection table, of an umbrella an a sewing machine. For this, he thanks his family.

Take a Moment for Thanks!
(Lori Paxton)

It usually starts the same old way
The rush, the stress of everyday
Buses to catch, deadlines to meet
Coats on the floor, the cat's at your feet.

The kids start to fight, the phone starts to ring
You're losing your patience with everything
You think life's so bad, there're bills to pay
Your sanity's going, another bad day

But just stop and think, for a minute or two
Be thankful that's all you're going through
Somebody out there has just lost someone
A parent, a friend, a daughter or son

No warning, just happened, the laughter is gone
It's *silence* and *sadness* that greets them at dawn
The yearning and heartache that they must endure
Death strikes with no warning, nothing's for sure

Take a minute and think before harsh words are spoken
It might be *you* next whose heart gets ripped open
Call a parent or friend or your kids near or far
Just hold them and tell them how special they are

Take a long hard look, not a casual glance
And tell them you love them, now that you've got the chance
So if life's free of grief and your loved one's not gone
Be thankful when two fighting kids greet your dawn!

To friends who left without "Good-byes" and to my Sons, my inspiration, my Life!

Morning Metamorphosis

(Heather Pearson)

The shadowed hulk—
Solid silhouette against morning's grey veil.
Motionless, poised for violence on the grass beside the sidewalk.
Grey slides through shades of purple
Snaked with orange and
Still he stands—
Elbows in,
Head turtled,
Waiting—
Yellow and white rush upward,
Bouquets tossed high into the morning sky.
He straightens,
Exposed—
Headless, with strong flat shoulders and
Sharp cornered elbows.
Metalled mugger
Awaiting mail.

To Daphne Marlatt, who taught me to write images.

Hatchet the VIII

(Neil Penner)

Henry, in a horrible tone
Henry, it was your chromosome
Darling, off with your head
You did not bear an heir and now you're dead.

Ms. Boleyn, I love you dearly
And the axe that could but Shirley,
Please understand why not a man
could put the blame on Henry.

Jacky boy, always coy
Whitechapel was the stomp
Snow white boy in a treacherous pomp
Weep for the women of ill repute.

Longish Liz, I love you dearly
And government that could but Shirley
Please understand why not a man
could put the blame on Jack.

And a man is not a man anymore
His general mentality is a historical bore
Shirley, I have to state you're quite within your rights
But still, must you, my toast is getting cold.

Age: 21
Born in Brandon, Manitoba. Studied and performed classical guitar. Lead guitar in high school jazz band. "Big Jule" in high school production of "Guys & Dolls." Goals: compose and record music.

Untitled

(Michelle Pental-Currie)

The builders of the ancient
pyramids heard
The music of the spheres
We interpret, knowing
seeing,
instead of feeling
what they knew
The state of shattered, mindful
being.

What Is a Cat?

(Mario Peretiatko)

A cat is a cat and that is that
It scampers around in my den
A fluff of fur
And a gentle purr
Who loves to play with my *pen* (shoo!)

A cat is a cat and that is that
It likes to be near me now and then
It nudges my nose
And bites my toes
And constantly plays with my *pen* (stop it!)

A cat is a cat and that is that
Possessive and unafraid to get into a tiff
Incredibly smart
But oh what a fart!
Should you have the misfortune to sniff (whew!)

"So what is a cat?" I ask you that
Does your opinion vary?
It's neither a bat
Nor a rat
Yet some people find them quite scary

A cat is love, a cat is joy
And to me nothing short of a god-send
A cat is a cat and that is that
But I wish it would stop playing with my *pen*

I Hear . . .

(Gabrielle Perreault)

Somewhere in the crashing waves
the sound of currents flowing
A sound that's like no other
without change, yet always growing

Among the floods that never stop
the light shines through one single drop,
a magic pure, that of a child,
the secret dream that never hides.

Somewhere in the roaring wind
a whisper comes from close behind,
"Though time may be an endless sea,
some seconds are eternity."

Born in Montréal 32 years ago, Gabrielle is a Renaissance gal who's still deciding what to be when she "grows up." She quietly admits a preference for keeping in touch with the ethereal as opposed to the general trappings of the "real world." Gabrielle has recently left Toronto behind her after 11 years as well as the field of graphics. She currently lives in Kitchener, Ontario.

Untitled

(Catherine Thomas Perrotta)

I hear my muffled soul—
It cries inside the bathroom
With the door shut.
I peer through the keyhole
And see a distorted image:
Part of an extreme close-up.
I cannot step back—
My flesh presses against the door.
I attempt to break the wooden barrier.
I smell oceans of tears in a torrent of sobs;
I drown.

Confessions of a Person Everyone Loves

(Kimberly Peterson)

Witnessed only by laughing seagulls
I dip tentative toes into
shimmering velvet waves
that soothe the stoic shore
sweeping sand castles away, polishing frigid stones

A playful breeze which waltzes
through my mind's timber-lands
stirs hushed whispers much
as gossips share at church
shaking loose leafy memories
that drift into consciousness
self-reproach washes over me with the endless waves

My nimbostratus grey eyes storm
with the terror of a rabbit
entranced by Medusan rays
slithering from headlights
as I am held by your expectations
and fear of quivering-squirrel quickness
that I will reveal my imperfections

The cool morning air whispers winter
when ice's thick crust
will capture this river's life
As I am entombed by my rules

Perhaps I will drill a hole
and fish myself out

The Bus Ride

(Olga Petrik)

The bus gains speed,
As it travels through the darkness.
All of us,
quiet and unassuming.

Don't look at him or her.
Don't speak!
Wrapped up on our own lives,
We avoid eye contact.

The bus,
with its velour seats
and carpeted walls
And a toilet
that smells of disinfectant.

Everyone passes judgement
on the others.
Look at him,
Look at her!

We are a society unto ourselves.

Until the bus reaches that final stop,
and we disembark.

Thanks to my family and to Chett, even though he never got on the bus!

Age: 20
I am currently attending Carleton University, majoring in Art History. I've never really thought of myself as a poet; it's something I've always enjoyed doing. Most of my work has been limited to school publications. My family and friends are my support and inspiration. Chett Bradley has my undying thanks for always liking my work! My future . . . I have so many plans and desires and so little time. But I'm young, with my whole life ahead of me, and only time will tell what can happen next.

Rain
(Santino Petrucci)

The lamppost shares its heavenly light
As I plod along the street this night,
A comfort found in the wind's cool touch
Caresses my cheeks to rose from white.

The sidewalk leads and I follow as such—
Like a lame man leaning on a wooden crutch.
The path dispersed by now flickering rays,
Neither left nor right can I sway so much.

My locks have aged from black to grey
As nights have drawn to let in day.
Now storm clouds gather to bless with rain
Those that stroll at night this way.

And I look not back from where I came
For this eve's show is mine to gain,
Since few things shake the weary alive
Only burrowed fools could then abstain.

The lightning cracks and soon will arrive
The roaring thunder that then will drive
The pelting rain to refresh the earth
And make the weary come alive.
And make the weary come alive.

Algonquin Reflection
(Tony Pignataro)

The cedars of Northern Ontario
(because of the base of Shield rock on which they grow),
are a magnificent example of patient endurance,
of the indomitable will to grow and flourish.
At any turn on the trail, one can find red tentacles
the size of tree trunks wrapped around granite boulders.
These long, tenacious roots grip the rock and extend
beyond it to sparse sources of nourishment and water.
Some literally grow on the rock face.
What threatened to be an insurmountable obstacle,
the cedar clasped and encircled.
What loomed as an immovable barrier,
the cedar used as a foundation,
adding to its own strength and stability.

One of the great paradoxes of life is this:
That the thing which most threatens to drive us away,
we must bring close.
That what sets us off in a panic,
we must learn to live with.
Escaping is not the answer.
Running is not the answer;
befriending is.

Untitled

(Laurie Pithouse)

As I begin to awaken
I can hear someone opening the door.
Then little feet hurrying across the floor.
I know this person is getting up from
A long night's rest.
Soon they'll want to get dressed.
I get up, pull on my slippers.
Knowing now they'll want to be fed
Oh, not yet, time to make the bed.
I turn on the cartoons,
Put on the tea,
Prepare some breakfast for her and
For me.
After, I prepare a bath and hop right in.
I know she wants one too, hearing
Her clothes thrown in the bin.
I know this is a clue
'Cause she now wants one too.
I start on with my housework.
But out of all that I do
It's worthwhile
Just when I hear "Mommy, I love you."

To my daughter, Amanda, and to my Mother, who was supportive.

Age: 23
Telephone: (905) 688-9820
Since I was a teenager, with those heartaches and lonely nights, I started to put my love and hurting on paper and began writing poetry. My mother always believed and taught me you can do anything you put your mind to. I now have a daughter, 3, she also gives me inspiration. I completed Grade 11 in high school.

Prime Red

(Valentine Planida)

RED…alert…danger…beware
…rage…violence…death
…stop
RED…scatters the wind in a field of poppies
…ribbons in my sun-lit chestnut brown hair
…wine kisses my lips like a lover
…blood…flow of life
HEART…pulsating…beating…like a jungle drum
…bringing love to a withered soul
PASSIONATE & full of DESIRE
RED-orange-magenta sunset ends the day
…in glory…as in forgiveness
RED-purple-blue sunrise heralds a new yawning
***
RED Sea…long ago history/legend/myth
…still unproven
nearly forgotten
like other floods, a killer
RED Square…not so far away…uneasy
still…pregnant blue/black cloud
on the brink of discharge

still misunderstood
even if you don't agree…you must simply
let me be…original…PRIME RED

To my beloved Father in Heaven, Mother Anna, Grandmother Puliosha, and Husband/best friend, Damian.

To Hound
(John M. Poole)

I had a little dachshund,
Of him I was quite "fund."
Now, if I had a Pekingese,
I'd have to say, "Speak Eng. please."
I could have had a Rottweiler,
But not while there
Are other dogs around.
Maybe a Basset hound?

-

Might I not be "true" Canadian,
If I had a Pomeranian?
But O.K. if I canoodle
With a beautiful French Poodle?
And might it be "de rigueur,"
To own an Irish Terrier?
At one time I had a yen
To have an elegant Afghan.

-

On other dogs the door I've shut.
I love the one I found.
Although he's just a "no-name" mutt,
He's mine!—I call him Hound.

To China's "Misty" poets—may their words see the light.

Address: 127 Dalhousie Court West, Lethbridge, AB, T1K 4C8
Telephone: (403) 381-7252
Married, with three children and five grandchildren. Retired former Ceramic Engineer. Hobbies: Water-colour painting, writing, paper-making, crosswords. Teaches Tai Chi Chu'an and Chi Kung classes. Erstwhile printer of, and contributor of articles to one-time religious magazine. Local newspaper articles and poetry well received. Published in two anthologies by National Library of Poetry. Charter Lifetime Member of International Society of Poets (Advisory Committee Member). His poetry, from serious to humorous, seeks to inform, make statements and entertain. Believes that poetry is best felt rather than analyzed.

Misplaced
(Paula Porrone)

There behind that desk,
        there is a man
    —different from me.
He hides his face beneath all his work.
     All the papers scattered around him
        appear to be meaningless;
But to this man, each sheet has a purpose
    Each sheet has a destination—
        it is a masterpiece.
And here I sit, at the other end of the room—
     with all my papers neatly arranged
       in straight eight by eleven columns
       with no destination.

To my Mother and Father for the gift of life. Franco and Cristina.

Age: 22
Address: 1811 Talbot Road, Kingsville, ON, N9Y 2E4
Telephone: (519) 256 6232
Presently, I attend the University of Windsor, in my third year of the International Relations program. My greatest desire is to help people on a global level by becoming a member of the United Nations. Life has treated me well, and I hope to return the favour to others.

Blue and Red Poem

(Melissa Pound)

Two people
see one another
through a haze
of heat
a curtain of heat

So hot and present
their hair starts to melt
and separate
from them and slide
down their tender backs

It burns them
and crawls
to the ground

On the surface of their feet,
these discoloured pools
float
shimmering like drops of mercury

A brilliant blue and red
catastrophe,

but it's gorgeous

To Harriet, who taught me so much, with love and gratitude.

Dreams

(Tanya Power)

He held me in his arms, and we continued to dance to the melodies of an unknown song.
Beautiful
And strong enough to shelter me from the ills of the world
In his embrace I feel graceful and infinitely precious
As we glide around in a strange and mystical light
Tears of golden fire begin to fall
With a comforting smile of such gentleness, he kisses my wet cheek
And turns into the mist of our ballroom and is gone
Having but a moment ago been so profoundly happy, I don't fully comprehend what has happened
The lovely protector of my dreams has gone
I close my eyes and begin to dance again, trying to recapture the feeling
Of being loved and happy as in no other time in my life
But I stumble and feel a chill steal over me
The unknown song of before now has recognizable words and isn't as peaceful
As I open my eyes to see the dawn of a new day through my window,
I realize that it was only another of my fanciful dreams
And that now I have awoke to the constant companion of reality
Except in my dreams, where in the still of night my companion is who I choose him to be.

The Spirit and the Warrior
(Carley Price)

handled and harnessed
the spirit chants to shadows named;
exposed in darkness,
naked and shamed.

branded and burdened
no longer bound to hold its size;
breaks the seal wide,
and learns to rise.

trembled and troubled
the lovers with their souls afire;
dance in soft curves,
widening gyres.

tearing and twisting
plucking tender tendon strings;
raging hearts with
ragged wings.

lifted and lightened
the frightened and the weary fly;
sigh and flutter,
spin and die.

timid and tiptoe
love lies with small and tumbled heads;
giggles into feather dreams,
and into fairy beds.

Carley Price is a Toronto-born student of English Literature. Currently, Carley is the Creative Director of *Freewheelin'* Magazine, and in her spare time, enjoys playing guitar, painting, and most of all, writing. "The Spirit and the Warrior" is her first published poem, and hopefully the first of many.

Toward the North

(Keith Proudman)

We come from all points south
we head towards the north,
and in our hearts we hold a flame
that keeps us on our course
From all the cities and the towns
the young and old as well
seeking out adventuring
in this frozen hell

Some come for fun and some for gold
but few will till the soil
and most are here for revenue
created by the oil
And some will stay a day or two
and some will stay a year
and some will live here evermore
their reason never clear

but I will be here for awhile
the flame inside still fanned
but when it's snuffed, I will leave,
back to my southern land
Where everything is easier
and most of life is fun
And I know I'll never forget
the land of the midnight sun.

To C.M., my true inspiration.

Happily Ever After

(Sheri Radford)

She stares at the last few embers of a fire she built
out of kindling she chopped from an oak that she felled
and listens (only slightly) to his often-told tale
of the dragons and serpents and giants (and so on)
he slayed (with such difficulty) for her much-coveted hand
and she darns his old socks as she listens (only slightly)
to his tale of his bravery and daring (and so on)
and she remembers the days when her evil step-sisters
dressed her in rags and made her clean chimneys
and she smiles (almost fondly) at this memory
in which she was young and was beautiful
and (most importantly) was not married to *him*.

Isn't this life?

(Safreena Rajan)

    water trickles,
    heaven giggles.
    kittens purr,
    humans stir.
stars glow,
that i know.
    no more fun,
    school's begun.
    the end seems far,
    oh, where's the nearest bar?
i am on my knees
oh, where are my keys?
    people leave,
    am i to grieve?
    people smile,
    laugh for a while.
some drink their sorrows away—
fools! they'll come back another day!
    no more tears,
    have you no fears?
    I am brave,
    it's chocolates i crave!!

To all those who have given, from wisdom to ice cream, thank you.

For November 2nd

(Benjamin Ramsay)

sitting stiff on the bus
flashing past broken down brick houses
unsalted streets and
teen girls freezing through their stockings

fields of felt poppies walk by
few fiery leaves hang on to regretful branches
i'm wearing mitts
it is november

365 crusty eyelids have passed
i've changed
listening to new music
talking with different voices

my brain is a bit fuller
my liver a bit sicker
i've got a different body
my muscles don't do what i say

but still
i hear your nose voice
feel your cold wire fingers
taste your greasy string hair

you're still around too much
pushing me off cliffs
laughing through my aching mind
dancing away with books, songs, clothes, make-up, soap
your eyes still bore holes in my
confidence when we talk

i'm smitten with another these days
but my chapped lips still bleed
unhealed from your kiss

Stop Requested
(Dean Ramsbottom)

As I peer through salt-lacquered panes,
The tune of "Jeremy" floats through my ears.
Headstone upon headstone travels by;
Lonely and desolate jutting markers, on and on.

Female, purple tights, black scuffed men's dress shoes.
Male, old beard, broken rimmed hat with make-shift twist-ties.
Born from death—only to return.
The sign reads, "C.D.s, Tapes, Records, and Posters."

Weighted speakers, piercing my ears.
Knees peaking from carefully structured orifices.
Overwhelming stench of bile, vomit, urine, and wine.
Police make another arrest.

As the spinning disc drains to rest
—directly correlating the journey—,
I look upward at the glowing indicator,
The sign read this, "Stop Requested."

To Bud O., Dan H. and my H.P.—your support has left me forever grateful.

Artemis

(Susan Ratkaj)

Last night I witnessed a passionate affair
On a horizon of rubies and mist;
Yellow fingers caressed tips of white foam
Then dropped diamonds to moon-eyed fish.

Wide waves licked and lapped wet lips
Against the bronzéd sun's,
While threads of white cotton weaved them a blanket
Stitched by the needles of gulls.

Those seamsters screamed with approval,
As they unravelled the last spools of day
I stared at those ruby limbs melted
Beneath an embroidered canopy.

It was not until the jealous throngs
Beating blue below the satin,
Had spit and hissed towards my feet
That I stopped. Awkwardly, I looked away.
Flushed and flustered, I carried my gaze
To where I stood, like a huntress,
In the sand
Upon a diamond strand.

"Though the leaves are many, the root is one." For A.R.

Prayer

(Randy Rauser)

May life never be so intense
that it bids a poem be written.

Migration

(Janet Read)

In the museum is a stone boat,
a umiak full of people who are larger than the boat
who push through the dead air of that place with huge oars.

The stubby mast and sail wait for the wind
to swirl up Dundas Street, bursting doors open
in a sudden Arctic gale.

The boat tilts on an imagined sea full of walrus and fish
where the sea goddess swims under dark sea roads.

She carries fish to the hunter in her arms,
receives tokens; each gift balancing harm.

Sedna has a mother's heart and the soul of a wolf
devouring the weak; all the fallen ones meet her,
are trapped in her hair, black as water, strong as ice.

The people in the boat lean forward,
their eyes huge with light from sea and sky.

Ivory walrus and soapstone seals arch their backs,
carved dogs stretch in leather traces,
the hunter shifts his feet, feels the harpoon weight his hand.

A small sound, like one breath drawn together,
escapes from the mouths of the people.

The wind picks up,
and, for a moment, the sail trembles.

Olga

(Helen Harris Reekie)

I knew a kind simple woman
Who was so rich in mind and heart
The shadows in the forest whispered
When she passed
The brook threw water diamonds
As she gave her happy laugh

The flowers mixed their best perfume
Surrounding her on the road
One sunshine day an angel came
They went together hand in hand
Maybe she left behind
Her rich heart and mind
For me to find

To Olga Whight, who passed away in 1992.

Address: R.R. #1, Parry Sound, ON, P2A 2W7
Telephone: (705) 746-2777
I have lived all of my life in the Parry Sound area. I have had 64 articles, short stories and poems published in different newspapers and magazines. I will have a childrens' book published next year by the Highway Book Shop in Colbalt, Ontario. I am currently writing a humorous column on farming for a newspaper called *The Georgian Bay Today*. I am currently the President of The Parry Sound Writer's Group and am studying to achieve my BA in English.

Sounds

(Kevin Reger)

The sounds that we hear from day to day . . . .
Sounds that touch our feelings
A child sobbing, the shuffling feet of the aged

The cry of the Loon on a northern lake
The freight train—lonely sounds

Many sounds only the quietness can hear
Aural artistry, painting a picture
Painting perfectly on the canvas of an imagination

Sounds . . . can you hear them?

Endings

(Debra L. Richardson)

The delicate miracle collapses
the perfect prayer is unspeakable
this tender silence will die on my lips
and with my words I contaminate.

Suicide
(Lee Richardson)

You've got some problems
that you can't solve.
No one wants to listen.
So you go into your own little world.
No one asks.
Maybe no one cares.

You don't care any more.
Now you're twenty stories
above the ground
on a small ledge.
Everyone's crying and screaming,
but you don't care anymore.

You want to die.
Everyone you cared for is still screaming
You jump . . . .

Everything is going by,
your life, friends and family.
You wished you hadn't jumped.
It's too late.

Out of Her Element

(Katherine M. Richmond)

The seasoned rush-hour bus rider
Is out of her element
When there are children aboard.
Children do not travel during rush hour.
This is not rush hour.
This is Saturday afternoon;
The children are boisterous
And act like fools
Like children
Who own the bus.
The seasoned rush-hour bus rider
Is relieved when she changes buses
Because the destroyers of peace
Do not follow.
They tear across the bus loop
To the mall to meet their friends.
The seasoned rush-hour bus rider
Is relieved that she does not travel
With them on the bus
Every day of the week.

Meeting
(Ralph Richmond)

Her honey-hued tresses wave in the morning mist,
    as rain-filled meadow mud
    sucks at her shoeless, fleet feet.

Was it my heart or hers
    cascading summer rhythms
    through the body's blood?

By the old stump,
    just inside the weathered woods,
    I crouch.............waiting?

From the tree's remnant,
    a fragile shoot emerges,
    straining for life
    amidst Hades' dry choke hold.

She's here now.
Hesitantly,
    I take her hand.

Indigo
(Sue Ridler)

The woman with black hair runs on the water
    my people   my people   my people

Bleeding men chase her beauty with scarlet hands
    Indigo   Indigo   Indigo

Evening dares to hide her path with darkness
    follow me   follow me   follow

But the stars forgive her fatal journey
    they will kill   my people my people   they will kill

Water carries her with forceful hands
    I can not   breathe I can not   breathe

The men's splintered fists dig into the water
    can not stop me   not stop me   can not stop

The end of the river trips Indigo into the sky
    wind   will catch me   I will catch   the wind

River hurls a hundred canoes to nearing rocks
    for my people   I kiss the wind   goodbye

To Gladstone Ridler and the magical art of storytelling.

Age: 23
Address: 26 Morewood Crescent, North York, ON, M2K 1L7
Telephone: (416) 223-0391
Imagine me in a black leather jacket, wearing a Latvian ring & carrying tarot cards while reading in a library somewhere. Creative Writing student at York who has always been told "no one will understand." Yet published in "Womyn's Words," "Existere" and now *Scaling the Face of Reason*. Amateur tarot and palm reader, who also enjoys dancing on beer bottles while listening to Tori Amos. My goal: To write without fear. Fatal flaw: Too nice for my own good. Greatest achievement: Writing anything at all.

I See You Too

(Cathy Riedl)

While waking from a restful sleep,
I rise to face a former dawn,
One in which had little hope.
I'm unaware of what may follow.
The year has passed like an aeon,
And a lifetime altered in twelve short months.
Today, I try to avoid reflection,
Avert my memory from haunting thought.

Now in a different time and place,
Removed from a tainted yesterday,
My space confines me without threat,
Free to move, think and breathe.

The words I speak are of conscious voice,
Not of a dark and murky haze.
My body functions unassisted.
My mind is free of invading fear.

To all who have stood by me and believed in me.

A Day in the Life
(John Ringrose)

From the depths of her sleep, his mother awakens,
Roused by his calling. No, she is not mistaken.
It is *her* hand he's pulling, *her* blanket he takes.
The day has begun, and he wants his Cornflakes.

His breakfast gets spilled, from his nose to his knee.
His mother just smiles, soothed by coffee.
He's loud and he's rough and he's so full of glee,
But after all, he is only three.

The day's full of questions, demands—never calm.
The house looks like it's been struck by a bomb.
But each night it happens, and her heart beats strong,
He cuddles his blanket and says, "I love Mom."

Hit and Run

(Kathryn Charlotte Rison)

"Soundprints" of your death still cover my heart.
    I dream your high metallic crushing, your glass breaking, tinkling inward—inward through that hole where wind and snow and cold night also poured in.

Hit and run . . . .
    your body distorted, skin torn, soul broken, all scattered on uncaring ground in this now silent, bitter winter darkness—and I, bearing two tiny scratches (that was all our assailant forced on me) departed you forever, surprised, on foot and suddenly
                                        very
                                            alone . . . .

I miss you like a friend, a lover. I spoke around you, spoke
    inside you often. It seemed I was my most profound because you silently approved. You hummed, moaned, purred approval . . . . You seldom hesitated, seldom argued the haste I forced on our relationship, the pace (the race?) I asked us both to keep.

You were the sanctuary I found peace and focus within.

I bought you gifts because you were my friend.

    And then . . . you died, saving my life.
        You stayed between me and the world one
                                                    last
                                                        time.

You loved me, too . . . .

A Man's Net Worth
(George Roberts)

Most cowboy friends that I still know
Their hair is silver or white as snow.
Strong faces lined by wind and cold
They are survivors and now are old.

At their age they've seen things change
As too many people have ruined the range.
Where horses and cattle once roamed free
Farm land and fences are what you'll see.

Back in those early days of the west
Clean water and air were at their best.
Friendship with trust went hand in hand
Now the greed and crime are hurting man.

My old pals don't like this modern life
With all its troubles and daily strife.
They have fond memories about the past
But those times are gone it couldn't last.

When the Big Boss calls them to come home
That one way trail, cowboys ride alone.
For that's the way it will always be
As they cross the divide to eternity.

He will be waiting with His tally sheet
To check them out, the strong and weak.
If some went wrong back here on earth,
The balance sheet will show net worth.

Age: 86
Address: Box 44, Arrowwood, AB, T0L 0B0
Telephone: (403) 534-2426
I'm now a retired farmer but have been a cowboy, rodeo contestant and boxer. In 1928 I rode in one of the last big horse roundups in Alberta. Then I worked at the Buffalo Hills Ranch, Arrowwood, for 14 years. I have written two books; the last one is still available at $12.00 plus $4.25 postage. It's called *Buffalo Chips and Prairie Grass*, has 137 pages containing pictures and over 60 poems—most of these relate to my life in some way. I am also a life-time member of the Alberta Cowboy Poetry Association.

The Tusket "Cranes"
(Louis Robinson)

'Tis my domain, these stretching moors,
A river, and a "Crane";
These sullen slopes, this solitude,
And softly falling rain.
'Tis my domain, and yet it seems
Usurped from creature tall,
Who stately, silent stands amid
The artery of all
That must in truth, belong to him,
For far superior he,
And more efficient to attend
The final touch of artistry.

Rooster's Melody
(Tina Rooney)

My Chinese year of the rooster
Arrives like a cyclone . . .
Tossing my life around.
Closest relatives treat me like a guest.
Old friends want to be lovers.
Funfairs turn erotic, as balloons pop around me.
My children bring me flowers, in the deep freeze of February.
I seem incapable of filling in simple forms.
My mind is frozen much like the snow.
Yet the same day, it's been announced I'll be a published author.
Around mc,
Old phantoms from the past
Demand my attention with their impending physical death.
The year has just begun; I will know later if I'll have
Something to crow about
And whether I'll be able to pick up the feather
And stick it in my hat.

All or Nothing!: (Lear's fetish)
(Kari Ross)

You and Me
And the spaces
in be tween
Nothing.
Pulling at me
Nothing?
Nothing.
Your words don't bite
They enter
andtwistandrip
—Loving is not enough.
It's nothing.
Across the room
On different floors
In different houses
Using different windows
You're throwing stones
bricks
I'm breaking
mirrors.
Why must the truth get in the middle
Push i n g u s a p a r t . . .

Feral

(Ronda E. Ross)

Once in a while, I feel a pull
    as I look to the sky;
        and the wind tries to lift me

Every now and then, I hear the wolves
    howl in the wind;
        and the trees whisper and wave to me

So many times, I see the sea
    rippling deep and blue;
        and the waves try to pull me

Sometimes, I wonder
    if I should be what I am
        and what I should be;
            and the wild keeps calling . . . to free me

To my Grandfathers: Dayson J. Quinlan and Earle Wickens.

Age: 28
Address: R.R. #1 Clarks Harbour, Shelburne County, NS, B0W 1P0
I live at the southern-most tip of Nova Scotia, Canada, on Cape Sable Island, with my husband, Jeffrey G. Ross. My parents are Horton Quinlan and Marjorie Quinlan (Wickens). I have written many poems and stories and enjoy sketching, reading, horse-back riding, and swimming. I have a poem published in the National Library of Poetry's anthology, *Tears of Fire*. I am currently the Accounts Payable Clerk for our County's School Board Office. I enjoy nature and hope we can preserve what God has given to us.

Untitled

(Jean-Jacques Rousseau)

There never was a day I was so sad
My tears blur my vision I'm so damned mad
The one I love has left me today
And there's nothing I can do to make her stay
Nothing or no one can ease my pain
Blood rushes my veins and clouds my brain
I only need to be alone
The only tears shed need to be my own
How I wish I didn't still
But I love her more and it drives me ill
If only I could reach out to someone
But I searched and searched and know there is no one

I seek the shadows but crave for light
Lord help me make all things right
I turn to you for there's no other way
I tried my own and it didn't pay

Lord, give me strength to live today
But brighten my tomorrow
For people see me smile but do not know
It hides the deepest sorrow.

Through the Eyes of a Child
(Renée Rousseau)

Little child, dry your tears away
Everything will be all right.
I promise that, with each day,
I will try not to fight.

Little child, you have so much.
Without realizing it, you have learned.
Love came into your life as such,
But love wasn't what I returned.

Little child, you cried so much,
You held on with all of your might,
Hoping that I'd respond to your touch,
And that I could hold you throughout the night . . .

The Walls
(Mike Rowbottom)

Yes, walls came down today
Spectacular though they be
Freedom replacing fear
Letting in love, fellowship and brotherhood
"Why now," we ask.
After years of being separated by walls.

The answer came as if in some quiet dream.
Walls are built around us all
To protect those within from that which lies without.
Ideas, truths, which in the end we can't shut out.

When I tore at the wall I'd built.
Pride, that barrier of the soul, gave way.
In its place, new life, hope, joy and peace.
Love came in, which once was shut out.

Crumbling walls no longer stand.
Differences of ideology are no more.
Yes, walls came down today.
So ended years of distrust and cold war.
East and west together meet.
Fellow citizens each the other greet.

To my wife, Linda, who helped rip down the walls in my life.

20th Century Fox

(Karen Rowe)

She is so chic
From Paris to New York
She is unique.
Cheekbones so high they intimidate
Silicone and dye to infatuate.
Creating awe when she walks
Radiating confidence when she talks.
Her beauty is timeless
but represents the time.
Her presence seems ageless
but will wither in the rhyme.
Her person is complex
but she doesn't reveal her mind.
Her smile penetrates the hearts of all men
but inside she despises and resents all of them.
She feeds on compliments and flattery as fuel
Then struggles to expel all she eats. Food is a tool.
The leaner her exterior
The meaner her interior.
Beneath the mask and costume
She is like the rest
She knows best
She dresses for success.

I Wanted to Write Home

(Stan Ruecker)

Dear Mom and Dad,
she kissed my neck
her tongue along the fringes of my hair
she brought me lilies
cheese with names I can't remember
a bottle that she opened with a towel

on the feast day of St. David
she went and found a leek for in my hat
my jaw hurts from so much smiling
I wake up and the day is new

how are you?

Dark Star Dark Star

(David J. Russell)

Dost thou laugh
O fallen star?
Dost thou laugh
at foolish mortals
who don masks
of painted light
and dance about
the altar
to scare away the night?
Dost thou laugh
O fallen star?
Thou who's swum
the skies
and walked
the coldest cosmos
Where no sun will ever rise?
Dost thou laugh
O fallen star?
Dost thou laugh
at prayers and wishes
that come flying
from mankind
to find a burnt-out star
that's cold and dark and blind?

To them who dare; thank you Sam.

Address: #12 Caramillo Road, Kelowna, BC, V1V 1B1

Carefree
(B. Salvin)

Do you ever yearn like me,
Just for a little while to be free?

Free from all the ties that bind,
Free to leave all cares behind;
To walk in fields and greenwoods wild
As I did when just a child?

Deep in a fallow field to lie
And see the grasses frame the sky;
To watch a beetle's wavering walk
As he climbs up a flower stalk?

To hear a skylark leave his lair
And climb through pollen-heavy air,
Pouring forth his glorious strain
Then plummeting to Earth again?

Do you never yearn, like me,
Just for a little while, to be free?

Oasis
(Lily G. Sather)

At
A Food Court
In a Mall,
Scores of people
Rest and reminisce.
It's noisy,
But
Still an oasis
In the desert
Of rush!

The Moor and the Fineland
(J.T. Sauntry)

I sit upon this moorish heath,
And welcome the light that comes from above.
I look at the stream that flows slowly,
As when nature and beauty fell in love and became one.
Its translucent waters, yellow, green, blue,
Its beauty resets my life, this beauty is so new.
The still house that is on the shore, not breathing, uninhabited,
Lay there for someone to start a new life.
A grove behind the hut, small but thick with vegetation,
And ready to make my dreams come true.
I wish to rest in the green grove
Or lie on the warm sands of the shore
And smell the fresh air of my mind.
I start to walk from this heath
And look back at the people who only wish for this.
And all I can say is:
"Just Imagine."

To those who still believe there is a power within the mind.

Age: 19
Address: 269 Mary Street, Newcastle, NB, E1V 1Z4
J.T. Sauntry's real name is Terry Sauntry, a 19-year-old who lives in Newcastle, NB. He has previously placed second in a provincial essay contest and received a $1,000 scholarship prize. Terry enjoys reading, writing, music, and basket ball. His main interest is writing, both poetry and fiction. He also wrote a 22-page children's picture book (unpublished).

The Creek

(George E. Savage)

A chance word stirs a memory.

A boy,
not yet a man,
though on that journey bound,
drawn, as are all boys,
to flowing waters.
A bridge,
ageless, decrepit, rusting.
Hours spent
along creek banks,
unaware of, yet absorbing
its sounds, its sights, its smells,
while my soul flies free.

. . .

The bridge is gone,
and in its place
a soulless concrete culvert.
Farmers,
whose fields I walked
and who shared words
as man to man,
are now all dead.
The creek still flows,
but the boy is gone.

Submission

(Sabina Savoia)

It was an immense night out there,
whirling and windy.
The lights in the church were helpless
against the black paved path.
Liberty came like an Angel,
from beyond the shadow of doubt.
The small luminating glare was welcoming;
but darkness rapidly stormed upon us.
The insane clock struck the uncountable time.
The villagers seemed huddled together,
afraid to move; one of all the rest.
The change was frightening; ease is found in what is known.
Towering on the roof was the dancing rain,
while the forest trees crackled in despair.
Tomorrow the sun will not shine,
nor a cell divide.
Above in the high cold night,
a mournful, unannounced tear was shed.

Survival

(Rick Savoie)

Humans are just like snowflakes
Each with our own pattern and style
We try to last forever
But will only last a while
On this planet earth
We call the rains our tears
Because our deaths are inevitable
Though we have lasted many years
Survival of the fittest
Has become our motto
But in the long run
We shall return to our own grotto
Animals have survived longer
And have adapted under our sun
Though as I look upon our wild kingdom
I have to ask, "What have we done?"
We, who are the smartest (HA!),
I believe are the most dumb
We have killed off many species
And let our hearts become numb
Keeping this up, we will kill ourselves
And all our weapons will turn to rust
And then the animals will return
But none will say, "Ashes to ashes
and dust to dust."

For my Mother and my Son, both of whom I love dearly and miss greatly.

Winter Storm

(Bessie J. Sawatsky)

North wind blowing fiercely;
Trees, bending to the ground,
Whirling, twirling snowflakes
Tumbling, rapidly, down.

Heaps of snow, piling up
In drifts, upon the road.
Snow-plows working vainly,
Trying to clear the load.

Slowly-crawling traffic,
Battling the wintry storm—
Watching from my window,
I'm feeling snug and warm.

T.V. for amusement,
Furnace, providing heat,
In refrigerator,
There is plenty to eat.

Must not be complacent;
It may not always last!
Could be power failure,
From any angry blast!

But, I'll count my blessings,
And pray, that God will be
Watching over others,
Less fortunate than me.

To my two Sons, twin Daughters, ten Grandchildren, and three great Grandchildren, with love.

Age: 71
Address: R.R. #1, Belmont, NS, B0M 1C0
Telephone: (902) 662-4111
Birthplace—Belmont, Colchester County, NS. Parents—Ethel and Bent Roode. Had seven sisters and two brothers. Grew up on a farm. Attended one-room school in Elementary Grades. Graduated from Col. Co. Academy and Provincial Normal College, Truro, NS. Taught in Elementary Schools for 32 years, retiring in 1982. Married Henry Sawatsky in 1943. Have two sons and twin daughters. Became a widow in 1989. Now live alone.

To Whom May Be Listening
(Anna Sawicki)

You think of me as old, brittle and grey
Who can't get out of bed each passing day
You think I have no friends at all
If I get carried away, I might fall
You feel that I can't get by
That very soon, I shall die . . . .
Well, let me tell, to whom may be listening
Your ways of thinking have something missing
I'm knowledgeable and I'm free
I can climb from my bed, I can even climb a tree
I can walk, I can run
And I certainly still have fun
So for those of you confused
Your words that are abused
Remember, you too will be old someday
And that you will be happy in every way . . . .

To my Grandmother, Anne Sawicki. My true inspiration for this poem!

Age: 27
I have always been inspired by the true emotions of others near to me. Writing poetry has also always been a personal therapy to me. I was born in Elliott Lake, ON, in 1967 and moved to Kirkland Lake with my parents, Alice and Horst Sawicki, and my sister, Tina, who now resides in London, ON. During my stay in Kirland Lake, I obtained my Diploma in Social Work. I have a beautiful four-year-old daughter named Sahara.

The Spider, the Fly and I

(Adelaide Schartner)

Today—
    I saved a spider
        but killed a fly.

Why was I—
    gentle with spider
        but ruthless with fly?

To kill a spider
    is flirting with doom.
But a *fly*? speed him on
    to oblivion.

But what of the spider?
What of the fly?
What about me?

Thanks to me,
    the spider still lives.
    Because of me—
        the fly is still dead.

But the spider and I
    will also die
        And what does it matter
            WHO killed the fly?

But—somehow—I wish
    it had not been I.

The Actor

(Jon Scheffer)

As the heart beats fast,
as the skin glistens when it is not hot,
and yet under the light I shine,
viewed by all as a reflection of what they want to be;
and I, delegated by known authority,
stationed here to control emotion,
as wind passes through me,
and onto that which others see, and know.

As what I wear transforms me, presents me to the unknown,
I shudder, not knowing the end
that will come to rapture me,
to find me blind and unwilling,
fighting off hands that appear before me,
grabbing for some piece of what they think is me.

Stares drive into me,
as the hands grab fragments of space.
I run, leaving behind that which
I was, for safety, for sanity,
for I do not want to remain in shambles, in partiality,
in the mind of those who want to be what I was.
I am what I was before that, I will be that which I want,
And I will not always be there to satisfy your desires.

Stalemate
(Chris Schmidt)

entrenched
in a relationship
as thick as blood
and almost as appealing
the heart
a battle field
scarred by accusations
torn apart
by unrelenting demands
perhaps surrender
graciously
would solve nothing
but at least
leave one survivor

The Lord Made Time Enough for Us All

(Michael Ross Schmidt)

On that cold winter morning in the shadow of the Truckstop
the old man sat at the counter with his keys in his hands;
"Well, I'll tell ya, you young guns got some tough times in front of you
and I'm ashamed to tell you this
but I don't think I'll be alive long enough to help you boys out.

My old man was a Hired-Man, Y'see
worked the threshing-machines
years back, when ownin' your own Quarter really meant something
I can remember the dirt-floor in the old house,
and how it got so dark when the snow piled up against the windows outside.
In those days we didn't have any car or even a radio,
just an old team of horses, and a pair of old cows.
Mother would sit up late, making butter
to take door-to-door
in Town, if the weather was good.

I watched him walk by my sports-car,
like the good Lord had made time enough for us all
and I thought about myself, a little.
At first I wondered if he was going to make out all right;
but I figured he would.
Then I wondered if it wouldn't have done my own parents some good
to have had to scrape by a few years,
and not just say that they did.

For Leon and Phil, my friends.

Age: 23
Michael Ross Schmidt is from Rollyview, Alberta. He is 23 years old. This is his first publication in a nationwide venue. "I grew up in Leduc during the heyday of the Alberta oil boom, in the seventies; for a long time, my home was the focus of attention for the whole world. Growing up that way pushed me to do two things—become a geologist and write about the things that went on here."

The Dance

(Janine Schoff)

As she moves over the floor
the music fills her mind, body, and senses
taking her far away to a land of
mystical, rhythmic beauty!
Freedom and perfection are alive here.
All her senses are filled with the
tingling movement.
It's a perfect high!
And as the waves wash over,
one,
after another,
her body takes to the rhythm,
and moves . . . .
All her senses are filled with unbinding freedom.
She is flying,
gliding,
diving,
life is but a blur.
The magic has taken over as the waves reoccur.
Life seems to vibrate through her,
from her,
around her,
for at this moment,
life is unattainably PURE!

To my Dad for teaching me to dance and Mom for my love of music!

My Magicians
(Monte Schooley)

Whether involves an alternative
which may, when
expressed precisely,
make perfect sense
without pretence.

Whether to go to work
or whether to rest in bed;
that thought winds spirally in my head.

Such are the stormy moments
cresting in my soul
when weather whether
casts her spell
should I be feeling well.

    Sir, I am a bit under the whether
    won't be in to work today.
    The whether's got me down.

To be indecisive
may be a disease
that requires some planning.
I rely on two letters
for the cure that will please.

Words. I love those magicians
which conceal
and let me lie in truth.

Address: 1109 East Puce Road, R.R. #3, Essex, ON, N8M 2X7
Telephone: (519) 727-6363

Broken Spirits
(Claudia Schwan)

Broken spirits cannot fly
Their fine and noble love
Crushed in cruel hands
Like glass broken into
A thousand pieces

Broken spirits cannot laugh
Laughter died and turned
Into an anguished scream
Can no one hear the pain
Does no one care

Can broken spirits ever be mended
Will a kind and caring hand
Come along and gently put
The splintered pieces back together

Remembrances—Thoughts
(Felix Schwarz)

I reminisce often and fondly
of the hours we shared,
but mostly they are more than memories,
at least they are not dead,
nor do they lie far in the distance.
No, they laugh, kiss, play, cry,
hug, and feel.
Like ostrich feathers they stroke my heart
and transfuse warmth and pleasant feelings
to my insides, and this inner happiness is visible
from the outside through my smile—
a smile
that tells the others the story about you and I.
A smile that represents "us,"
and it carries your name.
I reminisce often and fondly,
but more often and more fondly,
I dream about our future together,
which will be more than a memory.

To my Wife.

My Prayer

(Barbara-Ann Scott)

Dear God—the Father—I've barely known
I'm here before you all alone
I know you're here within my head
A life so empty, a soul so dead

I know you're out there, that's why I'm here
I'll try to listen when you are near
I've felt your warmth, your light within
I close my eyes, you're gone again

A sinner, yes I am for sure
This life is wasted, I need you more
To take my hand and lead the way
So I can hear you when I pray

I need you now and evermore
To walk beside along life's shore
My heart is hard, my spirit is weak
Your love can lift me back to my feet

Dear God, this is my selfish wish
To walk with you in loving bliss
I'll hold on tight to your guiding hand
To live the life that is your plan.
Amen

To all His children who have been filled with the Holy Spirit—born again of God.

Age: 39
Address: 55 Lavinia Drive, Apt. #3, Truro, NS, B2N 5N5

I was brought up the second oldest of eight children. I have been writing poetry, prose and song lyrics most of my life. After high school, I took a creative writing course. I have several small pieces in hospitals and recovery houses. I am now working on getting two original songs recorded. My lifetime goal is to win a Juno for Lyricist of the Year. I am also working on a line of greeting cards titled "Imagine"—in visual imagery.

Two Toothbrushes

(Chris Scott)

As I got out of the shower
One afternoon,
I noticed two toothbrushes
In the five-toothbrush holder

One Pink
One Blue
Both hard-bristled
From lack of use

The Pink one had its
Back turned to the Blue
For Good Reason
And if toothbrushes had arms
The Pink's would have been folded

Time for new toothbrushes?
Time to start brushing.

Age: 21
Address: 835 Grant Road, Kamloops, BC, V2B 6K7
I have a Bachelor of Arts with a major in Political Science and a concentration in English from the University College of the Cariboo in Kamloops. I love to write and hope to make it my profession. Poetry is a challenge, and I am honoured to have been selected to be published in *Scaling the Face of Reason*. To other struggling poets and writers: "Good luck and keep writing."

Untitled

(Christopher Scott)

When tomorrow's sun is set,
And the little boys and girls who are our children have been
safely tucked to bed,
When Fate, a soft-eyed matron, broods over her grey hairs,
And we . . . and we? Yes . . . we, well, yes again . . . O . . . we?

When the hustle and the bustle of all our years drop to the
depths of the timeless sea,
When Poseidon's bosom yields up the blade he wrenched from
ravished Ashtolot so long ago;
When the Muse's stone, now cracked with age, recites her
nursery rhymes in the dying gloom,
And when the Dryads come home to rest;
Then from the land beyond the dream shall rise a shadow
cloaked in white
And tiptoeing on the edge of the world, with his invisible
hand shall beckon us to partake in the dance of silence.

What then is the poet's art?
To knead the dough of human memory . . .
To stir the embers of a dying fire, lost in the mountains for
centuries,
To kiss Eternity on the cheek, and in her health
Drink deep the draught of dandelion juice.

To the one who knows.

The Evening Wolves
(Jane Scott)

In the evening
The wolves howl
The moonlight shudders
Liquefies
Turns to silver dew
And falls, with gravity
The smooth snakes
Of sound mournful
Arch upwards
Charmed by sorrow
So elusive
That shimmering moonlight
Transforms
To slake the soul thirst
Of howling mouths

White Sunshine, Green Gowns
(Ryan Seeley)

An angel is dying, so let him sleep
Peacefully amongst his family's tears.
While sunshine falls on days I long to keep.

Open eyes close and pain's river runs deep
Through a body I've known and held so near.
An angel is dying, so let him sleep.

He is not the only one who wakes to weep
In cold sweats that bring dreaded floods of fear;
While sunshine falls on days I long to keep.

All day his face is turned to God, who reaps
Souls from skies hanging infinite and clear.
An angel is dying, so let him sleep.

A green gown covers his frame, too weak to leap
Over grey evil that steals nights from his years.
Still, sunshine falls on days I long to keep.

I am a shepherd watching over one sheep.
I call out to him, but he cannot hear.
An angel has died, so please let him sleep
On sunshine that falls on days I long to keep.

Age: 19
Address: 40 Park Road South, Grimsby, ON, L3M 4E7
Ryan Seeley is 19 years old, a resident of Grimsby, Ontario, a graduate of Denis Morris High School, and currently an English Major student at the University of Guelph.

Decadence

(Lisa Seepersad)

Silently composing
Loudly writing
To decadence at its best
Damned be all the rest

Conscious or consciousless
I write and restore
Troubled beatings of yore
Vainly pretending to clean up the mess

Suggested ways are
Never realised or relevant
Fly, squeal, do all but mar
The power of pens, voice and rant

To end this decadence would be
Honourable virtue but curtailed glee!

Age: 21
I have been educated in Trinidad and in Canada. I am a graduate of the University of Toronto with a specialist in English. I won a scholarship in English from this university last year and was involved in university newsletters and various social groups. My interests include music, cooking and singing . . . . A part of me feels compelled to write, and a a part of me always trembles at the thought.

I Wonder Why

(Margaret R. Sell)

A little girl just four years old
is abandoned by her mother
A little boy just past ten
is looking for his father
A teenager just robbed a man
of everything he had
A hooker on the corner
just made a deal with dad
A man of the cloth just made a call
on the widow Brown
A woman for her gossip known
just spread it all over town
An angry man out of work
calmly pulled a knife
and robbed a liquor store in town
Another took a life
A young mother of tender years
is watching her baby starve
A soldier on the battlefield
just suddenly lost his nerve
A lady in pain and anguish
begs the courts to let her die
Seems the whole world has gone crazy
Me, I wonder why

To my loving Mom, whose love of reciting poetry has been my inspiration.

Address: R.R. #3, Pembroke, ON, K8A 6W4
Born in Bromely Township, Jan. 30th, 1939, to William C. Coleman and Edna P. Hartwick-Coleman. Married Elmer Sell, September 24, 1955. Mother of three sons and one daughter. Grandmother of six. First-place winner of two short stories and one poem. Two poems published in anthologies, seven published in local papers. Hope to publish a book of poems someday.

Birthing the Blue

(Dee September)

i sit peeling away silence
at the centre of naked stars
and bite the apple of my dreams

my hands move-moving
reach into earth's fullness
pull at a fragile budding
and the roots of first creation

my eyes are married
to this pure memory of birth
loving the innocence of beginnings

these fingers remember every detail
every trace of tear, of blood, of kiss
and vein of rushing water
with the quivering of insight

this weeping up brims with joy
quick trembles and ripples anew
at the pulse of my touch

i raise my head
shouting with the expanse of lungs
and empty my tears and laughter
into blue electric skies—waiting

Address: 201-309 Pridaux Street, Nanaimo, BC, V9R 2N4
Dee September was born in South Africa and emigrated to Canada. She has travelled to Africa, Europe, the U.S.A. and across Canada. Dee has read her poetry in Canada and abroad. Her poems have been translated into 15 languages and published in 21 countries. Dee's innate sense of justice, equality and love of humanity find expression in her poetry. Her poems have found wide acceptance because of the political and philosophical messages imbued in them. Dee is a member of the Multi Media Arts Resource Society. She resides in Nanaimo writing, performing and getting involved in the artistic community.

Pathway of Persuasion
(Aurangzaib Shaikh)

A candle in darkness,
Your smile lights the way.
Like lost times of youth,
In my memories you stay.

Just like the dusky sun
Summons the night,
Your sweet soft voice
Persuades me to write.

As others have tried
Through so many a time,
To reveal true thoughts
Through letters in rhyme,

With so much to utter
And no words to say,
I search for something
Which might lead the way.

But travelling alone
At some forgotten mile
I long for all of you,
Not content with that smile.

Age: 20
I have always been interested in the art of writing, especially fiction and poetry. Both my parents contributed and encouraged this interest. My father, a writer himself, has written and published numerous short stories, a novel and collection of poems. Therefore, I have always been encouraged in my literary pursuits. My first "literary" accomplishment came when I was in grade two. I received first prize for writing the best fairy tale. This moment was significant in encouraging my later "works." As I grew older my interest in writing began to expand.

The Voice
(Norma Doreen Shaw)

"Who am I really, why am I here?"
This was my question for many a year.
Everywhere Nature, encompassing me—
Softly, a voice said, "You are the sea."

Stars in their grandeur, bewitching my soul!
Guarding the waters that ceaselessly roll:
Was it the sky, or was it the earth?
"My child, 'twas the ocean that gave all life birth."

Thc rcd salty brine that pounds in my veins,
Makes me a part of the thunder and rains.
A part of the river that flows to the sea—
"Yes, I'm the ocean, the ocean *is me*."

To our son, Dan, whose love for the world of nature is my greatest joy.

Age: 69
Address: 673 Mountjoy Street South, Timmins, ON, P4N 7Z4
I was born in Toronto to nature-loving parents of British descent in 1924. This was still the age when conquering and exploiting nature was the most acceptable form of activity. Outside of having the most gorgeous garden in the neighbourhood, our secret love of nature was pretty secure. However, the inward joy that we felt was quite apparent. Girls were supposed to scream at 'creepy crawlers,' but I was too fascinated to be afraid of any living thing.

Inclusion

(Sybil Shaw-Hamm)

kindly he explains
HIM
includes her, dear.
MANKIND
includes you, dear,
and when she says she somehow feels invisible
he winks
slyly.

Turquoise Was Love
(T. Shea)

take my shoes

walk in them

it's easy

follow my footprints
through the dusty trainyard
one single set
to my door

my bedroom is robin-egg blue
call it turquoise
I have made love in it

turquoise was salty skin
your mouth on my lips
love

today turquoise is a cruel reminder
of salty skin
of lips
love

I cross you both off my list
the past and the future
and it's so unfair

take my shoes

walk in them

put them on the wrong feet

Death Hues/Death You; I Am

(Robert J. Shearer)

Everything breathes so vague
As nothing emanates violent colour anymore
It all sleeps in mundane death hues
And shallow boredom pervades my soul

The pot-holes in the road out there
And the low contrast salty pavement
Are uninspiring as this concrete suburbia:
Anarchic undisturbed slumber of modernity

(Don't tell me more lies . . .)
You're a fallen empire of words, hope and sand
And I forgot who I am

I reach to remember an ancient day
Before the personalities became solemn statues
Before the winter of reason invited the death hues
And the vagueness of the deadened mind sounds

(I can still remember when . . .)
You, the rapist of raped God and the now raped land
Begged me to forget who I am

And still I forget who I am

Too Late . . .

(Ann Shen)

There she stands . . . alone, afraid.
The warmth and security,
The caring and feeling
Are missing.

She thinks of how it was
Just mere days ago
When friends were around
And spirits were high.
But now . . .

There she sits . . . tired, weary.
The pain of the words,
The wounds of the fight
Are deep.

She covers her face with her hands
As tears well up in her eyes
To run down her cheeks,
To dampen her lap.
But why . . .

There she waits . . . forgotten, lonely.
For trust to return,
For friends to forgive,
Too late.

Age: 22
Address: 2039 Montcrest Court, Mississauga, ON, L5M 4X9
Telephone: (905) 542-1126
I graduated from the University of Waterloo this april with a Bachelor of Mathematics Degree. I hope to continue in school to pursue a medical career. I enjoy writing poems in my spare time as a way to express my feelings. My poems are written for certain people and about certain events in my life. My life goal is to have a happy family.

My Ageless Friend

(M. Shippey)

He is not old this man who walks towards me,
Eyes all alight, step slow, arms outstretched in glee;
For what is age but youth by age improved,
And what is youth but age five score removed.

REFRAIN
Oh! winds of time blow gently on my friend,
For he with me and I with him will mend
The scars, which only in the telling heal,
The thoughtless wrongs which man to man does deal.

What brings us here to meet and share our truth?
He apologizes for his faltering step, I for my lost
youth.
Each week we play this game, just he and I,
We meet in private conversation, we laugh, we cry.

He seeks to guide my life, to grasp that thread so thin
Which will bring him to life's circle once again.
I seek the grandfather that life has twice denied,
I look to him for timeless love, for joy, for pride.

"May I return next week?" I ask as in a dare,
While secretly I voice one small prayer:
Lord, let the wind of change blow softly and time
lightly tread,
Our time together has been short, so much is yet unsaid.

When all of my tomorrows have become life's yesterdays,
Of all the spoken and shared thoughts I'll tread the maze;
And catalogue each special dream, each lofty
thought,
And in my heart's treasure I'll remember all that you
have taught.

Pane Of Glass

(K. Shmyr)

Naked against a pane of glass,
I look to you.
In my heart, you've always lasted,
you remain true.
Naked in front of all,
nothing is to hide,
for nothing matters at all,
and I must survive.
So naked I remain in front of
my pane of glass
for all those to see,
but the heartache that remains
still continues to bleed.
Naked in front of the world,
where no one belongs,
I turn towards you and
see that you have gone.
It is this cold world
I reveal to,
Bleak as I may be.
It is this world I live in
that is naked to me.

For Mom, Dad, Lisa and the pain inside of me that led me to succeed.

Winter's Passing

(Jeanette A. Singh)

This morning I woke to the song of a bird.
It was the sweetest sound in a long time I'd heard.
Winter, her icy fingers had long held sway.
But today promised to be a different day.

I turned and listened and got up with a will,
Determined to find the source of this glorious thrill.
I knew then that I would never be bored
As up through my window the twittering soared.

Dreams of Spring had kept me sane
During January's icy blast.
When through the wind and freezing rain
Bundled up, everyone hurried past.

Now March is here
And with it comes
The early morning bird song.

Surely, surely, it won't be long
When Summer would right old Winter's wrong.
When colours and heat and noise and flowers
Would joyfully follow on April's showers.

To my Father (who never knew winter).

What I Am and Hope to Be
(Walter Slater)

I am dirt in the hand of the gardener
who planted the forests of the earth
to be used to nourish others.

I am a hammer in the hand of the carpenter
who built this universe
to be used to build up others.

I am a life-preserver in the hand of the captain
who separated the seas
to be tossed out to a drowning one.

I am a brush in the hand of the artist
who paints the sunsets
to be used to add colour to the lives around me.

And now I want to be a bowl in the hand of the chef
who feeds every living thing.
Pour into me your ingredients of love, joy, and peace
and stir vigorously forever.

To the glory of God, who, by his stripes, my soul has healed.

Age: 23
Address: 651 West Street, Simcoe, ON, N3Y 4K5
Born in Brantford, ON, 1971, raised in the Waterford area. Graduated from Waterford District High School. I plan to continue impacting the lives of area teens in a positive yet unstaunch manner. My greatest goal in life is to learn how to love the way love was meant to be in the beginning. I want to live a simple life and have a good steak now and again.

The Lady's in Shawanaga

(Michael McEvoy Smart)

Snow fell last night
Clinging to the rough-barked
Maples lining the dirt road.
Now cold winds harass
Their twitching limbs
Yanking the leaves off
And throwing them onto
October's carpet spread across
The homestead's tired ground.
Blackened sunflowers, their
Stooped bodies swaying in
Uncontrolled rhythm, play
Weary hosts to greedy
Bluejays who are undisturbed
By the day's depression, doomed
To be unbroken by
Cloudless laughter, sunny smiles and
Warm hugs because . . .
The lady's in Shawanaga.

To Ease Her Pain

(Clayton Smith)

With her feelings hurt,
    and bloodshot eyes,
Now she's all alone
    When she's sad and cries.
In her hand she grabs
    A bottle and swallows.
The whisky goes down,
    And her tears will follow.
With no one to talk to,
    She plays with her hair.
She's been waiting so long
    For someone to care.
She shoots up her life
    With a needle and some hate,
To ease her pain
    In this broken down state.
Smoke fills the room,
    And a candle burns slow.
Her face pure white,
    Like the falling snow.
She's walked through the door
    To the heavens above.
Maybe here she can find
Someone to love.

The Day I Met Her

(David John Montague Smith)

There stood a girl in shades and a kilt,
Her socks rolled down, her hands on a hilt.
The sword in her hand was tightly gripped
The bonnet on her head was slightly tipped.
Her hair was pulled back and tightly braided,
Her painted lips were slightly faded.
Her feet were wrapped in soft black ghillies,
The lace on her coat was as white as lilies.
Her beauty was incredible, she was simply shocking.
All I could do was stand there gawking.
She stood beneath a big oak tree,
And when I looked she smiled at me.
She came over and we started to talk.
It was time to leave when I looked at the clock.
She gave me a paper, it had her address;
She asked me to visit, I quickly said yes.
I asked her out, and she said okay;
I think that was my very best day.
One day she'll stand under that same oak tree;
I'll be in front of her upon one knee.
I'll give her a ring and she'll start to smile,
I hope she can't wait to walk down that aisle.
The day we get married might top all the rest,
But the day that I met her will always be the best.

Factory Sounds
(Wayne E. Smith)

Remember once the factory sounds,
through high-wire fences clear around,
of trucks, machines, and weighty things,
and muscled hands with union rings.

Recall the primed and pounding press,
as grinding steel on steel caressed,
the spark, the flame, to embers cried,
while smoke-borne death betook the sky.

An age when men were old so young,
by cancerous ills and blackened tongues,
when thermos dreams the whistle killed,
and shifting gears meant coffee spilled.

Upon their backs like sweaty mules
were flung the dreams of fossil fuel,
and year by year the pickets danced,
to greedy jigs and come-by-chance.

But now the whistle breathes no more,
and no more sweat bleeds through the pores
of labour grunts with collar blue,
who line the master's welfare pew.

I seldom miss those factory sounds,
through high-wire fences clear around,
but cold, so cold, for me to turn,
from those whose hopes in history burn.

To my fellow sentient traveller, who all along nurtured the gift, my Mother.

Sundog

(Carla Smithson)

The calf lay in the short pasture grass
—a black hump
From where we filled up the sprayer tank.
The herd came and stood around it:
A silent circle of mourning,
Trying to comprehend.
They drifted slowly from the open grave,
Leaving the mother
—a solitary weeper
Who moved away as we walked closer.
The calf was already partly devoured . . .
Coyotes and crows, delighting in
such an easy feast.
No way to tell how it died, really.
The ear with the tag was missing
—nameless
With no number to identify it.
The cow returned as we went back to work.
Lost our gloves somewhere, so
We handled the pesticide with bare hands
And each glance at the pasture,
At the cow who couldn't understand,
Held us at reality,
No need to
—philosophize.

Age: 23
Address: R.R. #1, Bittern Lake, AB, T0C 0L0
I grew up in Northern Alberta but moved to Central Alberta in 1987, when we took over my grandfather's farm. I earned a BA in English at the University of Alberta and am currently finishing my MA in Comparative Literature at the same university. I plan to do missionary work for a few years after I graduate.

The Storm

(John A. Smits)

The cottony grey clouds appear
The sun swallowed by their advance
Another storm draws near
It holds me in a trance

Now dark, the blue skies gone
The birds streak for their nests
The wind and rain rage on
These times I like best

The waves slap the shore like thunder
The mist is blown around
While fish stay calm down under
A gull knows where he's bound

The storm has gone away
The air is fresh as spring
The sun brings back the day
And life to everything

Age: 38
Address: 32 Helen Street, Port Colborne, ON, L3K 3N9
Telephone: (905) 835-8279
Born in Wainfleet, now living in Port Colborne. I was raised in a country setting. I have a great appreciation for nature. Living on Lake Erie has shown me what force nature can muster. With a number of poems and song lyrics already written, I strive to add to my collection. I would like to live long enough to see the band-aid holding our existence of humanity together removed, to reveal the wounds of life healed for all peoples.

The Fine Line

(Jennifer Snippe)

I want to sleep forever
in a bed
made of roses
and bubbles
and all things beautiful
                    (That I am not)

I want to live
in the luxury of love
fast kisses
long euphoric hugs
and neon lights in your eyes

I want something to hold onto
when I'm down
and upset
over life's continuous
lane of hurdles

I want all this
                    (and more)

I don't
want to reach out
to hold your hand
to find instead
a fistful of sand

For my Husband, Stephen, who helped me over the obstacles.

New Day

(Lynne Snyders)

'Tis dawn
The captive sun
Shakes free of shackling shade
To pierce with gleaming shafts of light
Night's gloom.

Feathered
Heralds proclaim
The triumph of the sun—
Piping his passage in trilling
Birdsong.

Mist wraiths
Mutely submit,
Raise spectral hands aloft;
Vanquished by the sun's pervasive
Power.

Pastels
Creep down hillsides
Ambush lurking shadows
And flood the land with radiant rays;
'Tis morn!

Awakc
Drowsing dreamers.
Gaze in rapt enchantment.
Embrace the passing pageantry!
'Tis day.

To my Husband—my finest critic, cheering section, and best friend.

The Upside-down Truth
(Nishi B. Sood)

Stars shine in the pavement
under a bloodless, faceless moon
who says,
"I'd cry if I could
but if I did, then who would
you swear by:
    'That's it,
    that's the last time;
    I've had enough
    of this cheap wine.
    Nothing's real
    but that stone in the sky.
    It can't cast any shadows;
    they're just lies
    from the lampposts,
    upside-down
    like a mirror in the sky'?"

For the stone in the sky and its and my Creator. Love, Nishi Es.

Highway Poetry

(Scott Sowerby)

Yes, show me the highway, friend.
But allow me to travel in the back seat.

Let me ride with childhood eyes, counting cows along the road
Let me satisfy my cherry greed at roadside stands; give me
one last taste
of that dense chocolate milk in the red windmill carton from the small-farm
    dairy
Roll down the window so I can hear the baffled wind roar by, then roll it up
    again
when the rain comes
so I can breathe on it and play a game of tic-tac-toe
Let me watch beads of water fill up and sl
                                        ip down the fogged-up glass
If I fall asleep on the journey home, carry me
softly to my bed piled with pillows and let me sleep
gently.

Gently without dreaming
There will be no need to dream;
Dreams will wait to begin afresh when the new sun shows its face.

Solitude
(Iris Sparling)

Alone on a hilltop and no one in sight;
A blue sky is edging the soft clouds of white.
Below me the grass waves when pleasant winds blow
Like infantry companies row after row.
There's sun on the wheat and long tapered corn,
And summer's a joy like the peal of a horn.

I have many loved ones; they do not know me—
They know but the features that age will not free;
The inner life, hidden and shielded from all,
Dwells deeply, serenely and heeds not their call.
It often walks darkly and comes very near
To uttermost depths of foreboding and fear.

But when on the hilltop the joy in me leaps,
And matches the great surging sea's wilder sweeps,
For deep tunnelled darkness there's not any room—
The high wind and sunlight wash from me the gloom.
Why then it's quite clear the real reason I'm here—
To praise and enjoy, rejoice and revere.

For you, Mom. I always knew you would be recognized someday.

Dream

(Robert Stanford)

She is bold and spontaneous,
With words as tough as callouses on time-worn hands.
But he watches her with patient comprehension.
His voice, both gentle and low, slips beyond the walls of her heart,
To what is hidden and vulnerable,
And real.

She caresses his face with strands of her long, auburn hair.
Soft, swirling strokes that playfully tickle their way to his ear.

He shares his food with her.
She shares her secrets with him.
Together they share a bed.

Sunrise fills their eyes, and a thousand yesterdays are forgotten.
Wounds of love are healed by love.
Though an ocean will soon separate them,
A single, silent tear speaks of tomorrow's kisses.

They will dream of each other when they are apart,
And they will dream of each other when they are together again,
In one another's arms . . . .

The Choice

(Charlotte J. Stanley)

Choose—as you will,
Life or death.
The animal? Well he is game!
To you it's just the same.

Choose—as you will,
The path you'll trace.
To bumble in the trees
Or kick up open space?

Choose—as you will,
Your horses fine,
To bear you, on, mute and knowing
(If puzzled by your crowing).

Choose—as you will,
Your hounds that can
Direct the ebb and flow
Of blood from fox to man.

When all is done, Who would know
That your face aglow, and vital eyes,
Bloom from shreds of matted fur—
A fox in plain disguise?

When all is said, it's much to think.
That a fox could pull the globe, and still
Escape the lethal course you chose.
Choose, choose as you will.

Maybe One Day

(Anne Stanton)

maybe one day
one day when peace lies within
when joy can come from that peace

then life
then life with all its beauty will be felt
hope will fill the mind
faith will strengthen the heart
and love of self
will ne'er depart

Two Little Girls

(John Steckley)

Sometimes,
you can think and reason all you want
but your words are merely
winter breath, chimney smoke, transport exhaust
looking like clouds
as you first approach them on the road,
but levelling low like vapour snowdrifts
as your car descends
into a cold-trapping northern valley,
so they fail to reach that place
where tobacco-fired prayers rise to meet
the grandfather spirits in the tallest sky.

In that way,
"Native issues" are sometimes not about cigarettes,
or borders, courtroom rights,
or anything else made visible by words,
but are two little girls
vulnerable like pale, brown skin
exposed to rays their grandmothers trusted,
two little girls who made me cast
a father's protective shadow
one summer I thought I was alone,
two little girls,
daughters of other men
children of another race.

To Amanda and Sheena.

Untitled

(Rose Anne Stephens)

My days are coloured black
covered by the dark, distant rain-clouds
shutting out any ray of sunshine
that tries to penetrate it.
But like all things it has a weakness,
and sometimes, on the coldest, bleakest
days of winter,
a ray of sunshine will break through
and rekindle my fading dreams.

For my dearest Robbie, who so often has rekindled my fading dreams.

Sounds of the Morning

(Jennifer St. Germain)

Sad and darkened by a bitter hand.
The sting of tears bites at her cheeks
Her hands wring her tousled hair.
They pull at her spirit and her self-esteem.
She laughs at her image in the water on the floor.
It spills across cold tile, smearing her bloodied lip.
The dog barks in the corner as the baby wails in its crib.
Her head hums with the ugly sound of a bruise.
She drags herself to her feet;
The dog needs to go out,
The baby needs to be fed,
And she wants to make sure he is gone.

Age: 23
Jennifer grew up in Owen Sound, Ontario, and she is proud to be of Métis descent. She attended McMaster University, where she majored in Political Science and History. She has enjoyed writing short stories since public school and hopes to pursue her literary interests as a freelance writer. She currently works in Hamilton, Ontario, and continues to write.

Life
(Karin Stieger)

Life is people
Life is a smile that
you see every day
Life is music
Life is the sunshine
that brightens everyone's day
Life is work
that has to be done
Life is being with others—
to get you through a dull day
Life is being alone—
to ponder over life's mysteries
Life is doing things
to keep busy
Life is depression,
just a state of mind
before you realize that
Life is happiness,
once you've found that special someone
Life is death, the end to all
so that we all can live again
Life is everlasting
to one and all.

Posted on a Fence

(Pamela St. Laurent)

big beaked,
crow freak—
a bulky bunch of
feathered hunch—
on the watch.
(unflappable, cussing ghouls)
for remains that be—
of animal fools . . .

To the memory of my Dad—Carl Oliver Lindberg—who showed me the animals.

The End of the Affair
(Marilyn Stock)

I am ephemeral
A flower
Plucked heedlessly from your garden
Left to dance on the wind ad infinitum

As I twirl towards oblivion
My colours flicker boldly
A neon sign gone awry
In its final supplication

I am somewhere in the distance
A blur across your mind
I have become without substance
A dalliance, a nuance in my femaleness
As tears flow from my very essence
I seek within you sublimation
And find only air

Kindred Souls
(Lisa Stoodley)

A single tree inhabits a field.
The tree needs the sun,
And the rain,
To help it grow and strengthen.
It does not ask to have
Its desires heard.
But if a lone man came along
And chose with his heart
To fulfill the wishes,
The tree would part its biggest branches
To welcome the man
And his kindness.

For Dale Sood, who showed me a different voice from the river that surrounds us.

The Brittle Girl

(Tami Stransky)

This is a photo of the brittle girl in the maze.
Back in the corner, playing mournfully
With frail arms, she is unaware of the camera.
Fury and dejection are seen in the brittle girl's eyes.
I look away, not wishing to remember.
As a true survivor, I have become impervious
To the shattered and secretive girl.
I want all the memories to vanish.
The brittle girl is struggling. She can only
Win the battle if she fights like a stubborn
Mule.
But she is with the rest of them,
All scuffling along.
None of them know how to find their
Way
Out
Of The
Maze.

They must be guided by someone they can trust.
I close the album.
Although her image fades, she
Will
Always
Be

There.

To Dr. Eudice Goldberg, who has made an incredible difference in my life.

Waves

(Laura Strong)

Waves
carry you with their gentleness
include you in their power
hold you with their strength
caress you with their rhythm

Waves
crush me
strangle me
pull me under
spit me out

Waves
like young spirits like yours
with childhood magic
and gleaming smiles
and optimism
and desire to go with their currents

Waves
do not like old spirits like mine
with practability
and sensibility
and cynicism
and desire to swim against their currents

Waves—will carry you to your dreams

Waves—will crush me to my death

To Greg.

Age: 23
Address: 4785 Tyndall Avenue, Victoria, BC, V8N 3S2
Laura spent her childhood years in St. Albert, Alberta, with her loving brother and parents. She studied classical piano with the Royal Conservatory of Music and achieved her grade 10 level with honours in 1989. Laura has spent the past four years at the University of British Columbia in Vancouver and graduated in 1993 with a Bachelor of Arts in English Literature.

Preferences
(Millie Sue)

We have irons
to make our clothes
smooth
but I find wrinkles
a lot more fascinating.

Untitled

(Michelle J. Superle)

I!
THE MAGICIAN!
was born to be a poet.
I become consumed with my poems
before they are born . . .
then cool, polished gems
tumble through my pens
and sparkle onto my pages.

I rub my magic stones together
until a poem forms,
from the soul to the frame.

I do not choose my poems;
they choose me
(the dark deeply disturbed poems
of summer arrive).

The madness of being cursed a bard:
what can I write
that has not been said
too many times already?

BUT
the triumphant triumph
springs from this . . .
when I have shifted
words and meanings
until I find them perfect.

The Ebb and Flow of Life

(Dr. Matt L. Sutcliffe)

Life can be full of pain and sorrow,
but every despairing night is vanquished by a fresh tomorrow.
Happiness and compassion will be found somewhere,
in a toddler's smile, a lover's kiss or a nurse's tender care.
Individual fortunes can change in a moment,
with a tragic loss or a kindly person's compliment.
It does not pay to brood or sink into despair;
better still, hold your chin up in the air,
and accept the ebb and flow of life,
with its periods of sheer joy and times of strife.

Reality

(Kimberley Beth Sutherland)

Idealistic thoughts that once crowded my head
Are now gone, forgotten, forever dead

Once I dared to wish and dream
Not now, I know the truth it seems

Is it life that has done this wrong?
Or merely experience playing its song

Maturity brings clearer thoughts
Of all the battles that have been fought

There really is no place for hope
Reality is how to cope

To a special little friend—my beloved Coopie.

Place of Birth: Truro, NS. Parents: Barbara and Ronald Fowler. Spouse: Robert H. Sutherland. Date of Marriage: October 17, 1987. Cat: Siamese named Cupid. Education: Cobequid Educational Centre, NS. Teacher's College

Winter Memories

(Ruth E. Swim)

I remember as just a child
How my family and I would go;
For a drive 'neath all the stars
To see the fresh fall'n snow.
The trees dressed in regal beauty
Stood silent, as if in awe.
My eyes were round with wonder,
To the sparkling world I saw.

Years have passed and things have changed
And I have long since grown;
Yet some things are just the same
Like the freshly fall'n snow.
The trees in regal beauty,
Stars dancing in soft moonlight;
Taking me back into memories
Of those long country rides at night.

To my Father, who has always believed in me; and my Mother—my inspiration.

Address: 130 King Street, Truro, NS, B2N 3L4
Originating with strong rural roots combined by family being a priority has conjured many fond childhood memories that are a pleasure to recant.

Fifty Below
(Sean Takacs)

Another face lost in the night,
fifty below,
a part of life?
A frozen expression—expressionless,
who? when? why?
it is anyone's guess,
for the tale is only told
through the deep-cut ravines,
maps of suffering,
maps of pain,
while time stands still
again and again.
Oh, the silent screams
of childhoods lost,
of innocence,
of death on a cross;
I hear them all each night,
so I wrap myself in warmth,
and I pour a drink,
I hear the cries
and the wind outside,
and I start to weep.
Fifty below
and I can no longer sleep.

Spring in Eastern Canada

(Susan Tannahill)

Warmth seeped into the wind
and a cloak of white lifted from the land
the sweet water ran, birds sang!
The earth calls us to employ
she offers us her bounty
we wait, silent, patient for the summer sun
our seeds clenched firmly in our hands
There is not time for idle words
we must be one with mother earth
water flows in gushing torrents, nature's mantra
Our hearts pound when we see
the wild field so alive
Our children shriek with glee
as they race outside
the frigid beauty of winter fades to verdant spring . . .
It's the passing of an age,
but we remain behind
if only to feel alive.

Untitled

(Katrina Tanne)

Little bird
Do they hear your cries?
An age of anguish
Captured in your eyes.
A drowning man's last gasp for air.
Little bird, will you still be there?

Little bird
In your nest alone.
What will you do
Now your heart's turned to stone?
A man on a cliff who leaps to fall.
Little bird, will you end it all?

Little bird
They loved you so much.
Was it you that they loved
Or the feel of your touch?
A man with a needle has died today.
They're here, little bird,
To take you away.

Panic Attack
(Katherine E. Tapley)

Pain is like spinach,
It's supposed to be good for you.
But this viper
In my breast
Continues to bite ferociously;
It curls inside viscera,
Sinking long fangs
Deep into tender tissues,
Until I writhe in existential agony.
Upon the side-walk I tread,
Trying to appear nonchalant
As an invisible giant takes
His oversized fists and wrings my heart muscle.
Suffocating pressure. Internal screaming.
I smile and say to a passer-by,
"Hello. How are you? Nice Day."

Re-birth of a Drifter
(David Taylor)

Standing on the beach of hope,
I see the Sun
Set over yesterday's untouched dreams,
While the moon rises in full-bloom glory
In celebration of tomorrow
And an end to sorrow;
I see, floating,
                flowing,
Visions of changes,
A ship upon the silvery water,
                the misty tide,
With its multitude of magical ways
In which I can re-arrange
                the paints that I use
To re-create my life . . .
Yes, I stand at a distance—
                a pirate in the wind,
                a drifter on the wing,
                a minstrel in the gallery,
                a ghost who longs to sing
With a broken voice mended only by
                artifacts of optimism
And token memories . . .
                of you.

To my Mother and to free-spirited people everywhere.

Some Will Read This—I Shall Write It

(Rick Taylor)

Those who bind me and blind me,
I shall not forgive.
Those who untie me and pry open my eyelids,
I shall not forget.

Those who come to sell me a tomorrow,
I shall turn away until tomorrow.
But until tomorrow,
I shall prepare for the purchase.

Some will pack all their yesterdays
In a dusty trunk in the attic.
I shall dust and polish mine,
And hang them on the wall.

Some will look for beauty in nature.
And while they gaze through open eyes
And indeed see it and smile,
I shall look for beauty
In the smile and open eyes.

Some will wander around, under the forest's trees.
They will watch as each foot falls to the path.
I shall thrust my feet to the forest floor,
That later I can turn around and see my footprints.

To Rob Finucan, Synnyside, and all the footprints we made.

Our Sunshine

(Tami A. Taylor)

"One dull gloomy day,"
My brother did say
As he stuck his head out the front door

"So much to be done
But no sign of the sun,"
And with that, he said not a word more

"I feel so depressed,
I don't think I'll get dressed,"
Sighed my neighbour from over the phone

"I know it will rain,
And I'm in constant pain,"
She complained as she sat in her home

Our days are all rosy
We feel warm and cozy
And that feeling comes not with the sun

All we need is Adam
Our precious wee lamb
Our baby, our sunshine, our son.

To all my "sunshines," Adam, Jacob and Tara.

Age: 35
Address: P.O. Box 791, Bancroft, ON, K0L 1C0
I am employed full-time as a Law Clerk, have been married to a dear man, Rick, for 15 short years, and have 3 wonderful children, Adam (8), Jacob (5) and Tara (3). I am presently enroled in a first-year BA course at Queen's University in Kingston, which I have been taking by correspondence. I have always had a keen interest in writing poems and stories, particularly children's stories, and enjoy creating my own greeting cards. It is my literary goal to actually have my work published and to be able to write full-time someday.

Anima [1]

(S. Taylor-Griffiths)

In the forest of the fight a sleeping
leopard dreams the dreams of primal night.
His claws, the talons of the flight,
tucked gently in the sacred earth
that generations of other kind have
deemed it so.
The dreams are clothed in colours
swift and camouflaged. The grip of
faint sweet smelling sky surrounding
the sweat of sunrise, and as the sky
blue sea tide stretches, an eagle flies,
behind the sleeping whitened eyes.
It starts and bears last witness to the
destruction of the land.
There is no choice but wait and sleep
against the throes of hunger sought,
but predator and prey are one, each
sucking stones to ease the thirst.
The sunburns and whitened eyes of sleep
our daily blindness comes, without hands
to shield or heart to care. Compassion I
know not of, but sorrows deep and searing
pain I understand, for once alone, our
passions spent, our friends not like
ourselves expired, this world will cease
to be, for wonders lost our souls cannot
soar free.

To those who sweep the path before walking.

Address: 233 Vercheres Street, Longueuil, QC, J4K 2Y4
S. Taylor-Griffiths is an environmental artist and consultant who holds a Fine Arts Degree from Concordia University and is presently completing a Post-graduate Diploma in Environmental Studies from McGill University. A researcher on endangered species, extinction and ethics, S. Taylor-Griffiths is the resident artist for Terra Gaea, a small gallery promoting art from an environmental and spiritual perspective. In progress, a collection of poems entitled "Anima, Dominus and Gaea" and an illustrated book for children.

anger and the innocent bystander

(antranik e. tchalekian)

walking through death
thousand eyes on me
judging
drag me across
a freezing beach
can’t seem to save
my eyes
from the sand
down my throat
go the hands
at my back the window
the ocean
try to swim but the tide
drags me across
the crowd
thousand eyes on me
surfing through death.

"No"
(Denise Tendall)

Thinking of yesterdays
Thoughts of tomorrow
Often bring happiness
Or tears of sorrow.

The winter is now finished
And spring is in the air
Cautious of our future
Will your promises still be there?

You promised your love
You promised your life
You promised a lifetime commitment
If I would be your wife.

Soon ends the warm weather
And back to the snow
I am too unsure of your promises
So my answer is . . . NO.

To those who have and continue to inspire me—many thanks.

Elms

(Christine A. Terris)

Look into my eyes and tell me
What you think you see.
Is it real? Do you know?
When you feel the sides,
Are you touching?
Down a road embraced with elms,
I see myself two paces behind you.
Pretentious, but not to the core.
You think too much to be truly ostentatious.
A benevolent smile,
A promiscuous hand.
What are you hiding from?
When you sleep, I almost think
You are at peace.
Touch me, know me, need me,
But most of all, want me.
I would say I don't care, but
That would be too close to the truth.
Run your eyes through my soul
And make a wish.
Eccentricity be my consort,
Spontaneity free my spirit.
Come . . .
Walk with me for a while.

To Peter Salah—thanks for helping me see this poem was really about myself!

Migraine
(Theresa Theobald)

A gloved hand wakes me
        crushing my left head

Reeling across a Dali landscape
        I cross the room

Smashing against the throbbing
        cacophony of a
 thousand primal drums

As the gates of chaos open
        and the demons begin to
                                dance

Harvest Moon
(Marina Thiessen)

twilight's feathered clouds gently
swab up moonbeams
whose golden fingers
reach out
to smooth wrinkles in night's blanket
leaving hints of
melting butter and scalded milk
ripe pumpkin and warm spices
a delicious path to
Harvest Moon

L'il Skunk
(Cheryle Thompson)

Swaggering, tail down, tiny white feet.
Through foggy headlights late at night.
Journeying from his woody retreat.
Deep in the mud; out of sight.
A four-lane highway down his back.
Nostrils twitching away in the other direction;
Unaware his privacy was under attack.
Quietly we follow—best not make correction.
Could it be that he knows and yet doesn't care,
Swaying to a four-piece band that we can't hear?
No, for all he knows the road is bare.
As the young gentleman in tails waits for his love to appear.

M.S. Haiku

(James S. Thomson)

My body says
I cannot run
I smile
And run free into my mind

Age: 48
Address: 222 Erie Street, Stratford, ON, N5A 2M8
Telephone: (519) 273-0375
Education: BA; MBA

Garboard Strake (for Marina)

(Ross Thomson)

It has brushed against bottom
the deepest of depressions
carrying the weight of life itself

It arches its back against burden
the deluge of regression
ferrying cargo dry without cry

I
your garboard
            strake bend to the
     grace under pressure
            and snap to
           give back to
                   the living coral
the corral
of

kept
      brute
            instinct . . .

Cosmos

(Robin Tilley)

Somewhere
Out there
There's something in the Cosmos
Trying vainly to reach
The dwellers of Earth
We lie blind to its research
One day we'll find
Its confetti on Earth
But since our birth
From supposed evolution
Or the mighty big bang
It seems we remain
Removed and refrained
From serious action
So we sit and stare
At the sky above
And think that
Maybe
Out there
There's nothing at all

The Night Before

(Caitlin G. Tillman)

    but she says: "Fine."
She's fine.
Making me want to scream
but what about the ambulance,
the convulsions,
the bruise on your left arm where they struggled
to put in the I.V.?
What about that?
Is that "Fine" for you?

    but I say nothing
because I am her sister, not her keeper,
and we know how to keep secrets.
Even if they kill.

Depression

(Dave Tonge)

Have you ever tasted a snowflake?
Or have you kissed the rain?
Nature's calling, the rise of passion
loneliness is paired with pain.

Despair it seems so distant
and blurred through water-coated eyes.
Yet it reaches out to embrace you.
Why, for God's sake, why?

Laughter is the best medicine.
A cure is then a bottle of mirth.
The laughter is killing you, can't you see that?
Run, run for all you're worth.

Its magic can change your emotions;
as they say, "drown your sorrow."
God I miss my family.
I'll just struggle for another tomorrow.

To my beautiful Wife, Jocelyn, and my Boys, Jeff and Garry.

Untitled

(Jacqui Touchette)

You lure me down towards the pond.
You slap your hate down on my back,
Push me in and watch me sink.
My quiet gods are subtle rage.

Feel the grey press down on my eyes.
I hook the clouds right off the stage
And wait for night, my eyes will break.
I see you fight me all the way.

Two years are gone and so am I,
Worn away against the grades.
I was the signpost or unseen
And you buried your head in the sand.

She

(Thao Tran)

She wears tight jeans and baggy
sweat-shirts. Conscious of her
earrings, hairdos, and toiletry.

Much too young
to know about
relationships.
Yet her heart is hardened
into cynicism,
indifference,
and scorn.

She talks about her parents making love.
She talks about her "clinical depression,"
of thinking of a gun through the brain,
but afraid of the pain.

She talks about her parents' divorce.
She smiles a fateful, relentless, arrogant smile.

Seemingly
challenging the world.

She's a brat.

She's a saint.

Or perhaps, her only

Defence?

Loose Woman
(Mildred Tremblay)

Old woman has let go of her sadness now.
She has shed her allotment of tears.
Nine hundred and ninety-nine million of them.
She has broken her sugar bowl, spilled her sugar
into the dust bin, collected her coins.
Is she angry? Yes, she is dangerously angry.
She no longer sits at her place by the chimney.
She is roaming the halls—this way and that.
Her hair is loose. Her tongue. She is dangerously loose,
shouting questions, rattling on doorknobs.
In the rooms the directors hear her pass;
the long table shudders, cracks split the wood.
Her feet have grown large, they say.
Their eyes slide sideways in fear.
She is loose, they whisper, we must burn her again.

The chairman speaks: there is no fire hot enough,
no rope strong enough.
She has gathered the winds at her back.
The serpent has leapt from the ground
to encircle her arm. Even now the trees
in the night whisper and plot to assist her.
The spirits of minerals have rushed to her side.
She has held council with the tribes underground,
with the wet clay and the roots and the stones.
Nothing can stop her. *She is loose.*

The Lament of an Urban Dweller

(Anastasios Triantafillou)

You buy and you sell
Guaranteeing your admission into Hell
I have lost more than this body can bear
Retracing my footsteps
Retracing my birth
This flat world is ready to fold
I meet with Passion
Like whores in the alley
Torn sails that can't catch the wind
And all the slick hucksters
That tear up the night
Are still aiming for one last shot at the moon
I hear Hank Williams and I hear Hank Snow
There's a haunting chill in my bones
If my heart has been broken
Don't tell me, I can't let it show

Discoveries

(Robert Trubenbach)

With nature's fury,
Come crashing waves
Upon the golden coast;
Though to the void
They seem to go.

The sun goes down again
On my sandy home,
With no moon to light the way;
I burn a path
Through night's black chill.

Through forest deep and dark and wild
I seek what must be;
But my flame has dimmed.
The way is lost
For senses are gone.

Night's creatures howl
And move about their world.
Pay me no heed;
I wish not to be,
That I might not be found.

I see the flame again,
Though none can claim it theirs.
It burns away the darkness and fear,
And lights my golden coast once more.
I feel the spray of the ocean.

To the beauty of British Columbia, my inspiration and my home.

Tears

(Mike Truscello)

Tears
I listen to the angels crying
Their celestial pain becomes my discomfort
Tears
The burden of sorrow
The proof of memory
Tears
They are mine; they are yours.
Do not speak.
Let me wipe away your
Tears.

Timeless Treasures

(Irene Stefania)

Cosmic dreams—
Light years' distance
. . . Twilight-thoughts
And
Star-dust rainbows

Galactic whispers—
Millenniums' moments
. . . Starlight-silence
And
Comet-crest skies

Universal stillness—
Earth-times' essence
. . . Dusk-dawn
And
Solar-mist moons

Gravital forces—
Lifes' measurements
. . . Transient-traces
And
Shooting-star stillness

To my Mother, Stefania, and to the mentally ill, their caregivers and mental health professionals.

A Special Person
(Rose Marie Tucker)

A mother is a wonderful person;
She's always there when needed.
She gives of herself and straight from her heart.
A mother is all of these and much more;
You couldn't ask for anything more.

For my Mom, the most important person in my life. From your loving Daughter, Rose Marie.

Imagine Being Imprisoned

(Randy R. Tunney)

Imagine being imprisoned, as a child through to adulthood—
Never understanding and no one understood.
Your mind, it was a prison with countless little cells—
Most held a tiny prisoner in whom the thought of freedom dwells.
Now life inside any prison can be a riotous affair—
All this human tragedy, most in total disrepair.
As at Jericho, the walls came tumbling down as time should have it be;
You walked anew in this world of ours, thinking finally I am me.

Now the bars are real—I feel their coldness in my hands.
Before, in my imprisonment, at least I walked the lands.
Sitting down alone quite tearfully, my face buried deep into my palms;
Humming hymns of Holiness, reciting verse from psalms,
Wiping away tears of happiness—each tear a memory of the past,
I look up, smile and thank the Lord; I know I'm free at last.

Now the philosophy of this poet, as you can plainly see,
"There are no greater prisons than trapped in conflict
with your personality."

To the countless thousands who suffer from the ills and abuses of this world.

Height of the Season
(Fran Turner)

Vines pump life juicy, ballooning
into tomato flesh smooth
and hot in my hand.

I pick alongside a trail of
baskets, half-bushels seasoned
by last year's harvest, now
brimming red and thoughtless:
my mother's labour so far today.

Noon heat shimmers as
her painter's cap bobs.
Her work-shirt flashes, bleached by sun.
Octopus arms stretch everywhere
fast and fluid into
sprawling vines. Tomatoes tumble
through her stain-encrusted
yellow rubber gloves.

Joy in her work, physical joy.
She loved to polka before I was born.

Sunday mornings the Czech program
crackles into our kitchen from Cleveland.
Solo, she glides around the table or
sweeps me around as her reluctant partner.

Next time we pick these rows,
the vines will curl and brown at the edges,
brittle with exhaustion.

Disturbed
(KPU)

"do not disturb
artist at work"
the sign on the door
the door that he carries
wherever he goes
he's mostly at home
at home
busily creating
the creative works
of the artist
not just any artist
unlike any other
abounding in insight
anxiously seeking adequate medium
to outwardly propound
the profound
to share with the world
a deeper understanding of itself
preoccupied in this endeavour
life passes
the artist
makes his final gesture
a clarification
of all he has said
and done

To Mother Nature and Father Time.

Address: Box 1087, Batawa, ON, K0K 1E0
"a simple man
of simple needs
a complex world
complexing me."

Blood and Pride
(Étienne Vaillancourt)

From what hand did this bullet flash
And from what canon did it crash
For who is right and what is wrong
The unknown soldier, the poet's song
To choose of freedom to kill the man
Fate for us and others damned
The brave young faces new of birth
Death for life is all it's worth
For those who fought with blood and pride
To those who live 'cause others died

Garden of Everyday II

(Marilynn Valby)

how do we take root in one another?
hold the bloom within each other?
are we nourished
by growing perfumes, rainlight or lightfall?
how is this continual surprise possible
upon our ordinary ground?
standing, surrounded, surreptitiously seeking,
we trust the garden we share together.
this garden, possibly glance, possibly greenery,
a vision in the light; ground
where our feet and hearts are firm.

McSex

(Henry Vandelinde)

Coupling frantically, just two backs,
Feeding hunger with Big Macs,
Empty of value, nutrition free.

In the dark, no faces only touch,
Not real, but a desperate clutch,
For what is supposed to be.

Before the grinning clown,
Two hearts kneel down,
And starve in sterility.

Completed
(John Van Dyk)

Lost, deserted
Nowhere to be found
Made, created
Heard without a sound
Spoke, said
Told all he knew
Alive, dead
Paid his due

To my Parents and Friends, always there making my life wonderful.

Age: 25
Telephone: (905) 436-3127
My poetry is a part of me, original, and composed in times of despair, happiness or contentment. Poems of love, death, religion and anything that was influencing my life at the time. I regret that my skill has not yet reached its potential, but I still have a long life to go and a lot more to experience. From a small town in Southern Ontario to the metropolis of Toronto, I am an accountant by trade with my own company, single, and embarking on travel plans.

A Survivor of the Holocaust
(Joris van Loo)

remember
the emaciated bearded figure
placed on the edge of the pit
of slain corpses
to say prayers for the dead
and that look   from those eyes
on you

standing
behind it
the young and healthy Nazis
blond and handsome
laughing   amused

before such images
that have made a grotesque of man
of life
the great works
of artists, poets   all masterworks
appear
          jejune

On a Suicide
(Martha van Loo)

Maturity a teeming brain of reasons,
explains away all failure and the broken sieve
of life through which all dreams fall through in season,
is mended and forgotten, for "a man just live."
Existence is resumed, the safe conventions,
(avoiding cautiously the pulsing winds in storm)
of marriage, children, scorn at old intentions,
the snug philosophy that all things feed the worm.

But Youth, with ever-clear eyes of a Galahad,
beneath whose mystic lashes burns the quest,
the Holy Grail, love, liberty and all the rest,
whose glowing aims are high, no matter what,
a life for a life or lost or won, no trivial breath,
for Youth when the dream is gone, there is only death.

My Husband
(Shelley VanSteeg)

He's my lifelong companion and my best friend.
Flowers, gifts and candy he doesn't always send.
Knowing I can count on him and he'll always be there.
His kindness and understanding show me his care.

Some said, "Getting married already? You're not old enough.
You'll have bills, hard work and all that stuff."
But instead I live with some quiet nights at home,
Happiness in knowing I'll never be left alone.

We just have fun walking, talking and enjoying life,
Satisfied in the benefits of husband and wife.
He's my lifelong companion and my best friend.
Flowers, gifts and candy he doesn't always send.

For My Friend

(Anne J. VanWyngaarden)

Come, wrap yourself
in my affection,
a feather-like cloak
no strings attached.

Come, warm yourself
in the affection
of a friendship
quite unmatched.

Come, my friend,
enjoy this gift
so freely given,
an answer to our prayer.

Let us wrap ourselves
in God's affection,
He promised us
His loving care.

And, when at times
we fail each other,
we will find peace
and healing there.

To Mary, for her encouragement and friendship.

Ablaze
(Carol Vautz)

She leaps into the darkness
like an arrow shot.
Her figure moves forward inside the deep, shady forest,
between the trees, where shadows hang.
Her eyes appear round and clear as marbles,
then switching to glowing fire-torches
that lighten the blackening woods.

She raises her devilish glare
to the treetops towering above her.
Her velvet paw comes to a stand,
her bone-white claw
ploughs the soil with leisure.
Leisure to open her monstrous jaw
to roar with cracking joints and razor teeth
dripping of ghostly whiteness.

She prowls across a musky floor
of forest leaves, bathing in a misty dew.
Shadows fall upon her,
Savage winds ruffle her pitch-black fur.
Her mission lies concealed in the tunnels of her eyes
as she moves with a slithering tail
out of the forest, towards the town,
shaking her palm of dirt.

To all my Friends from the French Language Program: In memory of a wonderful time.

Age: 22
Carol was born in Holland in 1971, though the greater part of her childhood was spent in Germany. She immigrated to Canada in December of 1984, commencing a new life together with her parents and two younger sisters. The years which followed were spent learning the English language, as well as becoming acquainted with a foreign culture. Carol is presently a student at St. Thomas University, Fredericton, pursuing a Language degree, which is to prepare her for Translation. She hopes to one day achieve her future goal of becoming a writer of fiction.

Breathless

(Colette Vincent)

Crisp brittle branches
A blanket of snow
See what I see
Know what I know

Sunshine glistening
Flakes on the go
Feel the warmth . . .
And know what I know

Smoke-filled sky
Storm winds blow
Chill in the air
Do you know what I know?

Romantic moonlight
Fireplace aglow,
Passionate hearts beating
Leave your thoughts go . . . .

The Side of the Road
(Erin Voegeli)

Walking on the side
Of the road,
The gravel screams hoarsely under my feet.
Trucks, cars
things made of steel
Hurtle past
Furiously,
Not knowing destination
delirious with speed.

Walking through
Lingering clouds of fumes,
Dust.
One day
I will
Reclaim
Them.

Upside-down Bosnia

(Zvezdan Vukanovic)

Nothing terrible can happen to you
I can see only one road
Which leads to nowhere
We are mirrors of personal destiny
Our punishment is damnation
Talking about nothing is not enough
For tired thoughts
Today is the same as yesterday
and Tomorrow will be the same as today
The gravitation of a fate is still very resistant
You sleep on the wrong side of destiny.

Now, everything is upside down like in puzzles
Unfortunately, this is not the end,
But the beginning of the end
NOTHING TERRIBLE CAN HAPPEN TO YOU
BECAUSE THE WORST HAS ALREADY HAPPENED!

To the victims of the civil war in Bosnia.

Age: 20
Address: Villa Camellia, Cordova Bay 5055 Road, Victoria, BC, V9Y 2K1
Telephone: (604) 658-5951
Zvezdan Vukanovic was born in 1974 in the former Yugoslavia. He was published in the Montenegrin Anthology of Modern Poetry in 1991 as the youngest Yugoslav poet. He published his own poetry book, *The Hymn About the Strange Things*, in 1992. He writes screenplays and plays. He lives in Victoria, BC.

Memories

(Marlene Waldron)

I remember old New Brunswick and all it means to me
Though I haven't been home in many a year
I have my memories

Skating on the old pond, swimming on the lake
Walking for miles on woodland hikes
What fun we used to make

Climbing up the apple tree; in fields picking flowers
Playing tag or just running 'round
They were such fun-filled hours!

Riding in the ferry from St. John to old Digby
Pretending we were pirates bold
Crossing the angry seas

Gazing in awe at Magnetic Hill or watching the Tidal Bore
Eating the large red lobsters
Along the New Brunswick shores

We have the longest covered bridge, Reversing Falls and tides
They have a beauty all their own
No matter where you bide

Exploring the caves at Fundy Bay, such wondrous sights to see
The hidden trail, the ebbing tides
What an exciting place to be!

There are so many splendid things, I cannot name them all
But if you're ever down our way
Don't hesitate to call!

River at Night
(Brian D. Walker)

Sometimes, when everyone else is asleep,
I rise from my bed,
pull on my coat and boots,
and cross over the road to the river.

On summer nights,
the river whispers a gentle lullaby
as it slides softly past
the slumbering willows.

In winter,
the windswept barrier shifts and cracks
while silvery moonbeams shimmer brightly
on jagged crests of broken ice.

High above, in the tranquillity of the night sky,
the myriad stars glow peacefully.

I stand quietly for a moment,
reverently drinking in the palpable solitude.
Then,
refreshed and contented,
I turn again for my home.

The Apple
(Rides At The Door)

I am like an apple
Red on the outside
White on the inside

I am a blood Indian
Raised the white way.

I lost my language, my culture.

But I went back to my reserve.
I saw that I was better off
where I was raised.

But I did learn a little of
my language and my culture.

So you see, Apples can brown.
I can be red on the outside
and my spirit can turn
the native way.

Survival
(John E. Walker)

She has outlived them all—
Sisters, brothers, husband, children, friends.
Each morning with weaker fingers
She breaks the crusts
And trembles crumbs
Along the window sill.
The cries of greedy sparrows
She hears as love
And from them gathers strength
To bear another empty day.

To Mrs. Ruth White, 1894-1985.

Paris Comes to Town

(Nicholette Walker)

Green hills dotted with woolly lambs,
bulbs stretching under warm starlight,
lovers strolling the Seine
beneath blossom-bending boughs

leave me cold

in this grit-sprayed slush
of prairie thawing.

In brown grass and puddled sunlight,
on a chilling metal bench,
two people hold one another's hands;

the sudden scent of lilac lines the breeze.

Born in 1971 in London, Ontario. Lived in Edmonton, Alberta, since 1976. Received BA in English Literature from the University of Alberta in April 1994. Studied French in Québec and did a year's study exchange to the University College of Swansea, Wales, in 1992-93. Currently working on Master's degree in 20th Century Canadian fiction.

Violets on the Lawn
(Rachel Wallace-Oberle)

Guarded by the noble oak
do the violets grow
tenderly in morning dew
their crowning petals show.

A faint illusion
oh sweet profusion;

of velvet green
of purple deep
where elf and sprite
their secrets keep.

Through morning mist
by sun's gleam kissed;

they sweep the knoll
embrace the trees
an undulating
petaled sea.

Winter Memories: A Step Back in Time

(Muriel Walowetz)

The Country Lifestyle is for me
No other place can e'er compare
Sharing memories with all my friends
Hospitality is everywhere!

Stretching out across the landscape
As far as one could see
Lay deeply laden sparkling snow
Awaiting winter memories

We made a handsome snowman
Then we gave him a top hat
Dressed him up in fine attire
I can still remember that!

We built a large block snow fort
For shelter from the cold
While we waited for the school van
Back in the years of old
The van was made of canvas
It was placed upon a sleigh
Proudly drawn by two horses
A sorrel and a bay

Yesterday is mine now
Today shines all bright and new
Tomorrow is for making memories
The future is for friends and you.

Sometimes

(Eva Walrond)

Sometimes when the wind
whispers through the air,
I think I hear.

Sometimes when the snow
blows so tenderly,
I think I see.

Sometimes when the rain
falls on cold dark days,
I think I feel the pain.

Sometimes when the sun
shines with a bright glow,
I think I know.

Someday when I hear, see, feel and know,
I will become more than a shadow.

Here's to Enlightenment
(Tawnya Walsh)

Up the trail the figure marched
Arm and Arm with the sun,
His shadow casting a vision
On steps yet to come.
As the quest continued
He felt the dampness in the air,
Awaiting the blankets of darkness . . .
Soon his shadow disappeared.
But still the figure marched
Oblivious to what came next
Rocks shifted under his feet
Scared of the pace that he had kept.
The figure continued climbing
Despite the comfort of the light.
He saw through the dampness
Fought the darkest of the nights
Soon he found himself
In the valleys of success,
Celebrating his enlightenment
With some shadows of the rest.
The figure being man
The shadow that person's soul
Now at one with its existence,
Yet few will march the road.

Enlightenment

(James A. Watts)

Melting of the souls, intertwined in mind.
Working together for common goals,
gently supporting, lifting each other into another plateau.
Like riding a wave through a sunset desert,
painting the world as you go on your journey.
A kaleidoscope of whirling colours, thoughts magnified.
Gently being kissed and loved, like you never have before.

To my Mother, who has a great outlook on life.

Address: Box 72, R.R. #1, Vittoria, ON, N0E 1W0
Telephone: (519) 428-2468

I am from a large family with three brothers and three sisters. In the past, I have enjoyed different sports and have won different medals and trophies. Currently, I am graduating from College in the Recreation Leadership Program. This is the first contest I have entered with any of my writings, and I am very happy with the results. I believe I am a good writer with a great imagination and, hopefully, one of these days I could develop this hobby into a livelihood.

Boredom

(Karla D. Weir)

Strangled thoughts,
bridled emotion,
churning anticipation,
time stands still.
Anger collides with apathy;
frustration lingers.
Life wasted . . . .

Wistful escapism.

Animal
(Brady White)

With each coming dawn
As I stretch my back and yawn,
The stage is set,
And like a giant net,
The curtain is drawn.

The things I have to do
Dancing, climbing, acting too.
Behind the glass
Is the huge mass
Of spectators, looking for something new.

There's no smell
But I couldn't tell.
For someone "behind bars"
(Not for stealing cars)
I'm looked after quite well.

Crash

(James White)

I can still hear the sounds
Of metal twisting and screaming in protest
Shivering.
I remember the road before and after
But in between is a haze.
The shame and hurt will linger forever
And memories will remain.
I could have stopped the car that night
But for a reason yet unexplained,
We hit the rail and went over, and over
And over and over.
Finally it stopped. Now all I have left
Are two legs and two arms.
Wouldn't be so bad if
They worked.

Reality
(L.J. White)

The downpour caused my banks to overflow,
I am dominant.
Sailing smoothly to a place I don't know.
I am dominant.

I talk and chatter so you can't understand.
I am determined.
I run my course over this sun-drenched land.
I am determined.

The foliage creeps by as if it were suspicious.
I know better.
The misty air, cool shadows, all seem fictitious.
I know better.

As I slip by, I read your mind.
I see everything.
Your dreams, your fantasies all combined.
I know everything.

Au Printemps

(Leah White)

The thunder crashes
And the lightning flashes,
In the battle that rages above.
The soothing sound,
As the rain pours down,
Is what dreams are made of.

Misty fog blankets the land,
Reach out and touch its hand
Before it slips away.
The soothing sight
Of veiled moonlight
Is the promise of another day.

When the fury is done
And Nature has won,
I will know deep in my heart
We are a sure thing,
Like thunder and lighting,
We'll never be far apart.

To those with enough freedom of mind to love life, freedom, Nature and themselves.

Through the Window of His Eyes:
(Bill Whyte)

The glistening snow below the stars
    encompasses Heaven's fringe.

The spoken words remove
    the beauty and its tinge.

The precious moments, those in time,
    the smell of burning wood,
    the frosted windows, eves so full,
        add to all life's good.

To my two dear Grandmothers, Betty Whyte and Mildred Fogarty.

Age: 31
I had spent 10 years with the Canadian Armed Forces from 1981 to 1991. Six years of that time was overseas. Having had so much contact with people from around the globe, I believe this prompted me to write poetry. Education: Grade 12 graduate.

Times of our Love

(Sherry Wick)

Like a warm summer breeze
as it spins to a swirl,
Like a strong swelling wave
as it builds to the curl,
Our love began.

Like endless passages
in an old Egyptian tomb,
Like bottomless quarries
host a shimmering moon,
Our love deepened.

Like a stagnant pond
on a hot, hot day,
Like a sullen child
who forgot to play,
Our love stifled.

Like a sinner's hope
when his test is done,
Like emerging buds
well nourished by sun,
Our love renewed.

Like a glowing ember
refusing to die,
Like dependable stars
return to the sky,
Our love continues . . . .

Age: 35
My husband and I own and operate a dairy farm along with our two children. I find poetry to be a great form of self-expression. I use varied formats in writing, but I especially enjoy the sound of rhyme and the challenge it presents.

Separate Shadows
(Carrie Wickman)

I will walk into your
    garden of shadows.

I will put my feet on the
    wet, cool grass.

I will smell the sweet
    stench of decaying roses.

I will embrace your
    total being.

But I won't give into your
    desires.

I won't be a string puppet.

I won't be a part of your
    ventriloquist act.

But I will love you
    as I want to be loved—
    as an individual.

Life Is Like a Candle

(Kaye Wieler)

A simple little candle stood on a window sill
Of a cottage by the wayside, just slightly on a hill.
The dazzling lights were beaming for passers-by to see
That the cottage by the wayside was filled with company.

There were sounds of merry making—with music, dance, and song,
But the simple little candle stood unnoticed by the throng.
"Why am I here," the candle mused, observing its formation,
Aware of no significance in life's gay celebration.

The clock on the wall ticked on and on as time was swiftly fleeting
In un-reluctant faithfulness—its hourly chimes repeating.
At last the cottage lights grew dim—the atmosphere was changing,
As shadows beneath the moonlit sky, their silhouettes were ranging.

The candle felt a gentle touch—its wick was lit in fashion!
With warm light glowing from within, it melted in compassion.
Life is like a candle—with a purpose to be spent.
Be it birthday, advent, or romance, the candle serves in sweet relent.
Not in wealth nor in position does life reveal its unique plan,
But in the heart's contrite submission—to love and serve one's fellow man.

The Yukon
(Donald C. Wigfield)

There's a land in the North that I've been to,
    A land with its own special charm;
It is north of most habitation,
    Of city and freeway and farm.

It's a vast land, wide open, empty,
    With fireweed, eagles, and shale;
It's a land that will draw you, then trap you,
    With no way to go back down the trail.

Ninety years after everyone came here,
    The gold is all gone from its creeks;
But there's something that people come looking for,
    There's something that everyone seeks.

They say that it still has a mystery,
    And a magic that goes with it too;
It's a land of the wildest country,
    Patient; and waiting for you.

To the people—past, present, and future—of the Yukon Territory, Canada.

Our Retirement Home

(Dorothy J. Willard)

Off where the hills are sometimes green
There where my heart has ever been
Away in the golden mists of time I see
A place where my dreams come true for me

Fields rolling gently, friendly too
A lake that is fresh and cool and blue
Friends gather round us in these later years
Some sharing memories, some share tears

The time will come and not too soon
When we'll be there, this afternoon

Clouds flowing by on wings of white
A sky where the stars are clear at night
Woods where all birds and creatures live serene
Would that it could be evergreen

Endarkenment
(R.A. Williams)

Shall I, then, speak and break my code of silence?
I might as well, to get it off my chest.
If you would know the reason for my violence,
You might as well remain to hear the rest:

The darkness came and touched my tender senses
Which wept, since light had gone and left them blind,
And broke its way through all of my defenses,
And left a message shrieking in my mind:

> "What is your life, which builds on faith and virtue
> And promises perfection when you die,
> When That-Which-Is was never meant to hurt you,
> And you have built your vision on a lie,
> And you have sold your soul to an illusion?"

Now pain explodes like lightning in my veins.
Enlightenment brought little but confusion,
And, now that Truth has vanished, what remains?

My Walk
(E. Willis)

As I went for a walk one day,
I stopped to watch the children play.
They laughed, jumped and played around,
Except one child, who sat on the ground.
His head was bowed, a tear in his eye,
I could see he was trying hard not to cry.
No socks on his feet and only one shoe,
His clothes were all muddy and torn, too.
His face had a bruise right under his cheek,
His hat was all mud and bent at the peak.
I looked at his hands all rugged and bare,
And thought I heard him utter a swear.
Then a man did appear, a beer to his mouth,
"Get up and come home," he said with a shout.
The boy jumped and walked real quick,
While the Father picked up a big stick.
My heart hurt and felt for this lad,
How could a Father treat him so bad.
It made me think of my Son and my Wife.
I'll treat them good the rest of my life.

Vaccinations Against Love and Other Diseases

(Deborah Wilson)

Beyond, behind the smile
She flashes to the world,
The serpent lies coiled
Around a bruised and aching heart.
A sudden pulse, and the serpent strikes,
Seeking out and finding the softest centre.

Slowly, so slowly,
The venom seeps into her system
To mix readily with the rich red arterial stream
That courses coldly through her body,
Feeling its inexorable way
To her extremities.

The pain, exquisite pain,
Flows out and back again,
Returning, only slightly diluted,
To inoculate the weary heart
'Gainst further woe.

After You've Gone
(John Wilson)

you were not here
to greet the tide
when it came sidling up
to lap around our door
and so it left
in slow sorrow down the shingle

the moon arose in solemn pomp
to pass the night-time hours
in talk of cheese and lunacy
you were not here
and so it left
upon its long-decaying arc

the continents no longer slide
upon the ocean plates
and glaciers cry milky tears
and sit upon the mountaintops
to wrap themselves in foggy loneliness

this morning my kettle made two cups of tea
to sit in accusatory silence
upon the desolation of my counter-top
you were not here
and so I drank them both

now I shall go down and sit
beside the crying waves
and see if the tide bothers to return

Surely, Giving Thanks

(Malcolm R. Wilson)

Surely, giving thanks
is the least exercised emotion.
When I feel poured out like water
it is due to the ravages of the emotions
of fear, hatred or desire.
When I feel blocked by stone walls
wherever I turn,
it is because I cannot get what I desire,
escape from what I fear,
crush that which I hate.
How easy by contrast to give thanks.
No obstacle external to me exists
to my giving thanks.
Who can stop me?
Who can refuse me?
Who can hurt me?

Pep Talk
(Elana Wolff)

"Dreamgirl:
It's all in your head.
You thought what he said was a sign.
Now you pine your days away.
You thought what he did
was a bid for your heart.
How you lead yourself astray.
You fabricate signs
from circles and lines.
A rose is a rose
is a rose sometimes,
Not a symbol of love or lament—
Just petals atop a long stem.
Look up. Glance around.
Your prospects abound.
You're not lost or bereaved.
You can give to receive.
So why grieve for the mythical green man?
Sometimes a smile is just a smile.
Sometimes a word is nothing more.
Sometimes the surface speaks for itself.
Accept it."

The Relationship
(Gayle Woods)

It's hot.
Why not,
It's summer.

We meet.
How sweet.
It's nice.

We grow.
Go slow.
It's better.

We care.
And share.
It's love.

I'm here.
You're there.
It's over.

It's cold.
I'm told,
It's winter.

It's Christmas Time Again

(Harriet Worden)

The scent of pine from the Christmas tree
The picture of baby on Santa's knee
The bells you hear all over town
The joy you feel to have loved-ones around

A dinner that mom is proud to make
The glamorous dress for the special date
The presents tucked snugly under the tree
The special something for you and me

And have you ever thought that the day would come,
when Christmas wouldn't be that much fun?

No lights on a tree, no turkey and trimmings,
No presents from loved-ones, no carollers singing

Have you ever stopped and, once in a while,
thought of the ones who never smile?
'Cause their tummies are empty,
And their bones are cold,
And there's no relief from troubles untold!

There are no boots or mittens or overalls,
No heat in the rad when the temperature falls.
Well think of all those who are feeling this way,
and give from your heart and may joy fill your day!

Freedom from Within

(Karen A. Woudstra)

Alone, a child sat on the stair
Bewildered, confused and so scared,
Tears were falling; it's so unfair
A child was beaten—her identity bared.

For what went wrong in the mind of a man
Whose temper flared without a cause,
A coward unleashing his stress; he can
As it was his home, his way, his laws.

The child grew up misled and hurt
She lost her roots, she lost her soul,
With no direction, she felt like dirt;
It took her years to set a goal.

Today she's recovered, happy and well;
The past is over, one can tell.

Address: 46 Walter Avenue, Newmarket, ON, L3Y 2T3
Karen is a freelance writer as well as a writer for a local community affairs magazine. When she's not busy at her PC, she delves into poetry for relaxation. Karen has had several poems published in American anthologies. Karen does most of her work at night as she is a full-time mother to her three pre-school children. Karen has taken several creative writing courses and is currently a correspondent student with "The Writing School."

This Is Canada

(Steve Wray)

The snow-capped Rockies
the plains of the Prairies
the Inuit of the North
the gold rush of the Yukon
the Great Lakes of Ontario
the French of Québec
the Bluenose of Nova Scotia
Signal Hill of Newfoundland
Anne of Green Gables
the tides of Fundy
the fisheries of the Maritimes
the red maple leaf
ice hockey, lacrosse, skiing,
curling, golf, and baseball
from Atlantic to Pacific
this land is terrific!

To all the people who are proud to call themselves Canadians.

Little Joys
(Anthony Wright)

Let me walk again like a child
see the world as a child sees it
let the simplest of things
be the most intricate
let me laugh and cry
feel cold and hot
let me burn myself
so that I may know
let me run and fall
and scrape my knees
let me learn from my mistakes
if I get hurt that's alright
and if I die
don't be upset with me
for having lived

Age: 31
I grew up in downtown Toronto. What fascinates me is the human condition and the answers to the question why. I have self-published two books of poetry titled *Who Here Is an Hercules?* and *The Precocious Fool*. At present, I am working on a fictional novel and a third book of poetry.

Mothers and Daughters
(Jone Wright)

Mothers and daughters
waging wars
between the smiles.
Laughing with
hardened fists
they cry together.
Very far apart
the tethered greetings
come.
Estranged goodbyes
and strangled hellos.

Create the pathos
of a love lorn pair.

The Gardens

(Eric Wuest)

The crowds cheer with a tumultuous roar
Like a dangerous tide crashing ashore.
They cheer for the men who live boyhood dreams;
For, this sacred match is more than it seems.
For it is a place to escape Fate's toss,
And, where the only heartache is a loss,
There's sure to be some revelry after
A hard-fought victory. Merry laughter
Carries us forth in our quest for the Grail
In Lord Stanley's name. Here, the banner hails
Proudly, like this monument built in our honour;
Victory be ours within the hour!
So come, play up, play up, and play the game
Here in the Gardens; it is here we reign.

Dedicated to the Toronto Maple Leafs in their quest for the Stanley Cup.

Age: 22
Address: 542 Barry Drive, Pickering, ON, L1V 1P9
Telephone: (905) 831-9498

I am 22 years old and a recent Trent University graduate with a degree in English Literature and History. I am not exactly sure what I want to do until I retire, but if I could make enough money just to live and write, I would be very happy. At 16, I wrote a story which was later considered for filming. As well, I am currently working on what will be my first novel and hopefully the first of many successes as I have several more ideas which I simply cannot wait to put onto paper.

Wilderness; Child
(Peter Wyns)

Wilderness face
Like infant face,
Innocent and inspiring.
Unknown, unpredictable,
Controlling those admiring.

Mystery
Irresistible,
Compelling exploration.
Studying its mood and ways,
But no reciprocation.

The crying wind,
The howling child,
Violence unexpected.
Tormenting rain and fearful strain
Anxiety projected.

Then screaming halts
To silent hush,
A breath, a sigh is taken.
'Tis strange the way it woos you back,
It must not be forsaken.

The sun slips down,
Black blanket wrapped around,
A holy time suspended.
Creation's wonder still unfolds,
Raw life, portrayed, perfected.

Moods

(Jim Yakemishyn)

Not unlike the clouds of Time so to caress,
One another upon her strident discourse yet fair,
Or as a turbulent wave to dance save confess,
The secret's not so hidden as a wanton stare.

And would we beseech an anchor of our tempest?
That cries may whisper or whispers cry,
A longing of wholeness that inspires best,
As a wandering but weary damsel by Love's gentle sigh.

The heart may question this uncertain sojourn,
Once at peace then not so much even less,
By eagle's will would a vision soar so stern,
Or falter beside twilight's grasp away from security's nest.

To feel is to us a timely gift from whatever kind force,
That shall govern creation's grace be sound,
Nor should it incur without a welcome by the source,
Which human hands do ascend yet unbound.

I dedicate my success to the success of the C.C.C.P. and to all Canadian poets.

Age: 42
Address: 150 William Street East, Oshawa, ON, L1G 1K6
Telephone: (416) 432-1105
Born in Oshawa of Ukrainian descent. I'm not an educated man but have travelled extensively and have learned much. I've a strong interest in the arts and spirituality. I also paint, act, and write short stories. This is my first publishing success. I've taken many workshops in enhancing humanness and have overcome strident challenges. I wish to upgrade my education and am currently taking an art course. I wish to assist others in maximizing their possibilities and gifts. We are more than we think. I attend A.A. and the Unity Church. I find these movements very nourishing and educational.

Hunter

(Jennifer Yee)

Chestnut Eyes
Capture my gaze
I am entranced
In your eyes I see
An image of you

An Eagle soaring
Through grey clouds
Daring to swoop down
To an unseeable surface

Snatching from the sea
All that you deem yours
Taking up to your retreat
The sustenance of your hopes

Enduring storms throughout your travels
To unknown territories
Gliding through gales at your leisure
In prey of Life's treasures
Forcing Nature to yield to your persistence

Chestnut Eyes
I am bewitched by your spell
Envisioning I am beside you
Unafraid and hungry
Eager
Too
For the hunt

For BRF.

Address: Apt. 3-4544 Lanes Road, R.R. #3, Cobble Hill, BC, V0R 1L0
Jennifer Yee is a West Coast writer currently residing on Vancouver Island. During her studies at the University of BC, she met an instructor named Jane Flick, who encouraged her to write form the heart; the result was one of Jennifer's essays being published in a 1990 anthology featuring works by Canadian university students. Jennifer is one of the founding board members of the Multi-Media Arts and Resource Society (MMARS) in Vancouver. Jennifer's latest project is collaborating with an illustrator to create a children's storybook.

Running to Montreal, Leaving Behind a Sink Full of Dishes
(Chris Yorke)

You thought you'd shared the Cakes of Pan
yet no brother as fast had ran
when the breaking of the fast was done
one brother dashed, thus leaving one
to guard and serve and mind the store
this he asked, and nothing more
and while he danced and drank and sang
he caught a glimpse of yin and yang
and all the girls were quite amazed
and all the men knew he was crazed
he gave his soul to strangers, fleet
they ate his soul as if t'was meat
and when his soul was done and gone
they asked him for his body warm

Untitled
(Elizabeth Zarnowiecki)

sparkling
intense
smiles
my heart   quickening pace
your eyes   meet mine
quickly   dart away
once
was our passion
now
belongs to someone else

Paradox
(Phay Zedd)

humble beginnings—it was her
motherless childhood—it was her
silent strength—it was her
crying at gladness—it was her
smiling through sadness—it was her
something from nothing—it was her
fixing when broken—it was her
teaching forgiveness—it was her
unconditional love—it was her
protecting—it was her
spanking for reason—it was her
silence in truth—it was her
grateful for living—it was her
laughing when beaten—it was her
suffering intensely—it was her
brave when lonely—it was her
supreme motherhood—it was her
lying in the coffin—was a corpse.

In memory of my Mother, Madeleine Denise Simard, 1929-1989—still with me in spirit.

I Fly

(Lili A. Zwart)

I fly over the wreckage of my past
My sins and the sins against me are there
I fly willingly and with a spirit of victory
For now my soul lives instead of survives
I fly over the breathing beauty that is my present
And see that even my limitations are beloved by me
Sweetest Friend of my soul, I invite You to soar with me
For it is Your Spirit that has led me to this wondrous place
I fly forward into the promise of my future
And see there glorious things unfolding
Will you fly with me there, my love?
Under your weary, burdened arms
Grow a strong pair of wings
Lest I fly ahead, leaving
you behind . . .

INDEX